CREATORS OF SCIENCE FICTION

Borgo Press Books by BRIAN STABLEFORD

Against the New Gods, and Other Essays on Writers of Imaginative Fiction
Algebraic Fantasies and Realistic Romances: More Masters of Science Fiction
Alien Abduction: The Wiltshire Revelations
The Best of Both Worlds and Other Ambiguous Tales
Beyond the Colors of Darkness and Other Exotica
Changelings and Other Metamorphic Tales
A Clash of Symbols: The Triumph of James Blish
Complications and Other Stories
The Cosmic Perspective and Other Black Comedies
Creators of Science Fiction
The Cure for Love and Other Tales of the Biotech Revolution
The Devil's Party: A Brief History of Satanic Abuse
The Dragon Man: A Novel of the Future
The Eleventh Hour
Exotic Encounters: Selected Reviews
Firefly: A Novel of the Far Future
The Gardens of Tantalus and Other Delusions
Glorious Perversity: The Decline and Fall of Literary Decadence
Gothic Grotesques: Essays on Fantastic Literature
The Great Chain of Being and Other Tales of the Biotech Revolution
The Haunted Bookshop and Other Apparitions
Heterocosms: Science Fiction in Context and Practice
In the Flesh and Other Tales of the Biotech Revolution
The Innsmouth Heritage and Other Sequels
Jaunting on the Scoriac Tempests and Other Essays on Fantastic Literature
Kiss the Goat
The Moment of Truth: A Novel of the Future
Narrative Strategies in Science Fiction, and Other Essays on Imaginative Fiction
News of the Black Feast and Other Random Reviews
An Oasis of Horror: Decadent Tales and Contes Cruels
Opening Minds: Essays on Fantastic Literature
Outside the Human Aquarium: Masters of Science Fiction, Second Edition
The Plurality of Worlds: A Sixteenth-Century Space Opera
Prelude to Eternity: A Romance of the First Time Machine
The Return of the Djinn and Other Black Melodramas
Salome and Other Decadent Fantasies
Slaves of the Death Spiders and Other Essays on Fantastic Literature
The Sociology of Science Fiction
Space, Time, and Infinity: Essays on Fantastic Literature
The Tree of Life and Other Tales of the Biotech Revolution
The World Beyond: A Sequel to S. Fowler Wright's The World Below
Yesterday's Bestsellers: A Voyage Through Literary History

CREATORS OF SCIENCE FICTION

by

Brian Stableford

THE BORGO PRESS

An Imprint of Wildside Press LLC

MMX

I.O. Evans Studies in the Philosophy and Criticism of Literature
ISSN 0271-9061

Number Fifty

Copyright © 1995, 1996, 1997, 1998, 1999, 2002, 2010 by Brian Stableford

All rights reserved.
No part of this book may be reproduced in any form without the expressed written consent of the publisher.

www.wildsidebooks.com

FIRST EDITION

CONTENTS

About the Author 6
Introduction 7

Frankenstein and the Origins of Science Fiction 9
Edgar Allan Poe's "Sonnet to Science" 20
Camille Flammarion's *Lumen* 24
Jules Verne's *Journey to the Center of the Earth* 47
H. G. Wells and his Time Machines 54
Hugo Gernsback 62
John W. Campbell, Jr. 73
Edward E. "Doc" Smith 83
Robert A. Heinlein 93
James Blish 111
Gregory Benford 121
Bruce Sterling 140
Ian Watson 155

Bibliography 170
Index 186

ABOUT THE AUTHOR

BRIAN STABLEFORD was born in Yorkshire in 1948. He taught at the University of Reading for several years, but is now a full-time writer. He has written many science fiction and fantasy novels, including *The Empire of Fear*, *The Werewolves of London*, *Year Zero*, *The Curse of the Coral Bride*, *The Stones of Camelot* and *Prelude to Eternity*. Collections of his short stories include a long series of *Tales of the Biotech Revolution*, and such idiosyncratic items as *Sheena and Other Gothic Tales* and The *Innnsmouth Heritage and Other Sequels*. He has written numerous nonfiction books, including *Scientific Romance in Britain, 1890-1950*, *Glorious Perversity: The Decline and Fall of Literary Decadence*, *Science Fact and Science Fiction: An Encyclopedia* and *The Devil's Party: A Brief History of Satanic Abuse*. He has contributed hundreds of biographical and critical entries to reference books, including both editions of *The Encyclopedia of Science Fiction* and several editions of the library guide, *Anatomy of Wonder*. He has also translated numerous novels from the French language, including several by the feuilletonist Paul Féval and numerous classics of French scientific romance by such writers as Albert Robida, Maurice Renard, and J. H. Rosny the Elder.

INTRODUCTION

Creators of Science Fiction was a title I first used on an occasional series of articles published in the British magazine *Interzone* in 1996-98, following a request from the editor, David Pringle, who thought that it might be a good idea to introduce his readers to the history of the genre. His readers were far from unanimous in their response to the series, which was eventually abandoned. Because some of the articles have already been reprinted in earlier Borgo Press collections, or have too considerable an overlap with others that have been reprinted, only four are reproduced here; the article on E. E. "Doc" Smith was number 7 in the series and appeared in issue no. 111 (September 1996); the article on James Blish was number 8 and appeared in issue no. 117 (March 1997); the article on Hugo Gernsback was number 10 and appeared in issue no. 126 (December 1997); and the article on John W. Campbell Jr. was number 11, appearing in issue no. 133 (July 1998).

It was probably not surprising that many of the readers of *Interzone* in the late 1990s were not much interested in the history of the genre, simply because it had become impractical by that time to take such an interest in any reasonably comprehensive fashion, at least in Britain. It was much easier in the early 1960s, when I began to read sf avidly. At that time the labeled genre had only just reached the end of the phase of its evolution when it was largely contained in magazines; second-hand digest magazines were easy to come by and relatively cheap, and much of the significant work from the pulp magazines was in the process of being reprinted in paperback by such publishers as Ace. The British Science Fiction Association had a postal lending library that included both books and magazines, and Sam Moskowitz had published series of articles in the magazines about the most significant writers within the labeled genre and their most important precursors, which served as an elementary guide to the most interesting materials. Anyone prepared to devote the time could, therefore, familiarize themselves with the entire history of sf, as well as keeping up with newly-published material, within a decade. Thirty years later there was not only twice as much historical material to catch up on, but the availability of the earlier material had been considerably reduced; little of it was being reprinted, second-hand bookshops were in steep decline and the half of the BSFA library that had not been consumed by fire had been removed to the vaults of Liverpool University Library as the nucleus of the Science Fiction Foundation collection, available only on-site to accredited scholars.

Given all that, it is not obvious that this collection, which attempts to put the remaining articles from the original series into a broader context, reaching back to the origins of speculative fiction and forward to more contemporary material, can be of overmuch interest to anyone but earnest academics. Indeed, now that textual science fiction no longer exists as a popular genre—save as a vestigial appendix of a fantasy genre that is itself in terminal decline—it is not obvious that there will be any significant further interest outside the groves of Academe in any of the material covered herein. Even so, I feel entitled to hope that it might qualify as something more than a mere elegy, if only on the grounds that text constains imaginative possibilities that TV and cinema will never be able to duplicate, by virtue of their inability to go beyond appearances, and will therefore always constitute a unique resource for the comprehensively alienated. If the comprehensively alienated are not willing to learn to read, in the full sense of the term, who will be?

"Frankenstein and the Origins of Science Fiction" first appeared in *Anticipations: Essays on Early Science Fiction and its Precursors* ed. David Seed, published by Liverpool University Press in 1995. the article on Edgar Allan Poe's "Sonnet: To Science" is based on an article in *Masterplots II: Poetry Series Supplement* edited by John Wilson & Philip K. Jason, published by Salem Press in 1998. The article on Camille Flammarion's *Lumen* is derived from the introduction to my translation of that work, issued by Wesleyan University Press in 2002. The articles on Verne and Wells both adapt material from other articles, but neither has been published in their present form before, although the Wells aricle was once read at a "conference" accompanying an exhibiton of children's books in Paris. The remaining articles first appeared in *Science Fiction Writers, 2nd Edition* edited by Richard Bleiler, published by Scribner's in 1999.

FRANKENSTEIN AND THE ORIGINS OF SCIENCE FICTION

Frankenstein is one of those literary characters whose names has entered common parlance; everyone recognizes the name and uses it casually. The recognition and the usage are often slightly uncertain—most people know the name from the film versions, which are significantly different from the book, and some people have to be reminded that Frankenstein is the name of the scientist, not the monster that the scientist made—but this uncertainty is not entirely inappropriate to a work whose implication and significance are rather problematic.

The popularity of *Frankenstein*, both as a literary classic and as a fuzzy set of ideas, bears testimony to the remarkable vividness of Mary Shelley's vision, but it also reflects the protean quality of its central motifs, which can be interpreted in several different ways so as to carry several different messages. The most common modern view of the story—aided and perhaps sustained by Boris Karloff's remarkable performance in the 1941 film version and its sequels—is that it is an account of the way in which "monstrousness" arises, involving diseased brains, inadequate control over one's actions and resentment against the unthinking horror with which most people react to ugliness. The most common view based on the book alone sees it as an allegory in which a scientist is rightly punished for daring to usurp the divine prerogative of creation. A closely-related interpretation regards Victor Frankenstein as an archetypal example of a man destroyed by his own creation; in this view the story becomes a central myth of the kind of technophobia which argues that modern man is indeed doomed to be destroyed by his own artifacts—and that such a fate, however tragic, is not undeserved. There are, of course, more convoluted interpretations of the text to be found in the voluminous academic literature dealing with the story. Among the most widely-cited are accounts that see the story as a kind of protofeminist parable about the male usurpation of the female prerogative of reproduction, and accounts that see it as an allegory of the evolving relationship between the *ancien régime* and the emergent industrial working class.

So far as can be ascertained, Mary Shelley does not appear to have had any of these theses in mind when she wrote the book, but champions of these various meanings are usually content to interpret them as the result of a coincidence of inspirational forces in which the author's role was that of semi-conscious instrument. Support is lent to this view by the fact that Mary Shelley was only nineteen years old when she completed Frankenstein, and by the fact that all her other books—with the partial exception of the majestically lachrymose jeremiad *The Last Man* (1826)—failed to excite the contemporary audience and are now rarely read or studied. However, the fact remains that *Frankenstein* is one of the most powerful stories produced in the course of the last two centuries and that it has better claims than any other to have become a "modern myth" (whatever one understands by that phrase).

* * * * * * *

Frankenstein is often called a Gothic novel, on the grounds that the popular horror stories of its day mostly shared a set of characteristics which justified that label, but it ought not to be thus classified on the grounds of its contents. Despite certain similarities of method and tone, its subject matter is very different from that of the classic Gothic novels. Horace Walpole's definitive *The Castle of Otranto* (1795), Ann Radcliffe's *The Mysteries of Udolpho* (1794), Matthew Gregory Lewis's *The Monk* (1796), and Charles Maturin's *Melmoth the Wanderer* (1820) all involve sinister ancient edifices, evil conspiracies, hideous apparitions (invariably interpreted as supernatural, though sometimes ultimately rationalized), the threat of sexual violation, and intimations of incest. The pretence that *Frankenstein*—which employs none of these motifs—belongs to the Gothic subgenre serves mainly to obscure the remarkable originality of its own subject-matter, which is broader and more forward-looking.

Victor Frankenstein might be regarded as a distant literary cousin of the seemingly diabolical—or, at least, diabolically-inspired—villains of the classic Gothic novels, but his personality and his ambitions are very different. Although he takes some early inspiration from occult writings, of a kind that the inquisitorially-minded might regard as the devil's work, he undertakes a decisive change of direction when he decides that it is modern science, not ancient magic, that will open the portals of wisdom for scholars of his and future generations. By virtue of this move, *Frankenstein* began the exploration of imaginative territory into which no previous author had penetrated (although that was not its initial purpose). For this reason, the novel is more aptly discussed as a pioneering work of science fiction, albeit one that was written at least half a century before its time, and one that does considerable disservice to the image of science as an instrument of human progress.

It is entirely appropriate that Brian Aldiss should have worked so hard in *Billion Year Spree* to establish *Frankenstein* as the foundation-stone of the modern genre of science fiction; the underlying world-view of the novel entitles it to that position. Its only significant competitor in terms of content is Willem Bilderdijk's *A Short Account of a Remarkable Aerial Voyage and Discovery of a New Planet* (1813), which is far less plausible and was far less influential, remaining untranslated into English until 1989. (The third book of Jonathan Swift's *Travels into Several Remote Nations of the World by Lemuel Gulliver*, 1726, must be disqualified on the grounds that its vitriolic parody of the activity and ambitions of scientists alienates it completely from the kind of proto-scientific world-view that Mary Shelley was ready to embrace, albeit in desperately anxious fashion.) On the other hand, given the nature of the most common interpretations of the text, it is by no means surprising that Isaac Asimov should have felt that the technophilic optimism of his own work—which was, of course, central to the historical development of genre science fiction—was framed in frank opposition to a "Frankenstein complex". The central myth of *Frankenstein* seemed to Asimov to be an ideative monster, which had to be slain by heroic and sinless robots for the benefit of future generations.

Ambivalent attitudes to science are not particularly unusual in works of speculative fiction. A great deal of the fiction nowadays categorized as science fiction is horrific, and much of it is born of a fear, or even a deep-seated hatred, of the scientific world-view, whose acknowledged intellectual triumph over older concepts of natural order seems to many observers to be unedifying and undesirable. Give this, it would not necessarily be inappropriate to trace the origins of the genre back to a science-hating ancestor—but it is not at all clear that the author of *Frankenstein* set out with the intention of attacking or scathingly criticizing the endeavors of science, even though many modern readers think that the text carries a bitterly critical moral.

Mary Shelley's life story suggests strongly that she was not the kind of person who might be expected to produce an anti-scientific parable. Her actions and the opinions she held in the years which led up to the writing of Frankenstein were such that one suspects that she might have been rather distressed to discover that so many readers interpreted her work in that way, although it must be admitted that she did little to discourage such an interpretation. If, however, one assumes that she had no such intention, there remains the problem of explaining how and why the book turned out to have such a semblance at all.

The full title that Mary Shelley gave to *Frankenstein* is *Frankenstein; or, The Modern Prometheus*. In attempting to assess the significance of this choice it is necessary to bear in mind her beloved husband's fascination with the character of Prometheus. To a committed atheist like Percy Shelley, Prometheus was a great hero whose condemnation to be chained to a rock throughout eternity while eagles came daily to devour his perpetually-regenerated liver was firm proof of the horrid unreasonableness and downright wickedness of godly tyrants. Shelley knew quite well that the atheism he proclaimed so loudly and the free love that he and Mary preached and practiced so brazenly were—in the eyes of his enemies—tantamount to Satanism, but like William Blake before him he was fully prepared to champion Satan himself, let alone the safely-obsolete Prometheus, as a revolutionary light-bearer unjustly slandered and condemned by a monstrous God. To Percy Shelley—and to Mary too, at least while Percy lived—no modern Prometheus could possibly be reckoned a villain, and any terrible fate a modern Prometheus might meet must be reckoned as a tragedy, not an exercise of any kind of justice, divine or otherwise.

Given all this, it is unlikely in the extreme that a book that Mary Shelley elected to call *The Modern Prometheus* was planned as an assault on the hubris of scientists, or as a defense of divine prerogative. It is true that Mary Shelley added a new introduction to the revised edition of the book issued in 1831, in which she seemed not unsympathetic to the demonization of Frankenstein, and also to the notion that she had been a mere instrument of creative forces for whose produce she was not to be held responsible, but this was nine years after Percy Shelley's death—which circumstance had forced her to compromise and make her peace with all the tyrannies of convention that he was able to despise and defy quite openly. (In Victorian times, even the most determinedly heroic woman had far less leeway than a man.) Even if the 1831 introduction can be reckoned sincere—and it almost certainly cannot—it must be reckoned the work of a person who bears much the same relation to the author of *Frankenstein* as the humbled Napoleon who came back from Moscow bore to the all-conquering hero who had set out.

The fact remains, however, that whether Frankenstein's fate was intended to be an awful warning to scientists or not, it certainly looks that way. How could this have come about?

* * * * * * *

The text of *Frankenstein* begins with a series of letters written by the explorer Robert Walton, who has been trying to navigate his ship through the Arctic ice in the hope of finding a warm continent beyond it, akin to the legendary Hyperborea. Modern readers know full well that this was a fool's errand, but that was not at all certain in 1818. Thus, although Walton's situation is clearly symbolic—one of the Gothic conventions that *Frankenstein* does adopt is that the weather is symbolic of human emotion, so his entrapment in the ice signifies that Walton's noble ambitions have unfortunately alienated him from the warmth of human companionship—it should not be taken for granted that Mary Shelley saw him as a lunatic who should have known better. Nor should we assume that Walton's encounter with Victor Frankenstein, who is similarly lost in the ice-field, and in whom Walton recognizes a kindred spirit, was, in her eyes, a meeting of damned men.

Victor's story, as regretfully told to Walton, is essentially that of a man who once had "everything" but lost what he had through desiring even more. The "everything" that he had included material goods, but its most precious aspects were friendship and love, embodied in his relationships with Henry Clerval and his cousin Elizabeth. He explains that his ambitions became inflated when he left home for university, where he became enamored of the grandiose dreams of Renaissance magicians like Paracelsus and Cornelius Agrippa. One of his teachers dismissed this fascination with frank contempt, but another pointed out that modern scientists were beginning to achieve results even more marvelous than those which the optimists and charlatans of earlier eras had claimed. Victor then made his crucial intellectual move, turning his attention to science—specifically to the science of electricity, the "vital fluid" whose implication in the mechanics of muscular movement had recently been demonstrated—as a possible means of achieving an unprecedented victory over the greatest of all tyrants: death.

(It is worth noting here that Mary Shelley, even at the tender age of nineteen, had good cause to be preoccupied with the oppressions of this particular tyrant. Her mother's glittering intellectual career had been cut short when she died shortly after bearing Mary, and Mary's first child by Shelley had already died before the fateful night at the Villa Diodati that set in train the sequence of events that ultimately led to the writing of *Frankenstein*. The death of Shelley's first wife Harriet—who drowned, probably by suicidal design, while Mary was engaged in the writing of the book—freed Shelley so that he and Mary could marry. This last episode presumably added an uncomfortably guilty ambivalence to her preoccupation with mortality.)

Victor explains to Walton that, while he was completing his experiments in resurrection, he became withdrawn and intellectually isolated, no longer able to find any joy in social intercourse. This process reached a frightful climax when the work was finally complete; the patchwork man that he had made had only to open a cold eye for Victor to be suddenly overcome by repulsion at what he had wrought. When the monster departed in confusion, Victor gladly reverted to type, renewing his relationships with his friend and his family—who gratefully nursed him back to health when he fell terribly ill.

One of the more ingenious academic interpretations of the plot suggests that, from this point onwards, much—if not all—of what Victor tells Walton is a chronicle of hallucinations, and that the monster who subsequently appears to him is a projection of his own personality: his own *doppelgänger*. Although this is, at least superficially, the most bizarre of the various academic reinterpretations, its adherents rightly point out that it makes condiserably more sense than a literal interpretation of the puzzling events that follow in Victor's narrative.

When Victor's young brother is murdered, Victor becomes afraid—and later becomes quite certain—that the monster is the murderer, and yet he proves curiously ineffective in preventing the wrongful conviction of an entirely innocent servant. The apparent immorality of this inaction is so striking as to have convinced some readers that Victor himself must be the true murderer, and that his subsequent account of the monster's activities, like his failure to speak up for the servant, is a pathological denial of his own guilt. Although this interpretation is certainly over-ingenious as an account of the author's intentions, and does not sit well with the conclusion of the story, it must be admitted that the monster's story is hardly more credible, and that the monster's explanation of his own motivation is, in its way, every bit as peculiar.

The monster tells Victor that he too has craved the fellowship and love that provided a safe refuge for the sick scientist, but that it was denied him absolutely. He was rejected by his creator at the moment of his first awakening, and was subsequently reviled by everyone who caught sight of him; even his desperate attempt to make a home with a blind man has inevitably come to nothing. It was, he claims, the madness born of this rejection that led him to kidnap a child, and the revelation that the child was the brother of his creator that drove him to murderous frenzy. In consequence of all this, the monster demands that a companion be made for him, given that he is too repulsive to be accepted into the community of men.

Victor initially agrees to this request, and sets out to accomplish it on a remote islet in the Orkneys, but he is no longer insulated by obsession, and becomes terrified of the thought that he is giving birth to an entire race of monsters, whose co-existence with mankind will be—to say the least—problematic. This prospect causes him to abandon the work, and no immediate repercussions ensue. In time, though, the monster sets out to exact his revenge, not upon Victor himself but upon his friends and loved ones. First Clerval is murdered—Victor is charged with the crime but eventually acquitted—and then, on her and Victor's wedding-night, Elizabeth. Isolated once again by these deprivations, Victor has little difficulty recovering the motive force of obsession, but this time his obsession is to rid the world of his creation.

All of this is mere hearsay, so far as Robert Walton is concerned, and too fantastic to be believed—at least at first. Victor explains to Walton that it is the consequent pursuit of the monster has led him into the Arctic wastes; he looks to Walton for aid, but when he learns that his host has already turned back from his own quest, and is now heading out of the ice-field, he realizes that he cannot carry through his purpose. He gives up and dies. The final confrontation with the monster—the only corroborative evidence of his actual existence—is left to Walton, and might simply be one more hallucination. At any rate, Walton finds Victor's adversary every bit as fearful as Victor led him to expect—but also confused, agonized and contrite.

One of the few books the monster has had the opportunity to read since he learned the uses of language by secretly observing a family at work and play is Goethe's Romantic classic *The Sorrows of Young Werther*, which waxes lyrical about the appropriateness of suicide as a solution for those bereft of any meaningful connection with their fellows, and it is hardly surprising that the monster, whether he is real or not, chooses to continue into the wilderness of the Arctic ice. "I am content to suffer alone while my sufferings shall endure," the monster says, regretfully, "when I die, I am well satisfied that abhorrence and opprobrium should load my memory."

Neither he nor his author could not possibly have guessed how prophetic these words would prove to be.

****

We are nowadays familiar with the circumstances of *Frankenstein*'s genesis, on the stormy night on which Lord Byron, Percy and Mary Shelley, Claire Clairmont, and Dr. Polidori amused themselves at the Villa Diodati by reading tales from a volume entitled *Fantasmagoriana*, which consisted of horror stories translated from German into French. They subsequently agreed that each of them would write a horrific tale of his or her own—although Polidori was the only one apart from Mary to produce anything substantial, and that was eventually published under circumstances that caused considerable embarrassment to him (and, of course, to Byron, to whom the work was at first falsely attributed).

The significance of the story's first inspiration to an understanding of the construction of *Frankenstein* is that its author was charged from the very beginning with the task of writing a horror story. The particular horror story she settled on grew from a fragment of an actual nightmare she experienced soon afterwards. If Mary's later claim is to be believed—and there seems no reason to doubt it—this nightmare displayed to her a creator's first and direly uncomfortable confrontation with his creation.

Thus, Mary did not begin the work of ideative elaboration with the premise of her story, but with its crucial image. The beginning and the end of the story are both extrapolations of that single instant, the one constructed in order to explain how it came about and the other to follow it to its implicit conclusion. Both are consistent, to a degree, with the visionary moment, but they are not really consistent with one another, in the way that they would have been had the author extrapolated an ending from the apparent premises contained in the beginning. Because the fact that the story was to be horrific was accepted as an axiom, much of what was eventually presented as the logic of the story—the "explanation" of how the nightmare confrontation came to take place—was formed by way of ideative apology, not as a set of propositions to be examined on their own merits.

Given all this, it is not entirely surprising that the logical patchwork leading to the true point of origination is somewhat ill-fitting. Had the author actually started to make up a story about a "modern Prometheus" she would surely have come up with something very different; that first awakening of the resurrected man might have been a joyous and triumphant affair, had it not been already set in place as the horrific *raison d'être* of the whole exercise. Alas for the modern Prometheus, his endeavor was damned before he was even thought of, let alone characterized.

The reason Mary made poor Victor Frankenstein a scientist, therefore, had nothing to do with a desire to comment on science as an endeavor. It was simply the result of wanting to do something different from the Gothic novels of supernatural horror that already become tedious and passé. The preface to the first edition, which was probably written by Percy Shelley on his wife's behalf, treads a delicate argumentative line in speaking of such matters. "I am by no means indifferent to the manner in which whatever moral tendencies exist in the sentiments or characters it contains shall affect the reader," 'Mary' says, "yet my chief concern in this respect has been limited to avoiding the enervating effects of the novels of the present day and to the exhibition of the amiableness of domestic affection, and the excellence of universal virtue". 'She' further insists that "the opinions which naturally spring from the character and situation of the hero are by no means to be conceived as existing always in my own conviction; nor is any inference justly to be drawn from the following pages as prejudicing any philosophical doctrine of whatever kind."

There is certainly some self-protective rationalization here—the author of the preface is shrewdly anticipating and trying cleverly to deflect the charge that the book promotes atheism—but 'she' is not trying nearly so hard to do that as she was later to attempt in the 1831 introduction, and it must be noted that "any philosophical doctrine whatsoever" includes science as well as religion.

If the build-up to the moment of confrontation between creator and creation is a fairly haphazard rationalization, then so is the subsequent unfolding of that horrific moment in the later pages of *Frankenstein*. What happens in the remainder of the novel makes little sense—rationally or morally—precisely because the horror of that moment can never be undermined or reduced, and thus can never undergo any kind of imaginative transformation, no matter how hard the unfortunate monster tries to find a solution. The machinery of the plot remains totally subordinate to that instant of revulsion, and revulsion remains the inescapable condition of the key characters, no matter how they may regret it. Victor and the monster are sealed within it and united by it, all possible avenues of escape being ruled out by the fact that theirs is, essentially and definitively, a horror story. It is only to be expected that the narrative expansion of the crucial moment should seem to some readers to be akin to a hallucination—especially to the kind of hallucination that allegedly packs a lifetime into the space of a single incident.

Thus, while the long prelude that precedes and sets up the visionary moment invents—more-or-less by accident—the modern genre of science fiction, the long coda that follows and expands upon it constitutes—again more-or-less by accident—a giant leap for the not-so-modern genre of delusional fantasy, which had recently been invented by E. T. A. Hoffmann. This double triumph assured that the book would become a landmark in the evolution of modern imaginative fiction as well as a popular success. It *is* a landmark, because rather than in spite of its inherent internal contradictions—because of its struggle to be something other than it is. It is a great book precisely because its author could not and would not settle for writing an ordinary book, which would hang together by reproducing some familiar pattern of clichés.

* * * * * * *

It would, of course, be foolish to regret that *Frankenstein* is the kind of book it is, or to wish that Mary Shelley had written another book instead. Life being what it is, we have to be grateful for whatever we have, and *Frankenstein*-the-novel is a book well worth having even if Frankenstein-the-myth is a nest of viperish ideas we could well do without. Given, however, that *Frankenstein* is a pioneering work of science fiction, it might be appropriate to wonder what Mary Shelley—doubtless with Percy's active encouragement and assistance—might have achieved had she decided, once the beginning of the story had been written, to cease taking it for granted that what she was writing was a horror story and cast aside the nightmarish seed.

So let us, briefly, wonder....

What if the scientific miracle that Victor Frankenstein had wrought had been allowed to be an authentic miracle, and the resurrected man no monster at all?

What if the monster, in spite of his ugliness, had been allowed to win the respect of others with his intelligence and moral sensibility? (Perhaps, like Remy de Gourmont after his face had been ruined by discoid lupus, he might have become a recluse illuminating the world with the wise produce of his pen!)

What if Victor, and Mary, had been allowed to proclaim that a Promethean man of science—a bringer of energetic fire and a creator of new life—would be the greatest benefactor imaginable by man, and that the day of such fire-bringers and creators was indeed at hand?

What if Victor, and Mary, had boldly proclaimed that there are no divine prerogatives except willful ignorance and vile intolerance, that the produce of scientific creativity ought not to be feared by religious men, nor by feminists, nor by political conservatives, and that such fear is merely the unreasoning electrical reflex of blinkered fools?

What if Mary had attached to her vivid romance the moral that Percy's preface would surely have delighted in celebrating: the moral that the only hope men have for any kind of salvation is that they might find the technological means to redeem themselves from every kind of earthly damnation?

What then?

The overwhelming probability, sad to say, is that such a book could never have been published in 1818. It would have been considered so horribly indecent and blasphemous that anyone who so much as read the manuscript would have screamed in horror. We may be reasonably confident of this conclusion because, sad to say, it is far easier, even today, to publish and find an appreciative audience for the ten thousandth rip-off of *Frankenstein* (*Jurassic Park*, to name but one example) than it is to publish and find an appreciative audience for the kind of novel that *Frankenstein* really should have been. The modern Prometheus remains a prophet without honor in his own country.

This is, in its way, a tragedy—a tragedy that has caught up in its toils the entire genre of science fiction descended, however inappropriately, from *Frankenstein*. The great bulk of modern science fiction still grows, by means of dubious patchworks of apologetic 'logic', from moments of nightmarish vision born of fear and dyspepsia, and fails to work the kind of imaginative alchemy that would be necessary to transform those moments of nightmare into something saner.

Let us be clear, though, about one thing: it was not our mad technological monsters that made the world the way it is, and murdered so many of the things which we ought to hold dear; it was us. To think otherwise is a delusion that might easily possess us until we are irredeemably lost in the icy wilderness of our own moral cowardice.

Mary Shelley knew that. It is a pity that those who are heir to the perverse produce of her imagination mostly do not.

EDGAR ALLAN POE'S SONNET TO SCIENCE

"Sonnet—to Science" was the earliest of all Poe's published works. In his later collections it appears with a footnote describing it as one of "the crude compositions of my earliest boyhood". The same footnote excuses its republication with reference to "private reasons—some of which have reference to the sin of plagiarism, and others to the date of Tennyson's first poems." Alfred, Lord Tennyson had been born in the same year as Poe and had also published his first volume of poetry, *Poems by Two Brothers* (in association with his brother Charles), in 1827.

The sonnet's rhyme-scheme follows the English, or Shakespearean, form rather than the Italian, or Petrarchan, form. Its substance, by contrast, has more in common with the Italian tradition, which characteristically involves the posing of a question, than with the English tradition, which tends to be more meditative. Where the Petrarchan sonnet would usually supplement an interrogatory octave with a responsive sestet, however, "Sonnet—to Science" maintains its enquiring tone throughout the three quatrains and the concluding couplet.

"Sonnet—to Science" addresses its object from a point of view solidly anchored within the Romantic Movement, likening science's keen-eyed inquiry to a vulture whose wings cast a shadow of "dull reality" upon the landscape of the imagination. It asks how the poet, having discovered such a predator "upon [his] heart" can possibly love the scientific revelation or concede its wisdom. It is only natural, the sonnet suggests, that poets should flee the shadow of dull reality in search of better and brighter pastures, lit by "jewelled skies".

The last six lines of the sonnet add detail to the charges laid in more general terms in the first eight. Like a prosecutor engaged in cross-examination the sonnet demands an accounting of specific sins. Has science not dragged Diana (a Roman goddess associated with nature and birth) from her "car"? (Diana was associated in Rome itself with moonlight, so the car in question is the moon.) Has not the Hamadryad (a type of nymph associated with oak trees) been "driven...from the wood" and the Naiad (a species of water-nymph) from her "blood"—the blood in question being the stream or spring embodying her spirit? Has science not banished the Elfin—the Anglo-Saxon fairy race—from its pastoral haunts? And has it not, in consequence, robbed the poet of the "summer dream" that might otherwise have visited him in the shade of the tamarind tree?

The accusative tone of these questions implies that they are rhetorical—that they do not actually require an answer, because it is obvious that each and every charge is correct. The fact remains, however, that no answer is given, and that the questions *are* questions rather than statements. The poem preserves a margin of uncertainty, which the poet's voice invites the reader to share. "Sonnet—to Science" is a poem that seeks to address a problem, and thus to define the problem's nature. As might be expected of a poem composed at the outset of an adventurous career, it is essentially open-ended. It is setting out an agenda rather than delivering a verdict.

Toward the end of his life, Poe was to expand greatly on his perception of the problem posed in "Sonnet—to Science" in the long poetic essay *Eureka* (1848). *Eureka* protests against the reductionist method of science while celebrating the magnificence of its revelations. Like "Sonnet—to Science", *Eureka*'s first concern was the astronomers who had dethroned Diana and the other deities embodied in the Heavens, but there remains a sense in which "Sonnet—to Science" was the more prophetic work, in that it proceeds to pay more attention to the disenchanting effects of biological science. Although Poe was well aware, in his later years, that he had been born in the same year as Tennyson, he might not have been conscious of the fact that he had also been born in the same year as Charles Darwin, whose theory of evolution was not published until ten years after Poe's death. It was Darwin's science that finally picked the bones of mythology clean, extrapolating in the process Tennyson's key image of "nature red in tooth and claw," contained in *In Memoriam* (1850).

Whether or not he was aware of Charles Darwin, however, Poe would certainly have been aware of his grandfather, Erasmus Darwin (1731-1802), who was renowned in his own day as a poet as well as a naturalist. Erasmus Darwin frequently reported his scientific discoveries in poetic form, and his earlier publications—including the collection reprinted as *The Loves of the Plants* (1789)—

were not ashamed to formulate such discoveries as news conveyed by nymphs and elemental spirits. The imagery of "Sonnet—to Science" implies a stark contrast between myth and science—a frank enmity, expressed in the violence with which it treats Diana and the dispossessed nymphs—but the implication is more tentative than it may seem.

By choosing the metaphor of a shadow-casting wing to represent science, Poe admits—and then re-emphasizes in the vital eighth line—that science has its own soaring imagination, and its own admirable courage. The first line, too, concedes that science is a "true daughter of Old Time", the time in question being that which brings self-knowledge and reveals previously-hidden truths—and perhaps also the time that heals wounds.

The concessions of the first and eighth lines would be more generous, of course, were it not for the fact that the shadow-casting wing of science is attached to a vulture: a bird of ill-omen more disreputable even than a raven. The third line makes it explicit, however, that Poe conceives science as a predator, not as a scavenger, and this is re-emphasized in the second part of the poem. Science drags, drives, and tears; it does not sit around waiting for myth to die of natural causes. It is, in fact, more like an eagle than a vulture. There is a hesitation here, if not an outright ambiguity.

Even in this early work, Poe seems to have been considering—albeit a little reluctantly—the possibility that he might align himself with those Romantics who celebrated the awesome revelations of the scientific imagination (among whom Percy Shelley was the most outstanding) rather than those who viewed the intellectual and industrial revolutions with mournful regret. He never did resolve that dilemma, and that was greatly to the advantage of his work. No other nineteenth century American writer fled as far as he "to seek for treasure in the jewelled skies"—and the flight in question began in the poem that follows "Sonnet—to Science" in his collected works: the brilliantly bizarre "Al Aaraaf".

The first footnote to "Al Aaraaf" links it to Tycho Brahe's "new star", which revealed once and for all that the Heavens were not fixed and finished, but the imagery of the long poem is as rich and exotic as anything Poe was later to produce. Other footnotes set classical references and scientific references side by side, but not as Erasmus Darwin might have done. Poe never lost the sense of a vital and violent struggle between the hallowed glories of mythology and the new revelations of science; he never could combine the two without a keen awareness that he was doing something paradoxical—but Poe was a very paradoxical man, and took pride in it. He conceived of his own self as something deeply divided, echoed that division in many of the characters with whom he populated his phantasmagoric tales, and saw it reflected in the war between Science and Romance for possession of the modern imagination.

"Sonnet—to Science" is a very modest poem by comparison with the works for which Poe is best remembered. It lacks all trace of the greatness of his best work, and might be held to have little merit by any standards, but it is certainly an interesting poem, both in the context of its time and in the context of the career which grew from it. Even as a teenager, Poe was aware of the overarching importance of the march of science, and was concerned to calculate its costs and rewards. "Sonnet—to Science" emphasizes the costs, but does not do so blindly or blandly; it has intelligence enough to acknowledge that the imaginative predations of science are not without a certain grandeur, as well as an ominous inevitability.

In answer to his own not-quite-rhetorical questions, Poe subsequently decided that, if science was neither lovable nor entirely wise, then the duty of the poet was to take arms against it and fight for the conservation of the Elfin and their Classical analogues, even if that meant establishing reservations far beyond the well-trodden bounds of the contemporary imagination. The heroic quality of that mission was never properly appreciated in his native land, where non-believers in science and technology preferred to besiege themselves within the sullen walls of religious fundamentalism. In the lands where the fugitive Elfin and the Dianic mysteries were still remembered, however, and their force still felt, Poe's progress from sonnet to epic—specifically, from "Sonnet—to Science" to *Eureka*, via the most scenic route imaginable—has been celebrated with all appropriate reverence.

CAMILLE FLAMMARION'S *LUMEN*

Nicolas Camille Flammarion was born on 25 February 1842 at Montigny-la-Roi in the Haut-Marne. His father had formerly been a farmer, but a series of financial misfortunes had reduced him to keeping a shop. Camille was apparently something of a child prodigy, forming an interest in astronomy at a very early age, fascinated by his observation of a solar eclipse on 9 October 1847. He observed a second eclipse on 28 July 1851, and contrived to retain a certain child-like sense of wonder in his contemplation of the starry firmament for the rest of his life.

He began to record his astronomical and meteorological observations at the age of eleven and began to write voluminously in his teens—another habit that remained with him indefinitely. The family's continuing financial difficulties caused them to move to Paris in 1856, where Camille was apprenticed to an engraver. He continued his studies in amateur astronomy alongside assiduous attempts to increase his education, and by the time he was sixteen had produced an unpublished "Voyage extatique aux régions lunaires, correspondence d'un philosophe adolescent" [A Visionary Journey to the Regions of the Moon, related by an adolescent philosopher] and a 500-page manuscript modestly entitled *Cosmologie Universelle* [Universal Cosmology], a version of which eventually saw print in 1885 as *Le Monde avant le création de l'homme* [The World Before the Creation of Humankind]. The latter was noticed by a physician called to treat him, who was sufficiently impressed to recommend the young man to Urbain Le Verrier (1811-1877), who was then in charge of the Paris Observatoire.

Le Verrier accepted Flammarion as an assistant, putting him to work in the Bureau des Calculs. Flammarion did not find this routine work to his taste, and was frustrated by the lack of opportunity to make his own observations; thus, when the publication of *La Pluralité des mondes habités* [The Plurality of Habitable Worlds] in 1862 gave him hope that he might be able to make a living as a writer, he left. Advertised by its subtitle as a study of the conditions of habitability of the planets in the solar system from the viewpoints of astronomy, physiology and natural philosophy, *La Pluralité des mondes habités* was a very successful work—it went through thirteen more editions in the next thirty years—and Flammarion also became a frequent contributor to several periodicals, but he could not support himself adequately on his writing income and he obtained a position in the Bureau des Longitudes, which allowed him to make further use of his experience as a calculator.

Flammarion did not allow his duties at the Bureau to impede his literary production. He may well have seen his next book, *Les Habitants de l'autre monde; révélations d'outre-tombe* [The Inhabitants of the Other World: Revelations of the Afterlife] (2 vols., 1862-63) as a companion-piece to its predecessor—he had met Allan Kardec, the French founder of "psychic research" while researching *La Pluralité des mondes habités*—but he must soon have been apprised of the fact that reporting alleged revelations from beyond the grave channeled by a spiritualist medium (Mademoiselle Huet) would not do his scientific career any good. His next book of the same kind, *Des Forces naturelles inconnues* [Unknown Natural Forces] (1865) was initially issued under the pseudonym Hermès, but he abandoned such subterfuges thereafter. He was always careful, however, to make it clear that his interest in psychic research was that of an open-minded scientific researcher; he was not a follower of the Spiritualist faith, and refused to consider the texts he produced during his experiments in automatic writing as anything other than the product of his own imagination.

Flammarion followed up his first work of speculative science with *Les Mondes imaginaires et les mondes réels* [Real and Imaginary Worlds] (1864). The first part of the book was a revisitation of the various worlds in the solar system, supplemented with a speculative note about planets illuminated by double stars, but the second was a thoroughgoing historical and critical survey of mythological, philosophical and literary speculations about the inhabitants of the planets and stars. His scientific work of this period included work for the *Annuaire de cosmos* [Cosmic Yearbook], and he began his own *Annuaire astronomique et météorologique* [Astronomical and Meteorological Yearbook], initially in *Le Magasin pittoresque* [The Illustrated Magazine].

Although he constructed a telescope of his own in 1866, Flammarion returned to the Observatoire in 1867 to take part in a project observing and mapping double stars. He also continued his meteorological observations, undertaking many balloon flights in order to observe atmospheric phenomena at closer range, resulting in his pioneering study of *L'atmosphère* [The Atmosphere] (1871). He continued, in the meantime, to produce popular articles and books with increasing rapidity, taking in vulcanology and climatology as well as astronomy. He was a frequent contributor to such periodicals as *Le Cosmos, L'Intransigéant* and *Le Siècle*.

Flammarion's greatest success as a popularizer of science came in 1880 when the publishing company in which his younger brother Ernest (1846-1936) had become a partner in 1875 issued his paradigmatic guide-book for amateur astronomers, *Astronomie populaire* [Popular Astronomy]. One admirer of his work, Monsieur Meret, was moved to make him a present of an estate in Juvisy-sur-Orge twenty miles south of Paris, to which Flammarion and his wife of eight years, Sylvie, moved in 1882. They constructed a new telescope there to facilitate his work. All these projects proved to be enduring: the Flammarion publishing firm still exists; the *Astronomie populaire* was continually updated by other hands after Flammarion's death; and the Juvisy telescope is still operational. Flammarion also founded the journal *L'Astronomie* [Astronomy], which took over his *Annuaire astronomique et météorologique* and became the definitive periodical for amateur astronomers. In 1887 he combined forces with other interested parties to found the Societé Astronomique de France, another organization that persists to the present day. The Societé supervised the construction of the first telescope for the use of the general public in the Latin Quarter of Paris.

Flammarion's most important endeavors in the popularization of science include a study of *La planète Mars et ses conditions d'habitabilité* [The Planet Mars and the Conditions of its Habitability] (1892; expanded edition 1909) which collated all observations of the planet made since 1636, including his own discovery (in 1876) of the seasonal changes affecting the dark regions—an observation as significant in its way as the "canali" publicized in 1877 by Schiaparelli. Even before the outbreak of the Great War of 1914-18, however, he had begun to concentrate his efforts increasingly on his studies in psychical research, holding regular séances at Juvisy in parallel with his astronomical observations. The famous Italian medium Eusapia Palladino was one of many who performed there, but he also entertained such visiting scientists as the American astronomer Percival Lowell.

After the war—which put an abrupt end to the continual reprinting of his early works—such new work as Flammarion published was almost all in the field of psychic research; the three volumes of *La Mort et son mystère* [Death and its Mystery] appeared between

1920 and 1922, and *Les Maisons hantées, en marge de la mort et son mystère* [Haunted Houses: On the Margin of Death and its Mystery] in 1923. Flammarion was deeply affected by the horrific casualties inflicted by the war—as was the English speculative writer Sir Arthur Conan Doyle, who became his friend after developing a similar interest in spiritualism—and his observations at Juvisy became something of a refuge from the world after 1918. He died there on 4 June 1925. His second wife Gabrielle—whom he had married in 1919—continued his work thereafter, assuming responsibility for further updates of the *Astronomie populaire*, which was by then his only work that retained substantial popular interest.

* * * * * * *

Although Camille Flammarion was not the first writer urged by a fervent missionary zeal to make the revelations of science available to ordinary readers, the sheer extravagance of his production—in terms of ambition as well as quantity—made him the figurehead of a growing movement of amateur and popular science. His journeywork as a cataloguer of stars, on the other hand, was soon absorbed into the ever-growing database of astronomical knowledge; like many another assiduous collector of data who never happened upon a particular discovery of charismatic quality or talismanic significance, he would soon have faded into obscurity had his name not been so widely advertised by his popularizations.

Much of Flammarion's work for periodicals was hastily-composed, and many of his books give the impression of being first drafts. Although he continually revised his most popular works as they went through consecutive editions, he almost invariably did so by inserting extra text rather than by rewriting existing chapters, further emphasizing an unfortunate tendency to repetition and only rarely contriving any stylistic improvement. He was never content to employ a useful metaphor or narrative device only once; certain key images and arguments recur throughout his work, appearing again and again with relatively little modification. These tendencies do, however, go with the territory; if Flammarion's career is compared with the heroic endeavors of such twentieth century popularizers of science as Isaac Asimov and Arthur C. Clarke one can easily find points of similarity in terms of method and idiosyncrasy as well as missionary enthusiasm.

Flammarion worked harder than any other man of his day to make the revelations of science accessible to ordinary readers, experimenting with every narrative device he could imagine in order to make his communications more effective. Although his reputation within the scientific community suffered, partly because of his success as a popularizer, partly because of his fondness for flights of wild fancy, and partly because of his unceasing attempts to apply the scientific method to studies in what would now be called the "paranormal", he did more to prepare the way for public acceptance of the cosmic perspectives of modern science than any other nineteenth century writer. The scope of his imagination was inevitably restricted by the limitations of the scientific knowledge on which he drew (especially in biology), but no one else matched his imaginative avidity or audacity.

In doing everything that he could to make people aware of a vast universe potentially filled with habitable worlds, whose life-forms must—by virtue of being adapted to different physical circumstances—be radically different from those found on Earth, Flammarion anticipated much of the substance of modern science fiction and helped lay the groundwork for its development. He was, however, writing at a time when the literary method of modern science fiction had not yet been perfected; the fact that his primary interest was in the didactic potential of his work directed him away from the story-forms that were to be developed by Jules Verne and H. G. Wells towards such hybrid formats as the philosophical dialogue and the dream-journey, and towards such artificial devices as crediting hypothetical intelligence and a voice to inanimate objects or symbolic figures. For this reason, most of Flammarion's adventures in speculative fiction seem to the modern reader to lie in an awkward grey area between fiction and non-fiction.

Although his early *voyage extatique* was his first experiment in romance, Flammarion first began to publish didactic fiction in popular magazines in the mid-1860s. *Lumen* is of particular interest to historians of science fiction not only because it comprises his first serious endeavor of this kind but also because it remained his boldest. It set out to dramatize the ideative content of two of his earliest works—*La Pluralité des mondes habités* and *Dieu dans la nature* [God in Nature] (1867)—but changed direction in mid-stream to take aboard a third: the translation he made in 1869 of Humphry Davy's *Consolations in Travel* (1830). *Lumen* is a manifestly shaky start to the business of constructing didactic fictions, the various "récits" (actually dialogues) comprising it having been composed in three separate batches between 1866 and 1869, but once the text finally hit its stride, it enabled Flammarion to produce a new and truly spectacular vision of the universe, which laid the groundwork for an entire tradition of modern visionary fantasy.

Lumen's first book publication was in the collection *Récits de l'infini* (1872; translated as *Stories of Infinity*, 1873), where it was supplemented by his next two endeavors of a similar kind: "Histoire d'une comète" (1869; tr. as "The History of a Comet"), which views episodes in the history of the Earth from the viewpoint of Halley's Comet; and "Dans l'infini" (1872; tr. as "In Infinity"), which describes the decoding of a cryptic communication from the spirit world. *Lumen* was first issued separately in 1887, although it also continued to feature in new editions of *Récits de l'infini*, which had attained its thirteenth edition by 1892. The final version of the French text—which incorporated some new material composed for the 1897 English translation—was a separate edition that was reprinted several times more before 1914 (its final printing was advertised as "seventieth thousand", presumably counting editions of *Récits de l'infini* as well as separate editions).

* * * * * * *

The record of *Lumen*'s predecessors is comprehensively set out in the second part of *Les Mondes imaginaires et les mondes réels*. Thanks to this essay, we know the titles of almost all the relevant works that Flammarion had read before setting out to write *Lumen* in 1866, and can easily judge the extent of their impact on his imagination and influence on his method.

The first two chapters of this critical review are a survey of ideas contained in oriental and occidental mythologies, while the third covers the development of theological and mystical images of the universe in the first millennium of the Christian era. The fourth moves from Thomas Aquinas's *Summa Theologica* to the literary images of Dante, Ariosto and Rabelais, by way of the speculations of Nicholas of Cusa. Chapter Five describes the Copernican revolution, and the significance of such supporters thereof as Giordano Bruno, Montaigne and Galileo. It includes a description of John Kepler's *Somnium* (1634), a visionary fantasy that attempts to make the Copernican system accessible to the imagination by describing cosmic events as an observer on the moon would see them—and which digresses, in its final pages, to address the question of what lunar life might be like, given the necessity of its adaptation to extraordinarily long days and nights.

The sixth and seventh chapters are devoted to imaginary voyages to the moon, including those of Francis Godwin and Cyrano de Bergerac, and such speculative essays as the 1640 supplement to John Wilkins' *Discovery of a World in the Moon* (1638) and Pierre

Borel's *Discours nouveau prouvant le pluralité des mondes* (whose composition date Flammarion gives as 1647, although it was not published until 1657). From Cyrano's bold (but unfortunately incomplete) *Histoire des états et empires du soleil* (1662) Flammarion moves on in the eighth chapter to more extravagant and wide-ranging cosmic voyages, including Athanasius Kircher's *Itinerarium Exstaticum* (1656), but it is not until the ninth—entitled "Les grands voyages" that he reaches the crucial work that is now recognizable as the foundation-stone of the tradition of the popularization of science, and which provided the model for *Lumen*: Bernard de Fontenelle's *Entretiens sur la pluralité des mondes* (1686; translated under various titles, the most accurate being *Conversations on the Plurality of Worlds*).

* * * * * * *

The first edition of *Entretiens sur la pluralité des mondes* consisted of five conversations, allegedly taking place on successive evenings between the first-person narrator and the Marquise de G***. Although a sixth evening was added in the second edition, its conversation served merely as a summary, and such revisions as were made as it passed through many other editions before Fontenelle's death in 1757 were mere tinkering, as much for the purpose of stylistic adjustment as to incorporate a handful of new discoveries. The work is conspicuously light-hearted and deftly witty; unlike previous works of natural philosophy employing the dialogue as a form of discourse—most notably Galileo's—it does not set up assertively opposed positions to dispute the truth, but establishes an innocent in search of both amusement and instruction, and an informant equally skilled in both.

The first conversation explains and justifies the Copernican model of the solar system. The second argues that the moon is a world not unlike the Earth, perhaps inhabited. The third prevaricates ingeniously, first taking back the suggestion that the moon might be inhabited by arguing that, because no clouds can be seen moving across the face of the moon, conditions on its surface must be very different from those supporting life on Earth, but then taking leave to wonder whether life-forms quite different from Earth might exist there, perhaps living beneath the surface.

From this specific case the narrator moves swiftly to the proposal that life in the universe might be infinitely various, and the fourth conversation elaborates this idea by wondering what life might be like on the other planets of the solar system. The fifth conversation introduces the notion that the stars are suns like ours, with their own families of planets, and wonders how various life might be beyond the solar system.

The fourth and fifth dialogues also go to some trouble to explain and elaborate the imaginative implications of René Descartes' theory of vortices, which asserted that space is not really empty, because all aggregations of matter—from atoms to stars—are constantly revolving, establishing "etheric whirlpools" around themselves, by means of which they constantly interact with one another even though they may appear to observers to be separated by vast distances.

The content of Fontenelle's light-hearted conversations seems quite innocuous to the modern reader, and even his educated contemporaries—those, at any rate, who had read John Wilkins (whose *Discovery* had been translated into French in 1655)—could not have been overly surprised by the casual proposition that the moon is a world that human beings will one day be able to visit, when the technology of flight is sufficiently improved. Fontenelle was, however, writing in a Catholic country, not long after Louis XIV's revocation of the Edict of Nantes, which had withdrawn from Protestants the right to pursue their religion in their own way, forcing many of them to flee the ensuing persecution. In providing a direct challenge to the Church's cosmology, the conversations were trespassing on dangerous ground—and in making their key ideas more easily accessible to ordinary people, with plausible and commonsensical supporting arguments, they provided an active and powerful antidote to blind faith.

Fontenelle's previous works had included a dramatic comedy, *La Comète* (1681), inspired by the comet of 1680—whose display had been far more impressive than the one put on in 1682 by Halley's comet—which had made much of the importance of comets in disproving the Aquinas-endorsed Aristotelian notion that the heavens consisted of a series of crystal spheres with the Earth at their centre. The *Entretiens* employs a similar lightness of tone and delicate wit to conceal its seriousness, but there could be no doubt that the narrator's protestation that the Marquise and his readers need not believe the ideas featured in the conversations is a protective device.

In the same year as the *Entretiens* Fontenelle produced an *Histoire des oracles* [History of Oracles], in which the myths and legends of the ancients are clinically analyzed as a record of the gradual development of a better understanding of nature, whose central progressive thread is the disposal of supernatural explanations and belief in magic. Although he carefully omitted any specific commentary on the prophecies and miracles that were key items of Christian faith, it was open to any reader to place them in the same sequence and subject them to the same skeptical scrutiny. It was, however, the *Entretiens* that became a huge best-seller, widely translated and continually reprinted. It helped secure Fontenelle's admission to the Académie Française, but he was not satisfied until he had also won admission to the Académie des Sciences, whose secretary he became in 1697. It was in that role that he produce a long series of *éloges* (eulogies) celebrating the work and achievements of every newly-deceased member of the Academy, collectively championing the notion that the scientific investigation of nature was not merely a solemn duty and a significant realm of heroic achievement, but also a source of great delight.

Fontenelle continued to produce *éloges* until he died, a mere month short of his hundredth birthday. He was not only Camille Flammarion's great hero and chief inspiration but the principal influence on the subsequent development of science-based speculative thought and the methods used by its boldest pioneers. Like Flammarion, he is more-or-less forgotten today, but as in Flammarion's case that is because he achieved what he set out to do in making once-problematic ideas seem so obviously true that no further dispute was necessary or possible.

* * * * * * *

Flammarion's chapter on "les grands voyages" in the *Revue critique* also includes descriptions of Gabriel Daniel's *Voyage du monde de Descartes* (1692) and Christian Huygens' *Cosmotheoros* (1698). The following chapter tracks the rich tradition of "voyages imaginaires" through the eighteenth century, including Jonathan Swift's *Gulliver's Travels* (1726), Ludvig Holberg's *Nils Klim* (1741), Voltaire's *Micromégas* (1752), and several less familiar items.

The next chapter begins with the observation that while imaginative travelers' tales grew ever more numerous and extravagant in the 18th century, attempts to imagine what conditions on other worlds might actually became rather stagnant by virtue of the failure of observation to maintain a healthy flow of new data. Even so, Flammarion concedes that some valuable precedents were set by Emmanuel Swedenborg, Imannuel Kant and such flamboyant cosmic expeditions as *Voyages de Mylord Céton dans les sept planètes* [Journeys by Lord Seaton to the Seven Planets] (1765) by Marie-Anne de Roumier.

Roumier's work, in particular, must be reckoned among the more important influences on Flammarion, because of the extensive use it makes of the notion that the other worlds of the solar system are arenas into which souls embodied in the Earth are routinely reincarnated, according to a definite scheme of moral propriety. Roumier's Mars is a "temple de la Gloire" [temple of glory] where cadavers are heaped up in a kind of Hell; its inhabitants include many great generals and conquerors, including Oliver Cromwell and Attila the Hun. The sun itself is the realm of truly great men: philosophers. One solar country accommodates a company ranging from Thales, Anaxagoras and Pythagoras to Cassini, Descartes and Newton; another's inhabitants range from Homer, Plato and Sophocles to Pascal, Montesquieu and la Rochefoucauld. Although the bodies of the violent retain their vulgar corporeality, the reincarnate philosophers are diaphanous; the thoughts in their heads and passions in their hearts can be clearly seen. *Voyages de Mylord Céton* was one of many works reprinted in a thirty-six-volume series of *Voyages imaginaires* produced in Paris by Charles Garnier in 1787-89.

The twelfth chapter of the *Revue critique*, which brings the story up to date by considering nineteenth century works, is oddly slight, giving only brief mention to numerous works of fiction and non-fiction. The most elaborate consideration is given to Edgar Poe's "Unparalleled Adventure of one Hans Pfaall" (1835). Later editions of *Les mondes imaginaires et les mondes réels* added a thirteenth chapter to the second part, which listed and annotated interplanetary voyages and speculative works touching on the subject of life on other worlds published after 1862. This includes thirty-one titles published between 1863 and 1876, but Flammarion gave up trying to keep track thereafter, and no further titles were added to the editions of the book published in the 1890s (by which time the number of such editions was in the mid-twenties). Rather perversely, however, he never went to the bother of revising any of the earlier chapters. Given the unsatisfactory nature of the chapter on the early nineteenth century, this omission is regrettable, all the more especially because he subsequently became acquainted with a number of key works published before 1862.

Three such works, in particular, are relevant predecessors of *Lumen*: Nicolas Restif de la Bretonne's *Les Posthumes* [Posthumous Correspondence] (1802; but written 1787-89); Humphry Davy's *Consolations in Travel; or, The Last Days of a Philosopher* (1830); and Edgar Poe's *Eureka—An Essay on the Material and Spiritual Universe* (1848). *Les Posthumes* is an epistolary piece in which the letters from a dead nobleman include an account of a cosmic voyage modeled on and perhaps satirizing Roumier's. It is possible that Flammarion never read it, but he certainly read *Consolations in Travel; or, The Last Days of a Philosopher*, which impressed him so profoundly that he was moved to translate it into French; his translation appeared in 1869, the year in which he resumed work on *Lumen* after a two-year gap, and it was obviously fresh in his mind when he wrote the remainder of the text.

* * * * * * *

Consolations in Travel consists of a series of six philosophical dialogues, whose hypothetical narrator is eventually given the name Philalethes ("love of truth"), although he remains unnamed in the first, which describes how he sat alone in the ruins of the Coliseum in Rome by the light of the full moon, ruminating on the transitory nature of human endeavor. These ruminations give rise to a vision in which a "superior intelligence", which he elects to call the Genius, carries him away on an educational voyage through time and space.

The narrator first reviews the history of humankind, observing the abrupt transition—a literal re-creation—of the species from brutal wildness to the birth of civilization and the subsequent intellectual, social and technological progress of that civilization. The Genius then begins to explain the cosmic perspective into which the career of humankind needs to be set:

"Spiritual natures are eternal and indivisible, but their modes of being are as infinitely varied as the forms of matter. They have no relation to space, and, in their transitions, no dependence upon time, so that they can pass from one part of the universe to another by laws entirely independent of their motion. The quantity, or the number of spiritual essences, like the quantity or number of the atoms of the material world, are always the same; but their arrangements, like those of the materials which they are destined to guide or govern, are infinitely diversified; they are, in fact, parts more or less inferior of the infinite mind, and in the planetary systems, to one of which this globe you inhabit belongs, are in a state of probation, continually aiming at, and generally rising to a higher state of existence."

The Genius tells the narrator that the spiritual essences that were once Socrates and Newton are "now in a higher and better state of planetary existence drinking intellectual light from a purer source" and conducts him to the planet Saturn, so that he might see its alien inhabitants:

"I saw moving on the surface below me immense masses, the forms of which I find it impossible to describe; they had systems for locomotion similar to those of the morse or sea-horse, but I saw with great surprise that they moved from place to place by six extremely thin membranes, which they used as wings. Their colours were varied and beautiful, but principally azure and rose-colour. I saw numerous convolutions of tubes, more analogous to the trunk of the elephant than anything else I can imagine, occupying what I supposed to be the upper parts of the body."

The Genius explains that each of these trunk-like tubes "is an organ of peculiar motion or sensation" and that their superior sensory apparatus and intelligence have allowed the Saturnians to discover far more about the universe and its laws than humankind ever could, and to become far more virtuous. He reveals that the other planets in the solar system are inhabited by beings at various levels of intellectual and spiritual development, and that the "higher natures" that exist elsewhere in the universe make use of "finer and more ethereal kinds of matter" in their organization. After death, therefore, men—among whom scientists are those most ready for rapid advancement—will make heavenly progress by slow and measured degrees, through a series of extraterrestrial incarnations: "The universe is everywhere full of life, but the modes of this life are infinitely diversified, and yet every form of it must be enjoyed and known by every spiritual nature before the consummation of all things."

The narrator is permitted to glimpse one other mode of existence, when he observes cometary "globes...composed of different kinds of flame and of different colours", containing figures that remind him of human faces. Although they were once incarnate as men, these beings can no more remember their humanity than men can remember life in the womb. The only "sentiment or passion" that the spiritual essence or "monad" carries forward through all its successive metamorphoses is the love of knowledge, whose ultimate extrapolation is the love of God. If this love is misapplied to worldly ambition or the pursuit of oppressive power, the Genius explains, a spirit "sinks in the scale of existence...till its errors are corrected by painful discipline" but the narrator is not insulted by any vision of such subhuman modes of existence. The Genius concentrates on celebration of the progressive aspects of the post-human situation, insisting that the cause of progress is not merely the highest good but the source of the greatest joy of which any imaginable being is capable.

Flammarion must have thought this vision wonderful, but he must also have regretted that the five dialogues following the first did not extrapolate it further, preferring instead to remain on Earth to debate matters of more immediate and intimate concern to the dying scientist. Although the first three parts of *Lumen* seem to be taking up where Fontenelle left off in his carefully-structured and calculatedly casual representation of a universe filled with infinitely various forms of life, the fourth manifestly takes up where Davy left off in elaborating his cosmic scheme.

* * * * * * *

As in Fontenelle's *Entretiens*, the narrative voices that Flammarion employs in the dialogues constituting *Lumen* are not disputants but a willing teacher and his eager pupil; like the Latinate characters in Davy's *Consolations*, however, they are as much symbols as actual human beings. Although the teacher, Lumen, gives an elaborate account of his life on Earth, his name declares that he is also light itself: the light of the stars, as observed and analyzed by astronomers. His interrogator, Quaerens, is partly Flammarion and partly his imagined reader, but his name signifies "Seeker" (of Knowledge).

It has to be admitted that the first dialogue, which labors long and hard to establish its elementary ideas, is rather slow, stodgy and repetitive. Flammarion—or perhaps his editor—seems to have been exceedingly doubtful as to the readiness and ability of his readers to take aboard the simplest corollaries of the limited velocity of light. The most interesting idea that the first dialogue raises—the principle that time and space are not absolute, but only exist relative to one another—is left stranded, and never properly developed. This is bound to seem disappointing to the modern reader, who might be inclined to wonder what Flammarion thought of Albert Einstein's special theory of relativity when it was published in 1905, and whether he cursed himself for not having extrapolated his own version of the idea more carefully and more boldly.

The second dialogue, whose central idea is that a viewpoint moving faster than light would be able to see events in reverse order, suffers from the same faults, partly because Flammarion did not take the trouble to remove from the collected version material that originally served to recap the basic thesis for the benefit of new readers.

It is only at the end of the second dialogue that the author picks up the pace and begins to broaden his imaginative horizons to take in wider vistas in both time and space, but, once having done that, he fails to carry the extrapolations of the third dialogue very far forward. He might have cut it short when it had hardly got going because he simply ran out of steam, but it seems more probable that the editor of the periodical in which the serial version appeared aborted it—in which case, Flammarion's decision to keep the first dialogue simple and to labor every point it made might have been wiser than it now seems.

The first three dialogues might be seen, collectively, as an extrapolation of a remark made by Fontenelle's narrator near the beginning of the *Entretiens*: "All philosophy," he tells the Marquise, "is based on two things only: curiosity and poor eyesight; if you had better eyesight you could see perfectly well whether or not these stars are solar systems, and if you were less curious, you wouldn't care.... The trouble is, we want to know more than we can see." Better telescopes and brand new spectroscopes had improved the sight of the naked eye considerably by 1867, but Flammarion was eager to demonstrate what a really powerful eye might see, and it was for that reason that he gifted Lumen's spirit self with a power of vision that proved troublesome to explain and protect from criticism.

Although the slight gap between the first and second dialogues made no evident difference to Flammarion's outlook, he seems to have emerged as a changed man from the two-year interval between the third and fourth. Perhaps the marked change of attitude and tone merely reflects the fact that he now felt free to express himself more freely and say what he really thought about such matters as the human tendency to war and French prevarication over the principles of republicanism, but it might be that he really had undergone a change of heart. Were it not for the testimony of the footnotes, a modern reader might easily wonder whether the crucial gap had been from 1869-71 rather than 1867-69, given that the Franco-Prussian War would have provided ample excuse for the hardening of his attitude to "great statesmen" and their warlike tendencies. It seems more likely, however, that he spent two frustrating years casting about for an editor willing to allow him to extrapolate his ideas as boldly as he wanted to—and that once having found one, he conceived an ardent ambition to make the most of the opportunity.

The crucial point in Lumen's discourse arrives when he explains that the form of the human body results from its adaptation to a specific set of physical circumstances rather than divine design, and that sentient beings elsewhere in the universe are likely to be very different, by virtue of being adapted to a wide variety of environments. Fontenelle had made a similar point, but the arguments backing up his insistence that the life-forms on other worlds must be different from men had been conscientiously playful, giving a higher priority to the likelihood of divine versatility than the necessity of adaptation; his examples had been calculated to amuse, and none too specific. Lumen, on the other hand, also insists that physical forms are the products of slow and never-ending processes of evolution, and thus steps up his argument by another gear.

It is at this point that Davy's example becomes more crucial than Fontenelle's. Flammarion's evolutionary theory is thoroughly Lamarckian, and its extrapolation from an earthly to a cosmic scale easily assimilates Davy's insistence that evolution is moral as well as physical, so that souls are subject to their own evolutionary process as they move through successive incarnations. In moving on to this larger stage, however, Flammarion is determined to keep hold of the key element of the earlier dialogues: the insistence that human curiosity is confounded and confused by "poor eyesight". He remain deeply preoccupied with the idea that our image of the universe is conditioned by the particular properties of our senses—and this is the notion that fuels his exploration of the multitudinous possibilities open to alien life.

The one significant respect in which Flammarion flatly refuses the influence of Fontenelle is that he considers Descartes' theory of vortices hopelessly outdated. Even so, he holds to its essentials; like Descartes and Fontenelle, Flammarion clings to the idea that the emptiness of space is an illusion of poor eyesight, and that it is actually full of connections binding visible entities together. Today, alas, Flammarion's talk of *ondulations* [undulations, or waves], and his contention that light might have hundreds or thousands of analogous "vibrations". seem just as primitive as Fontenelle's talk of Cartesian vortices—and yet, even though modern physicists have pared the number of fundamental forces to four, and have disposed of the outdated "luminiferous ether", they have retained the notion that "empty" space is a seething sea of potential particles, replete with hidden and seemingly-unexpressed energies.

It is, perhaps, ironic that the most striking anticipations in *Lumen* have little to do with the testimony of light, and that they rest on the discredited foundation of Lamarck's theory of evolution. The historian of science might dismiss them as mere folly, but to the historian of science fiction they are very important. Flammarion was the first writer to apply the theory of evolution to the wholesale construction of authentically alien beings, in so doing he established one of the ideative foundation stones on which modern science fiction is built. Although he continued to take an interest in hypothetical aliens, especially Martians, he never again exercised this kind of invention on the scale that he did in the fourth and fifth parts of *Lumen*; that is why *Lumen* remains a uniquely interesting work, and an astonishing product of its era.

We have grown so used to the idea of alien beings since H. G. Wells found a melodramatic role for them to play in *The War of the Worlds* (1898) that it is hard to imagine a time when the idea was new and wonderfully exotic. Kepler and Fontenelle deserve the credit for coming up with the idea that the life-forms existing on other planets must be very different from those of Earth because they would need to be adapted to very different physical circumstances, but Flammarion was the first man to attempt to extrapolate that notion to its hypothetical limit, and to fill that range with examples by the dozen.

Perhaps Flammarion decided subsequently that he had been far too ambitious in *Lumen*, in that he kept his imagination under a much tighter rein after 1869—and the modern reader can hardly help forming the impression that he could have been far more ambitious than he was—but the fact remains that the last two parts of *Lumen* represent an amazing feat of the imagination, which no one dared to emulate for more than a generation. Although the decay of Spiritualism and its associated researches has robbed *Lumen* of a significant pillar of the ideative foundations that Flammarion constructed to make the account plausible, modern readers should still be able to recognize that the fourth and fifth dialogues constitute a remarkable triumph of pioneering imaginative exploration.

* * * * * * *

Perhaps *Lumen* would be even more original than it is had it not been for the fact that its ambition to produce a coherent vision of the new book of destiny that had been opened by the astronomical discoveries of the early nineteenth century had been anticipated by Edgar Poe. Flammarion had not had the opportunity to read Charles Baudelaire's 1864 translation of Poe's *Eureka* when he wrote *Les Mondes imaginaires et les mondes réels* in 1862, and probably had not yet got around to it when he wrote *Lumen* in 1866-69, but he certainly discovered some time thereafter the extent to which he had been anticipated. He must have been pleased to discover that the most adventurous element of *Lumen*—the attempt to imagine and map the potential range of alien life-forms—had not been part of Poe's project.

In other works, Poe had also anticipated many of the other strategies that Flammarion was to try out in the service of the popularization of science, and had certainly deployed them to far better literary effect—but the real triumph of *Eureka* was that it construed certain aspects of the testimony of light more ingeniously and more accurately than *Lumen*, although the extent of its cleverness did not become obvious until the 1920s. Although it is the least read of Poe's prose works, *Eureka* provides a magnificent example of the role that the creative imagination has to play in the interpretation of scientific data, and the extent to which the science-fictional imagination can assist the serious business of thought-experimentation. What it does not do, however, is to populate the universe it imagines in the way that the fourth and fifth dialogues of *Lumen* fill the universe with wondrously exotic life.

Poe was the first writer fully to grasp some of the key implications of nineteenth-century astronomy, particularly the realization that the stars were mortal—in consequence of which, whether it was infinite in space or not, the universe could not be infinite in time. Gravity, he therefore presumed, would determine the ultimate fate of the universe. *Eureka* imagines moons falling upon planets and planets into suns,

> "…and the general result of this precipitation must be the gathering of the myriad now-existing stars of the firmament into an almost infinitely less number of almost infinitely superior spheres.... But all this will be merely a climactic magnificence foreboding the great end.... While undergoing consolidation, the clusters themselves, with a speed prodigiously accumulative, have been rushing towards their own general centre, and now, with a thousandfold electric velocity, commensurate only with their material grandeur and with the spiritual passion of their appetite for oneness, the majestic remnants of the tribe of stars flash, at length, into a common embrace."

Having attained this climacteric, Poe reaches further still, suggesting that this achievement of unity surely ought to be followed by a new expansive Creation, part of an eternal sequence that he characterizes as the pulsation of the "Heart Divine"—which is, by some essential analogy, also the beating of our own hearts. Poe probably means to imply more than the obvious analogy here; he was influenced considerably by Blaise Pascal, whose famous dictum that "the heart has its reasons which reason knows not" refers to a kind of apprehension identical to the "intuition" which Poe cited as his guide in the speculative adventures of Eureka. Flammarion was eventually to borrow all of this, but he did not produce his own version until he wrote the second part of *La Fin du monde* [The End of the World].

Had it been more widely read, *Eureka* might have made as great an impact on the evolution of speculative fiction as Flammarion did, but there is no doubt that *Lumen* is the work that had the more profound impact on the development of European scientific romance. It is certainly arguable that other French writers who were heavily influenced by *Lumen* and its derivatives had little further influence outside their own country, but it is arguable too that this was unfortunate, and that the evolution of American science fiction might have benefited had the Wellsian image of the alien as a monstrous competitor in a cosmic struggle for existence in which only the fittest would survive been more adequately supplemented by a Flammarionesque image of the alien as a precious element in the infinite variety of life in the cosmos. Despite the overarching example of Wells, British scientific romance did benefit to some extent from that kind of example in the first half of the twentieth century, and was the better for it.

Flammarion continued to experiment with the formats he had road-tested in Lumen and "Histoire d'une comète" throughout his career. He wrote only one more-or-less orthodox novel, the *bildungsroman Stella* (1897), which draws extensively on Flammarion's own experiences, although its eponymous protagonist is female. His most successful works of speculative fiction after *Lumen* were, however, *Stella*'s predecessors, *Uranie* (1889) and *La Fin du monde* (1894). *Uranie* was surprisingly successful in the short term (although it was not reprinted as frequently as *Lumen*) and its best-seller status caused three different translations to be made in the USA within a matter of months. Although advertised as a novel it is actually a portmanteau piece reminiscent of *Récits de l'infini* in more ways than one, comprising three pieces that must have been written separately and were presumably first published in periodicals.

The first part of *Uranie* is a *voyage extatique* in which the seventeen-year-old Flammarion, in his first year with Le Verrier at the Observatoire, is visited by the muse of astronomy, Uranie (Urania in English, although one of the three translations leaves the name in the French form). She takes him on a celestial voyage to view life on many other worlds, including a planet of the multiple star Gamma Andromedae, where androgynous dragonfly-like "humans" live in a symbiotic relationship with mobile plants. The catalogue of aliens included here is a straightforward extension of the one offered in the fourth dialogue of *Lumen*, and the entire piece is effectively a supplement to that dialogue.

The second part is also an appendix to *Lumen*, but to the pseudobiographical elements of the first three dialogues rather than the substance of the fourth. It describes the life and early afterlife of a friend of Flammarion's, here called George Spero. The third is another *voyage extatique* in which Flammarion makes an unaccompanied dream-journey to Mars, which he explores in the company of two human-seeming Martians, who lecture him extensively on the follies and moral weaknesses of humankind—especially war. After awakening on Earth Flammarion is visited by Spero's spirit just as the narrator of *Lumen* had been visited; Spero reveals that he was one of Flammarion's guides on Mars, having been reincarnate there as a female, but explains that Flammarion had been deluded into seeing the Martians as humans rather than the six-limbed winged beings they really are. Uranie then reappears to restate and amplify some of the points made in the first dialogue of Lumen, summarizing them in a series of aphorisms.

La Fin du monde (1894) was less successful than *Uranie*, although it is considerably bolder in imaginative terms. It too is a portmanteau work, whose first part, "Au Vingtième siecle: les théories", had appeared separately as a serial in the previous year. This first part begins as a cautionary tale about the panic that might be expected to follow the news that the Earth is about to be struck by a comet—a possibility that Flammarion had popularized in a number of magazine articles. The story veers away from the sensational, however, when it is revealed that the close encounter will only inflict light casualties, and a conference of savants meets to discuss alternative ways in which the world might end. The eventual glancing contact is spectacular, but the world survives.

The second part of the story, "Dans millions d'années", consists of an ambitious future history of life on Earth: a counterpart to the past history contained in *Le Monde avant le création d'homme* and dramatized in the second dialogue of *Lumen*. The concluding section displays the influence of *Eureka* as clearly as the fourth part of *Lumen* had shown the influence of Davy:

> "Mankind had passed by transmigration through the worlds to a new life with God, and freed from the

burdens of matter, soared with endless progress in eternal light.

"The immense gaseous nebula, which absorbed all former worlds, thus transformed into vapor, began to turn upon itself. And in the zones of condensation of its primordial star-mist, new worlds were born, as heretofore the earth was.

"So a new universe began, whose genesis some future Moses and Laplace would tell, a new creation, extraterrestrial, superhuman, inexhaustible...."

Stella attempts to take up where *Uranie* had left off, but failed to please the same audience, presumably because its mildly satirical depiction of contemporary French society left something to be desired. Having been wooed away from the fashionable *haut monde* (where she mingles with such characters as M. Aimelafille [girl-lover] and M. Pièdevache [bovine charity]) by reading a book entitled *L'affranchissement de la pensée par l'astronomie* [The Liberation of Thought by Astronomy] and subsequent dialogues with Flammarionesque savants, Stella d'Ossian falls in love with the young astronomer Raphaël Dargilan. Her nearest relatives, the Comte and Comtesse de Noirmoutier (*moutier* is a colloquial term for monastery, so the name's nearest English equivalent would probably be Blackfriars) do not approve, but she marries him anyway. Shortly afterwards Stella and Raphaël are fortunate enough to be caught up in a bizarre electrical storm, which leaves them both dead, but she contrives to get a posthumous massage back to Earth to reassure those left behind that he and she are deliriously happy, having made sufficient progress in their Earthly incarnation to be worthy of reincarnation on Mars.

Flammarion continued to produce shorter works in which factual material was dramatized by fictional devices until his production finally began to falter in the last years of his life. A few hybrid works produced in parallel to the books cited above can be found in *Dans le ciel et sur la terre* [In the Sky and on the Earth] (1886) and *Clairs de lune* [Moonlights] (1894). The last and best of several derivatives of Lumen is the longest item in *Rêves étoilés* [Starry Dreams] (1914), the *voyage extatique* "Voyage dans le ciel", which can be found in an English translation in E. E. Fournier d'Albe's translation of the collection, *Dreams of an Astronomer* (1923). Another equally-derivative piece, which appeared in the first French edition of *Rêves étoilés* but not in reprints or in the English translation of the book, and which appears to have been written in the wake of the success of *Uranie*, was translated into English as "A Celestial Love" in the December 1896 issue of *The Arena*.

Flammarion's last collection consisting entirely of fiction—*Rêves étoilés* is a mixture of fiction and non-fiction leaning more toward the latter—was *Contes philosophiques* [Philosophical Tales] (1911), whose six items include "Conversation avec un Marsien", a discourse on the folly of war in which the narrator dreams of meeting an inhabitant of Mars, and "Dialogue entre deux Académiciens et deux insects stercoraires", in which two dung beetles offer an appropriately contrasted view to that of two academicians on the subject of the conditions necessary to allow life to flourish on other worlds. The only sense in which these last revisitations carry the relevant arguments further than *Lumen* is that they are here expressed with a subtler and more playful irony.

Such work as this was perceived, even in Flammarion's own day, as something essentially second-rate, but there is a certain injustice in that judgment, and in the way that his name has been gradually erased from twentieth-century reference books. By 1945 the commentary on his career contained in the encyclopedic *Nouveau Petit Larousse* had been reduced to two seemingly dismissive words—*séduisant vulgarisateur* (seductive populariser)—but it is a description that he would surely have worn with pride, and rightly so.

* * * * * * *

The writer who absorbed the imagery of *Lumen* and its successors most fully, and redeployed that imagery most productively, was the Belgian writer Joseph-Henri Boëx (1856-1940), who signed himself J. H. Rosny aîné (he and his younger brother Justin had shared the pseudonym J. H. Rosny between 1893 and 1907, and divided it in two when they went their separate ways). In the novelette "Les Xipéhuz" (1887), prehistoric men encounter and exterminate inorganic aliens of an exceedingly strange kind, which might well have been drawn from a Flammarionesque catalogue. Rosny adopted a Flammarionesque method as well as a Flammarionesque visionary daring in the "fictionalized essay" *La Legénde sceptique* [The Skeptical Lenged] (1889), which served as a foundation for much of his subsequernt speculative fiction, although nothing that he wrote subsequently reproduced the casual daring of its speculations about the "planetary physiology" uniting the universe into a single super-creature. Although "La Mort de la terre" [The Death of the Earth] (1910) owed more to *La Fin du monde* and *Les Navi-*

gateurs de l'infini [Navigators of Space] (1925) seems to owe its direct inspiration to the final part of *Uranie*, they both assume the same kind of exotic evolutionary schema that Flammarion had sketched out, and to which Rosny had added his own higher level of organization. In the 1920s Rosny began a series of earnest philoshophical essays attempting to popularize the notion that the seemingly-empty space between the stars and within the atom could not really be empty, but must conain an infnity of parallel universes currently imperceptible by human senses—an imaginative leap of which Flammarion would surely have approved.

Both Rosny brothers served, under the chairmanship of Joris-Karl Huysmans, on the jury that awarded the very first Prix Goncourt, so it is not entirely surprising that the prize was won by a book of a kind that would have stood no chance of winning the same competition at a later date: the striking visionary fantasy *Force ennemie* [Hostile Force] (1903) by John-Antoine Nau (Eugène Torquet). *Force ennemie* employs Flammarion's notion of serial reincarnation in a far less optimistic fashion, afflicting a contemporary human with a kind of demonic possession by a soul whose present incarnation on another world is a perpetual torment. The most extravagant extrapolation of the notion of interplanetary reincarnation can be found in the two "planetary romances" that comprise the "Martian epic" of Octave Joncquel and Théo Varlet, *Les titans du ciel* [The Titans of the Sky] (1921) and *L'agonie de la terre* [The Death-throes of the Earth] (1922; translated in an omnibus edition as *The Martian Epic*). Although the prefatory material to these melodramas acknowledges a debt to H. G. Wells's *War of the Worlds*, the aftermath of the interplanetary war described therein is a further crisis caused by the fact that the souls of the Martian casualties seek reincarnation on Earth, as they believe is their due.

To trace the imaginative legacy of *Lumen* outside France would be a highly speculative process, but the kinship with it of two important British scientific romances is worthy of comment, even if no direct influence can be proved. The cosmic vision contained in William Hope Hodgson's *The House on the Borderland* (1905) is Flammarionesque while it deals with the fate of the Earth and the dying sun, but in the same way that the eponymous house is an allegory of the human mind, the whole universe is transformed by Hodgson's narrator's dream into an allegory of all that the mind must endure and contemplate. As with so many sons of clergymen who were converted to freethought by the discoveries of nineteenth century science, Hodgson took a gloomy view of the tacit moral order of the Christless universe, and his cosmic vision is far less optimistic than Flammarion's. A similar element of gloom is present in the twentieth-century work that has most in common with *Lumen*, and might be regarded as a definitive updating of it: Olaf Stapledon's *Star Maker* (1937).

Whether Stapledon ever read *Lumen* or not, *Star Maker* sets out to do a very similar job in presenting an image of the universe revealed by early twentieth-century telescopes, and imagining the many kinds of life that might be contained within it. Like Flammarion's cosmic schema, Stapledon's is a product of design, which has a progressive process built into it at the most fundamental level, and, like Flammarion's vision, Stapledon's is haunted by the idea that humankind's role in the cosmic plan is cursed by the self-destructive tendencies exhibited by a predilection for war. Although Stapledon cannot in the end consider the designer of his schema anything more than an incomplete artist, who still has a great deal to learn about the craft of creation, he still concedes that progress is being made, and hopes that it might one day be made more rapidly. Camille Flammarion—not to mention Lumen, George Spero, and Stella d'Ossian—would surely have approved wholeheartedly of the "two lights for guidance" offered to the reader in the final paragraph of Stapledon's novel:

> "The first, our little glowing atom of community, with all that it signifies. The second, the cold light of the stars, symbol of the hypercosmical reality, with its crystal ecstasy."

JULES VERNE'S *JOURNEY TO THE CENTER OF THE EARTH*

Jules Verne's *Voyage au centre de la terre* was initially published in 1864 and reissued in a revised version in 1867. Although it was preceded into print by *Cinq semaines en ballon* (1863; tr. as *Five Weeks in a Balloon*), which featured a balloon larger and more capable than any that actually existed at the time, the earlier novel now seems to many readers and critics to be too modest to count as science fiction, and it is, in consequence, *Voyage au centre de la terre* that is more often held up as a breakthrough text in the history of sf. It was also recognized by some contemporary reviewers as an important and ground-breaking text, and hailed as a potential pioneer of a genre of *romans scientifiques* [scientific novels].

Verne had not started his literary career with the aim of pioneering a new genre of adventure fiction. He had initially moved to Paris in the 1850s in the hope of becoming a playwright, and had shown enough signs of promise in that regard to be adopted as a protégé of Alexandre Dumas (who considered his own theatrical work to be far more worthy of critical attention and acclaim than his popular *feuilleton* novels). When Verne began to work in prose, he soon produced the allegorical complaint against the soullessness of technology "Maître Zacharius" (1854), in which a clockmaker is seduced by the Devil, and his career as a novelist might have developed differently had he been able to publish a much more elaborate complaint of the same sort, *Paris au XXe siècle* (1994; tr. as *Paris in the 20th Century*, 1996), which he write in the early 1860s—but he was instructed by his publisher never to let it see the light of day, and meekly obeyed.

The publisher in question was P.-J. Hetzel, one of the great pioneers of children's literature, for whom Dumas had done a good deal of work before both of them had been exiled from Paris in the wake of Louis Napoléon's *coup d'état* of 1851. Verne had offered Hetzel some non-fictional articles on ballooning, but Hetzel had persuaded him to use the material as the basis for an advenrure novel—the novel that ultimately materialized as *Cinq semaines en ballon*. Hetzel was sufficiently impressed to offer Verne a contract to produce similar aventure stories on a regular basis for the "family magazine" he founded in 1864, *Le Magasin d'Éducation and de Récréation*, and Verne accepted gratefully. Hetzel, however, was in two minds about Verne's tendency to let his imaginative run wild, and gradually reined him in. Verne followed *Voyage au centre de la terre* with *Les aventures de Capitaine Hatteras* (1864; tr. as *The English at the North Pole*), another novel that does not seem very fantastic nowadays, although it must have seemed more adventurous at the time, when the pole was still mysterious and out of reach, but he continued to produce even bolder exploratory works over the next few years.

The other Verne texts that may nowadays be considered important foundation-stones of sf include *De la terre à la lune* (1865; tr. as *From the Earth to the Moon*), which described the building of a huge gun for the purpose of firing a manned missile into space, the classic *Vingt mille lieues sous les mers* (1870: tr. as *Twenty Thousand Leagues Under the Sea*), which introduced the enigmatic Captain Nemo and his ultra-sophisticated submarine *Nautilus*, and a sequel to his space gun story, *Autour de la lune* (1870; tr. as *Around the Moon*), in which the missile orbits the moon before returning to Earth. Alongside these novels, however, Verne wrote far more modest adventure stories: *Le désert de glace* (1866; tr. as *The Desert of Ice*), *Les enfants du Capitaine Grant* (1867-68; tr. as *In Search of the Castaways*), the two novellas collected as *Une ville flottante suivi Les forceurs du blocus* (1871; tr. as *A Floating City* and *The Blockade Runners*), *Aventures de trois russes et de trois anglais dans l'Afrique australe* (1872; tr. as *The Adventures of Three Russians and Three Englishmen in South Africa* and *Measuring a Meridian*) and *Le pays des fourrures* (1873; tr. as *The Fur Country*), and the work that brought him to the peak of his celebrity, *Le tour du monde en quatre-vingt jours* (1873; tr. as *Around the World in Eighty Days*).

Although Verne subsequently ventured into space again in the unconvincing *Hector Servadac* (1877), and reproduced the narrative template of *Vingt mille lieues sous les mers* in *Robur le conquérant* (1886; tr. as *The Clipper of the Clouds*), substituting an airship for the submarine, he never returned wholeheartedly to the imaginative extravagance of his early novels, becoming so moderate in his inventions that the genre of *romans scientifiques* faltered somewhat, and did not make much further progress in Frane until the example of H. G. Wells provided an inspirational boost in the 1890s. There is a sense, however, in which that half-heartedness, and a marked reluctance to "go too far", was evident even in the works that were subsequently hailed as landmarks in the history of speculative fiction. Nowhere was that half-heartedness more manifest, in fact, than in *Voyage au centre de la terre*, although history has obscured the fact by consigning its first edition to oblivion; all subsequent reprints in France, and all translations, employed the 1867 text rather than the original, and the difference between them was significant.

The narrator of the story, Axel, witnesses the discovery by his uncle, Professor Lidenbrock, of an encrypted runic manuscript contained in a copy of the *Heimskringla* (a record of Icelandic kings) bought from a second-hand bookstore. The professor, a polymathic teacher at the Johanneum—a prestigious college in Hamburg—deciphers the cryptogram, which proves to be the work of a celebrated (fictitious) alchemist, Arne Saknussem; the resultant text claims that the center of the Earth might be reached means of one of the several craters of the extinct volcano of Snaefells in Iceland. When Lidenbrock suggests that they should follow in Saknussem's footsteps, Axel is initially horrified, but is persuaded to risk the enterprise by a girl named Graüben, whose affection he craves, and who judges that it will make a hero of him. Axel and his uncle then set sail for Reykjavik, eager to get there by the first of July, when the angle of the sun's rays will indicate the relevant crater.

After conferring with local scholars, Lidenbrock hires a taciturn guide, Hans Bjelke, and assembles an extensive collection of scientific instruments. The members of the party then make their way to Snaefells, where a sign specified by Saknussem's manuscript informs them into which crater they must descend. As they do so, they make various geological observations, but the expedition seems doomed to failure when they run out of water. They are saved when they find a hot spring, the downward course of which they begin to follow.

Eventually, the expeditionaries reach a series of caves beneath the Atlantic Ocean, at a depth previously believed to be the lower limit of the Earth's crust; instead of encountering the molten rock of the mantle, however, the travelers follow the mazy series of galleries down to an interior sea illuminated by a wan light produced by some natural electrical phenomenon. On its shore they find a fungal forest and other vegetable relics of the Earth's Secondary Epoch. When they set sail upon the sea on an improvised raft they witness a contest between a plesiosaur and an ichthyosaur in the water. By mid-August they calculate that they are somewhere beneath England.

It is at this point in the text that the two editions of the novel begin to differ significantly. In the now-familiar version, when their raft is wrecked by an electrical storm the three travelers find further relics of eras long past on the Earth's surface, including a giant humanoid skull that was absent from the 1864 edition. This discovery is followed by a remarkable sequence in which Axel appears to glimpse of a living creature of the kind represented by the skull, tending a herd of mastodons—although the possibility is carefully left open that this is a mere dream incpired by the first discovery. The two versions reconverge when the travelers repair their raft; subsequently, they try to blast a way through a rocky obstruction but provoke a major seismic disturbance and are nearly killed. Instead, though, they are borne hectically upwards by a flood of water and eventually expelled from the Italian volcano Stromboli, from which location they make their way home.

It ought to be pointed out that the first English version of *A Journey to the Center of the Earth*, initially published in the U.K. in 1871 by Griffith and Farren and reprinted by numerous U.S. publishers from 1877 onwards—in spite of the availability by then of a much better translation, initially serialized in the *Philadelphia Evening Telegraph* in 1874—is atrociously corrupt. It substitutes "Jack" and "Professor Hardwigg" for the names of the two main characters and distorts the text out of all recognition, to the extent of improvising melodramatic incidents absent from Verne's text and quite out of keeping with his project. The persistence of that version, even when much more accurate translations had become easily available, undoubtedly helped to give English readers the impression that the original is a more fanciful text than it actually is, even in the 1867 version.

The reason for the text's revision was that much of the geological and paleontological information contained in the first edition of *Voyage au centre de la terre* was borrowed, sometimes almost verbatim, from Louis Figuier's *La Terre avant le déluge* (1863; translated into English as *The World Before the Deluge*)—but Figuier issued a new edition of his book in 1867, which incorporated a crucial change of perspective. Whereas the first edition of Figuier's book had located the origins of humankind in the Garden of Eden, accepting that human beings were the product of a relatively recent special creation, the second came to a very different conclusion, substituting an evolutionary account in which primitive humans equipped with stone tools had lived alongside mammals that had since become extinct for hundreds of thousands of years. It was Figuier's change of mind that led Verne to add the scenes involving the discovery of the giant humanoid skull and the vision of the herdsman to the second edition of the novel.

Figuier's conversion, and the subsequent transmutation of Verne's novel, was occasioned by the discovery by Jacques Boucher de Perthes of a human jawbone in a quarry at Moulin-Quignon, near Abbéville, which had occurred too late in 1863 for him to take account of it in the first edition of his book. Boucher had been arguing fervently for more than thirty years that hand-worked flints he had found in the same area must be evidence of human habitation—which, if geological estimates of the age of the rocks could be trusted, must mean that humankind had existed long before the beginning of the six-thousand-year chronology suggested by *Genesis*—but he had not yet convinced his opponents. The Comte de Buffon and Georges Cuvier had already accepted that the history of the world itself must be much more ancient than six thousand years, and that the six "days" of Biblical creation must each have been tens of thousands of years long, at the least, but that was a minimal concession, and many scholars continued to insist long into the nineteenth century that the findings of geology and paleontology were still compatible with the account of human origins offered in *Genesis*. Such scholars contended that the apparent evidence of hand-working on Boucher' flints must be accidental, and they had backed up this claim by asserting that if the flints really had been hand-worked, then actual human remains should have been found too; the absence of such remains had become a crucial pivot in the argument, so their actual discovery made a tremendous impact on some waverers—including Figuier—who promptly changed sides. Those die-hards who refused to change sides were compelled to shift their ground, insisting instead that the flints themselves could not be as old as the evidence implied, and must be post-diluvian.

The most ironic twist to this story is that the particular jawbone found by Boucher de Perthes was not what it seemed; it was actually of modern origin, and had actually been planted as a hoax, much like the famous skull of "Piltdown man". Genuine human remains were to be found subsequently, not merely in Europe, but in distant parts of the world, gradually accumulating into the basis of a highly elaborate story of human evolution and migration extending back for millions of years to a remote "African genesis", so Figuier's conversion turned out, in the end, to be a step in the right direction—but it was launched from a shaky foundation, and Verne might well have been wise to leave the possibility open in his own story that what

Axel saw might have been a hallucination rather than a reality. Even so, his incorporation of the herdsman scene set his novel firmly down on the side of the evolutionists: a step that might seem small now but was, in the context of the time, a bold leap—too bold, perhaps, for Verne to feel entirely comfortable with it. It would be a long time before he was prepaed to match it, but that should not be allowed to obscure the fact that he did make it, and that it turned out to be a wise move. Hesitant or not, the revised text really was a landmark in the history of imaginative fiction, and does entitle *Voyage au centre de la terre* to be considered a key work in the evolution of modern speculatve fiction.

Incidentally, Figuier, who was later to edit *La Science Illustrée*—a popular science magazine that featured a good deal of early French science fiction—made no objection to Verne's borrowings, and seems to have been delighted that his popularizing work was being reproduced and amplified. Curiously enough, though, a plagiarism suit was launched against the first edition of *Voyage au centre de la terre* by one Léon Delmas, who had published a story about a subterranean descent provoked by a cryptogram in the September 1863 issue of *La Revue contemporaine*, entitled "La Tête de Mimers" [Mimers' Head], under the pseudonym René Pol-Just. The suit was eventually abandoned, presumably because it was hopeless, given that cryptograms and subterreanean descents were both commonplace in the popular fiction of the era.

Hetzel sent an advance copy of *Voyage au centre de la terre* to "George Sand" (Baroness Aurore Dupin), who had produced some juvenile fiction for him in the past, and was to continue doing so, but the hollow earth story she was inspired to write by Verne's novel, *Laura*—in which the Earth is imagined as a gargantuan geode filled with crystals—went to another publisher. Sand remained convinced, however, that it was a suggestion she had made to Hetzel, which was doubtless relayed to Verne, that prompted the author to write *Vingt mille lieues sous le mers*. Sand was by no means the only writer inspired by Verne to produce *voyages extraordinaires* of their own, but few of his other imitators took such extravagant imaginative licence as she did, and most "Vernian fiction" embraced the same careful hesitancy that held him back. Even so, the authentically sciencefictional notion of survivals from prehistoric eras continuing to thrive in protected enclaves—which is included in the 1864 version as well as the 1867 version—was to be re-employed many times over. The idea that the Earth might be at least partly hollow was by no means original to Verne, having been suggested several times before—most notably by the astronomer Edmond Halley—as a real possibility, and featured in numerous previous literary texts, but his version of it boosted the plausibility of the notion considerably.

The geological and paleontological "discoveries" made by Professor Lidenbrock in the course of this descent through the Earth's strata were as firmly based in the science of the day as Louis Figuier could contrive, but that science made a considerable leaps after the mid-1870s, and even the amended account was, inevitably, bound to be far surpassed in later years. For that reason, the text's scientific content has become an artifact of mainly historical interest, but the novel is still uniquely important in the context of the development of imaginative fiction, becaue of the earnest determination with which it depicts the methodical process of observation and deduction undertaken by the professor, with the aid of then-modern scientific instruments. Scientific inquisitiveness, served by ingenious technology and logical expertise, is located at the heart of the endeavor—although Verne was wise to choose a relatively naïve viewpoint character, ever-ready to receive enlightenment from his older and wiser uncle, to perform the narrative function of standing in for the reader.

Because Hetzel had made his reputation publishing collections of books and periodicals for children—although the new *Magasin* was not as restricted in its intended appeal as his earlier ventures—the fact that *Voyage au centre de la terre* employs a youthful narrator encouraged the notion that it ought to be seen as a children's book; its early translations were certainly marketed in that fashion in Britain and America. Verne did not intend it to be a children's book, however, and certainly made no attempt to tailor the tenor of his didactic discourse to younger readers. Although some of his translators did that in his stead, in a more-or-less brutal fashion, the fuller and better translations give a much better idea of the extent of the author's research, the scope of his speculations and the originality of his literary method. That narrative method, even more than the brief visionary glimpses of the potential wonders that might lie at the heart of the world, entitles Verne to be considered the most most important creator of speculative fiction of his era, and a writer who set an exceedingly valuable precedent.

H. G. WELLS AND HIS TIME MACHINES

A century has passed since H. G. Wells first began to play with the idea of a machine for traveling through time, in a series of essays that he wrote while he was training to be a schoolteacher. A similar span of time separated Wells's day from the era in which the works of men like the Comte du Buffon and Georges Cuvier had first proved, beyond all reasonable doubt, that the history of the Earth had to be reckoned at least in hundreds of thousands of years rather than in mere thousands, and that man was a very recent arrival on the prehistoric scene.

Wells was one of many people who realized that these discoveries about the past must make us think anew about the possibilities of the future, but he was one of the first to set out boldly to explore the possible futures that could now be glimpsed in the mind's eye. He argued that, if the human race was the recent product of a long process of evolution, then it would surely continue to evolve; and that just as the past history of the earth had extended far beyond mankind's beginnings, so its future history would probably extend beyond mankind's end. It was in order to explore such possibilities as these that Wells came up with the ingenious idea of equipping the hero of his story with a machine to transport him through time.

In 1893, two years before he published the final version of *The Time Machine*, Wells wrote an essay called "The Man of the Year Million", in which he tried to guess what our remotest descendants might look like, when they are on the point of becoming extinct. He imagined that they would have huge heads mounted on small bodies, because mental ability would be far more important in their lifestyle than physical strength; that they would live in underground caves because the cooling of the sun would have made the surface of the Earth too cold for comfort; that they would be extremely intelligent but emotionless creatures; and that their food, which would no longer need to be digested in their stomachs and intestines, would be distilled by chemists from the surrounding rocks.

The story told in *The Time Machine* offers us a more complicated picture. The Time Traveler finds not one but two future human races. One, the Eloi, enjoys a peaceful and leisurely existence on the surface. The other, the Morlocks, lives in much poorer circumstances underground, tending the machines that support the Eloi. In these two races the Time Traveler finds the ultimate development of the divided society of Wells's own time, in which poverty-stricken laborers toiled to support a leisured aristocracy—but Wells, who was an ardent socialist, inserted a dire warning into his vision of the future, by describing how the hideous Morlocks emerge from their underworld by night to pursue and devour the gentle Eloi. When the Time Traveler goes further into the future, however, the imagery of the essay and the story converges again. In the end, the cooling of the sun renders the surface of the Earth utterly desolate, mankind disappears, and all life ultimately becomes extinct.

Wells continued to write essays and stories in great abundance for the next fifty years, but he never again ventured as far into the future as he did in *The Time Machine*. The Time Traveler promises at the end of the story that he will come back again one day, in order to tell the people who have listened to his story about his further adventures, but he never did. Wells never used his fictitious machine again; he had no need to, because he had come to understand that he already had a real time machine at his disposal, in the power of the human imagination.

Wells was one of the first men fully to appreciate that if we are careful enough in our reasoning, and bold enough in our vision, we might be able to calculate what possibilities and threats lie ahead of us, as technology advances and the world changes. He was quite right to think so. Although the future is yet to be determined by the combined effects of our ambitions, our actions and our discoveries, and cannot possibly be foreseen as would-be prophets hope to foresee it, we can certainly investigate its possibilities. We can try to work out how today's technological discoveries will help us to transform tomorrow's world. The possible futures mapped out by this time machine of the imagination require constant revision and updating to take in our real discoveries, but it is vitally important in a world like ours that we never lose sight of them.

* * * * * * *

Wells was to use the time machine of his imagination to produce many more visions of the future after *The Time Machine* itself, but their range was narrower; they dealt in hundreds of years rather than hundreds of thousands. He became rather less interested in the ultimate fate of mankind, and much more interested in the near future: the world that the people of his own time were making for their children and their children's children to live in.

One question in particular came to dominate Wells's thinking about the near future: could the nations of the world form a single great community, dedicated to the ideals of liberty, equality and fraternity, or would the rivalry between nations, and the inequalities within nations, produce wars so violent that civilization would be wiped out? That was a question he explored again and again with the time machine of the imagination, constantly trying to find reasons for hoping that a better world could and would be made, and trying to identify the threats and dangers that would have to be overcome.

It is Wells's account of threats and dangers that seems more impressive today than his hopeful endeavors. In a short story called "The Land Ironclads," published in 1903, he produced the first account of tank warfare. In *The War in the Air*, published in 1906, he became one of the first writers to explore the role of aeroplanes in war, imagining great fleets of bombers destroying cities. In *The World Set Free*, published on the eve of World War I in 1914, he imagined the destruction that might be caused by atomic bombs. These stories now seem much cleverer than the Utopian stories in which he constantly revised his vision of the ideal state, and they are more interesting to read, because it is so much more exciting to read about bombs and battles than education systems and town planning, but it is to his credit that Wells always wanted to rebuild the world after he had blasted it to smithereens, and rebuild it better than it had been before.

In a book written in the 1930s, *The Shape of Things to Come*, Wells produced a history of the future in which the world gradually recovers from a devastating war to produce a single world-wide state. In a film-script based on that book, *Things to Come*, he chose as a climax the launching of a spaceship whose journey to the moon could be seen as the first step in the exploration and conquest of the universe—a great adventure, which, he suggested, might allow mankind to evade the extinction that he had thought while writing *The Time Machine* to be inevitable. That image was to become and to remain one of the central images of modern science fiction.

* * * * * * *

Wells was a very influential writer in Britain; he was the outstanding figure in the tradition of British scientific romance. Scientific romance first became established as an identifiable genre in the popular periodicals of the 1890s. The early successes of the genre were mostly future war stories: George Griffith was a prolific writer of such stories, having launched his career with *The Angel of the Revolution*, and M. P. Shiel's first novel was *The Yellow Danger*.

This preoccupation with the possibility of war is easy enough to understand. As a tiny nation with a large worldwide empire inexorably in decline, Britain harbored a strong sense of threat, especially in respect of the imperialistic ambitions of the newly-consolidated German nation. The Great War of 1914-18 was visible on the imaginative horizon for many years before it actually broke out. Anxiety about this prospect was mixed with a determination to triumph, a desire to make permanently secure that which was under threat. Much future war fiction before 1914 was therefore belligerent and bloodthirsty. When the war did come, it arrived having been advertised for many years as a war that would end war, and Britons were all the more eager to fight it because of this pre-established mythology. The actual experience of the war, though, betrayed these expectations in no uncertain terms. It turned out to be the vilest of wars, horrific in its cost in human lives, which achieved nothing, except the destruction of Europe as the economic heart of the world.

All the writers of post-war scientific romance had to come to terms with this betrayal of their hopes and dreams, and it is entirely understandable that their futuristic imagination thereafter focused in large measure on what they considered to be the historical lesson of the Great War: the belief that a new war, fought by air fleets that would bomb defenseless cities with high explosives and poison gas, would wreak destruction of a more horrific kind, and on a more terrible scale than was readily imaginable. Wells, as usual, had been the first to display such images, in *The War in the Air*. Later works of the same kind include Edward Shanks' *The People of the Ruins*, Cicely Hamilton's *Theodore Savage*, Neil Bell's *The Gas War of 1940*, and John Gloag's *Winter's Youth*.

Scientific romance was continually enlivened, and thereby saved from being entire gloomy, by input from essays in speculative science. Wells, in his early work in this vein, was carrying forward and strengthening a tradition that was as much intellectual play as anything else—a toying with ideas that was largely abstracted and amused; a variety of modest armchair philosophizing. After the Great War it extended through the works of such writers as J. B. S. Haldane and Julian Huxley. Some of the most imaginatively adventurous scientific romances, which include John Beresford's *The Hampdenshire Wonder*, E. V. Odle's *The Clockwork Man*, John Gloag's *Tomorrow's Yesterday*, and Murray Constantine's *Proud Man*, tend to be rather dreamy works even when they are not, like Olaf Stapledon's *Star Maker* or John Beresford and Esme Wynne-Tyson's *The Riddle of the Tower*, actual visionary fantasies. They frequently begin in country villages, and very often return full circle, with the initial circumstances restored, so that the world remains essentially undisturbed by the flight of fantasy.

Wells dubbed the period following the end of the Great War "The Age of Frustration", and scientific romance between the wars can be regarded as an extraordinary elaboration of that spirit of frustration. It shows up not merely in the pessimistic fantasies of destruction by war, and in such cynical analyses of perverted Utopian dreams as Muriel Jaeger's *The Question Mark* and Aldous Huxley's famous satire *Brave New World*, but also in the supposedly optimistic works of the period. When hope for the future is offered in postwar scientific romance it is usually tied to the idea that there might be some kind of miraculous transcendence of the human condition—that a new race might appear, freed from the awful psychological hangups that have prevented ordinary men from creating a just and satisfactory social order. Images of these "superior beings" can be found in the Amphibians of S. Fowler Wright's *The World Below*, the cat-people of John Gloag's *Tomorrow's Yesterday*, the Utopian supermen of John Beresford's *"What Dreams May Come...?"*, the "Young Men" whose anticipated advent was celebrated in M. P. Shiel's last novel, the "elevator man" of Gerald Heard's *Doppelgängers*, and many of the future species in Olaf Stapledon's epic future history *Last and First Men*. Such superhumans are always contrasted with our own kind, and the reader of such books is usually invited—indeed, commanded—to feel humiliated and debased by comparison.

The fashionability of scientific romance lasted only as long as the experimental phase of the middlebrow popular fiction magazines—they had virtually abandoned their enthusiastic championship of outré material as early as 1905. From then on scientific romance was considered a matter of minority interest, too outlandish to be widely popular, and it was forced to seek a place in more rarefied strata of the market—it filled a spectrum extending from the cheerfully middlebrow to the earnestly highbrow; even its imaginatively adventurous works were weighed down by their philosophical pretensions, to the point where the paperback reprint of *Last and*

First Men was released as a Pelican book, packaged as though it were non-fiction.

In America, by contrast, the new genre of science fiction appeared as a byproduct of a curious kind of brand warfare, instituted when the major publishers of popular pulp magazines began to multiply the number of titles they produced, diversifying and specializing their contents, in the hope of filling up more space on newsstands and hence crowding out their less powerful rivals. Much of Wells's work was reprinted in the early sf pulps, but even his most extravagantly imaginative work seemed staid by comparison with the company it kept. American science fiction was much more colorful and extravagant than British scientific romance, much more interested in space travel, wild adventures on other planets, and monstrous alien beings. Although one magazine editor, John Campbell Jr., presided over a gradual sophistication of the genre from 1938 onwards, the bulk of American sf consisted of futuristic costume drama and extravagant adventure stories until the end of the century, and still does.

After the end of World War II American sf achieved a rapid and pervasive penetration of the British popular fiction market, and the rather esoteric tradition of scientific romance was completely eclipsed, save for a few exceptional works like George Orwell's *Nineteen Eighty-Four*. The cream of the science fiction that eventually became dominant both in America and in Britain, however, combines the best elements of both the prior traditions, and has recovered much of the scope and daring of Wells' early scientific romances, which he wrote before the horizons of his futuristic imagination began to shrink.

* * * * * * *

We are the children of the children of the people of H. G. Wells's time, and we know how good his powers of foresight were. We live in a Europe whose cities have, indeed, been bombed by fleets of aeroplanes, but which has recovered from its devastation to set itself on the road to becoming a true European Community. We live in a world that possesses huge stockpiles of nuclear weapons, but whose leaders now seem to have a reasonable determination not to use them. There are men in today's world who have already set foot on the moon, and have told us what a giant leap for mankind that step was.

The question that is asked over and over again in Wells's essays and stories of the future still lies before us: can the nations of the world come together in a single community, dedicated to the ideals of liberty, equality and fraternity, before our conflicts, expressed in war and civil strife, tear down all that we have built in the last thousand years? If we can be slightly more optimistic in confronting that question now than we could be fifty years ago, that is partly because we have used, and are using, the time machine of the imagination to such good effect.

We also know now about the mistakes that Wells made in trying to figure out what the future might hold. We know, for instance, that he was wrong to assume that the sun would cool as quickly as he thought, because we know—although he could not, in 1895—that its heat is produced by a nuclear reaction and not by gravitational collapse. We also know that an atomic bomb produces a single big bang and not a series of explosions, like the bombs in *The World Set Free*. But we should not think of the time machine of the imagination as a prophetic device that intends to tell us in great detail exactly what will happen; it is much more useful than that, because it tries to show us a whole range of things that might happen, most of which certainly will not.

It is far more useful to know what *might* happen than what *must* happen, because knowing all the things that might happen offers us a chance to choose which of those things we want to happen, and which ones we desperately want to avoid. It is, in fact, more important to know about the things which we definitely do not want to happen, but which might if we cannot take steps to avoid them, than it is to know about the things which we would quite like to happen. We must first of all avoid destroying ourselves, or allowing ourselves to be destroyed; only when we have done that can we think sensibly about making the world better. This is why so many of the futures glimpsed through the time machine of the imagination are horrible and frightening—their purpose is to frighten us into taking care that we will not let such futures sneak up on us while we are not paying attention.

In the pages of modern science fiction stories, the time machine of the imagination is now operated simultaneously by thousands of writers working in dozens of different languages. It has to be, because, as time goes by, the pace of change speeds up, and many more possibilities come into view: many more dangers and many more threats, but also many more opportunities.

We already know, a mere hundred years after Wells wrote his classic essay, that his man of the year million is a mere phantom, because the evolutionary future of mankind is no longer subject to the dominion of natural selection. We now know the secrets of the genetic code, and we have every reason to suppose that we will become masters of our own future evolution, and of the evolution of all life on earth. The great adventure in which our children, and our children's children, will take part, is greater than anything H. G. Wells could imagine; but because he showed us the way to do it, we can imagine it, and we should certainly try as hard as we can to foresee all of its possibilities, good and bad.

HUGO GERNSBACK

According to the account of his life given by Sam Moskowitz in *Explorers of the Infinite* (1963), the man after whom the Hugo Awards are informally named, was born on 16 August 1884 in Luxemburg. He completed his education after the turn of the century at a technical college in the Rhineland town of Bingen, not far from Wiesbaden. He claimed that the book which first fired his imagination was a German translation of one of Percival Lowell's books on Mars, although he later became an enthusiastic reader of Jules Verne and H. G. Wells. He emigrated to the USA in 1904, allegedly because he was refused patents in France and Germany for a new kind of electrical battery. I say "allegedly" because everything that Sam Moskowitz wrote about his boyhood hero and sometime employer came directly from the great man's lips in the 1950s, by which time Gernsback was seventy-five. To the extent that what he told Moskowitz has been checked by other researchers, it appears that Gernsback's account was not entirely reliable.

Gernsback went to work for William Roche, a manufacturer of dry-cell batteries, but was dismissed after being found in Roche's office with confidential materials in his hands (he explained to Moskowitz that Roche had jumped to entirely the wrong conclusion). He found a partner and went into business manufacturing dry-cell batteries himself, but soon withdrew from the partnership (because his partner was leaching away the profits, he told Moskowitz). He continued as sole proprietor of a similar business, but it went bankrupt in 1907.

In 1904 Gernsback and a fellow-lodger had set up The Electro Importing Company (TELIMCO) to import scientific equipment from Germany and sell it on through mail-order catalogues. The star item was what Moskowitz described as "the first home radio set in history", although it was actually a wireless telegraph apparatus for sending and receiving Morse code. TELIMCO was investigated by police who thought that its ads were guilty of fraudulent representation, but no charges were brought (another mistake, Gernsback explained to Moskowitz). Gernsback was, however, trading in goods that were about to enjoy a spectacular boom, and his experience of publishing promotional catalogues provided him with a further opportunity to branch out.

Modern Electrics, founded in 1908, was essentially an advertising tool, whose editorial content was primarily geared to the promotion of Gernsback's other stocks-in-trade. A significant number of its readers were radio enthusiasts and would-be inventors, and Gernsback wasted no opportunity to flatter this constituency with promises that they were the coming men, who not only had their fingers on the pulse of progress but stood to make fortunes. In order to ram this message home Gernsback wrote a fictionalized tract that offered a vivid picture of the inventor of the future: *Ralph 124C41+*.

* * * * * * *

Ralph, whose punning surname hardly justifies Moskowitz's opinion that Gernsback was possessed of a "rapier-like wit", is one of only ten mental giants permitted to use the plus suffix in the year 2660. As he moves through his world, Gernsback offers lavish descriptions of the technological gadgets around him. In the book version published in 1923 and reprinted in 1955 these include the telephot (a video telephone), television, electric cars, wireless power-transmission, the electrical stimulation of crop-growth, radar, microfilm, antigravity, the hypnobioscope (for sleep-learning), the menograph (a thought-reading device), weather control and space travel, but some of these were probably added in when the serial was being revised for book publication.

The plot of the story involves Ralph falling in love by telephot and then performing a series of Herculean labours in order to save his beloved from various natural disasters (including death) and the dastardly attempts of two rival suitors—one of them a Martian—to kidnap and ravish her. The story bears far more resemblance to the fiction of contemporary pulp magazines and "dime novels" than to anything Verne or Wells might have written, although it does anticipate the similarly-inspired cinema serials that Hollywood had not yet started cranking out. The plot was, however, merely a convenient device. As Gernsback said in his introduction to the serial version, the story was "intended to give the reader as accurate a prophecy of the future as is consistent with the present marvelous growth of science".

Gernsback's original introduction went on to assure his readers that, no matter how improbable the devices featured in the story might seem, "they are not impossible, or outside of the reach of science". Many later commentators have been impressed by the truth of this judgment, but it is arguable that the most significant thing about the "hits" scored by Gernsback's story is that all of them were, indeed, straightforward applications of the scientific knowledge of his own day, with a minor contribution from contemporary pseudo-science. One thing that is absent from the image of 2660 inhabited by Ralph 124C41+ is any conspicuous advancement in science.

For a mental superman, Ralph is decidedly uninterested in theory; he is an improviser of gadgets; the "laboratory" in which we find him as the story opens is an assembly-shop. The hero on whom he is modeled—who must have been Gernsback's own hero—is clearly Thomas Edison, the very model of the practical experimenter and accumulator of patents. Edison—who did not die until 1931, although his greatest triumphs were already behind him in 1911—was the presiding genius of the contemporary American *zeitgeist*, the shining example held up before all the clients of Gernsback's mail-order business.

Gernsback continued to feature fiction in *Modern Electrics*. Jacques Morgan wrote five stories, presumably to commission, which appeared between October 1912 and February 1913. When *Modern Electrics* became *The Electrical Experimenter* later that year Gernsback began to broaden the range of contributors, eventually taking up his own pen again to contribute thirteen accounts of "Baron Muenchhausen's Scientific Adventures" between 1915 and 1917. These were narrated by one "I. M. Alier", a radio ham of genius who also happens to be a flagrant opportunist and an argumentative churl; he also seemed to have served time in jail. We can, of course, only speculate as to where Gernsback might have found the inspiration for such a character, but it might be worth noting that he is the only character in Gernsback's entire canon possessed of some literary semblance of life. The second Muenchhausen adventure took care to establish that the exiled Baron was on the side of the Allies in the Great War, although he had removed himself to Mars by the time America got involved. Most of the other fiction published in *The Electrical Experimenter* was not considered sufficiently fantastic to warrant inclusion in Everett F. Bleiler's magnificently comprehensive study of *Science-Fiction: The Early Years* (1990), but it did include an early two-part space opera by R. and C. Winthrop, "At War with the Invisible" (1918). This was illustrated by Frank R. Paul, who was by then—and was long to remain—Gernsback's most prolific illustrator.

In 1920 another title-change converted *The Electrical Experimenter* into *Science and Invention*, presumably because part of its area of concern had been shifted into a companion magazine founded in 1919, *Radio News*. In the next ten years *Radio News* published more than a hundred short stories and novelettes, although most of them—according to Bleiler—were not speculative. In the same period *Science and Invention* clocked up a similar wordage of fiction, almost all of it far more extravagant than the material featured in its sister publication. The August 1923 issue was entirely given over to what Gernsback called "scientifiction", and one of the contributors to that issue, Ray Cummings, was to become a regular contributor of serials. The most prolific contributor of all, however, was Clement Fézandié, whose series of "Dr. Hackensaw's Secrets" ran to more than forty items.

Like many other contemporary heroes, Hackensaw was clearly modeled on Edison, but Fézandié seems to have been much better-informed about matters of science than his rivals and was certainly more adventurous than other writers of such series. Many of Hackensaw's exploits involved biological inventions—the first item in the series dealt with possible aspects of cloning and genetic engineering, while the third extrapolated "the secret of suspended animation". The second had probed "the secret of the atom" with rather more intelligence than Ray Cummings was wont to display in his microcosmic romances.

Most historians of science fiction imply that these dabblings in fiction were a gestation period whose inevitable climax was *Amazing Stories*—an impression greatly encouraged in the 1950s when Sam Moskowitz offered Gernsback heroic status as "the Father of Science Fiction". There is, however, no conspicuous evidence that Gernsback had must interest in science fiction as fiction, rather than a means of popularizing technological gadgetry and the possibilities of future technology. Gernsback did indeed launch *Amazing Stories*, after fifteen years of dabbling in fiction, but it cannot really be regarded as a natural progression from the work in his other magazines; very few of the authors featured in *The Electrical Experimenter* and *Science and Invention* produced original work for *Amazing Stories* and Gernsnback's initial intention was to use the magazine as a vehicle for reprinting the popular works of Jules Verne and H. G. Wells, using other reprints (including a few from Gernsback's other magazines) as fillers.

In 1926 the American pulp magazine boom was at its giddy height, and many pulp publishers were employing the tactics of brand warfare, multiplying titles in order to occupy more of the limited space available on the newsstand racks. *Weird Tales*, founded in 1923, was using a considerable amount of science fiction, although other magazines that had flirted with the genre, like *Thrill Book*, had already gone broke. It seems likely that *Amazing Stories* was a purely commercial venture, which Gernsback undertook because he thought his existing subscription lists might help establish a secure commercial base for such a magazine. He seems to have believed that he could reprint the entire works of Verne and Wells without paying any fees, and when he went in pursuit of original work he did not call on his own stable of fiction-writers; he attempted instead to cash in on the enormous popularity of the exotic romances of Edgar Rice Burroughs and A. Merritt, who were among the most successful of all pulp writers. He had already persuaded Merritt to rewrite "The Metal Monster" as "The Metal Emperor" for use in *Science and Invention*, and he got Burroughs to write *The Master-Mind of Mars* for the 1927 *Amazing Stories Annual*, which preceded *Amazing Stories Quarterly*. The only writer featured in *Science and Invention* who did new work for *Amazing* was Fézandié, who did two more Dr. Hackensaw stories for it before abandoning sf forever.

Gernsback had little to do with the actual running of *Amazing*; he hired T. O'Conor Sloane to act as associate editor, and book-collector C. A. Brandt to identify and supply copies of suitable stories for reprinting. His main interest at this time was radio; he had been a prime mover in founding the first organization of radio hams and he had written one of the first books on radio broadcasting. By 1926 his empire had expanded to include two radio broadcasting stations, W2XAL and WRNY, and these were the primary focus of his entrepreneurial concerns. WRNY conducted an early experiment in television broadcasting in 1928 to publicize the launch of yet another new magazine, called *Television*. In February 1929, however, a petition was made to render two companies owned by Gernsback and his brother Sidney—including the Experimenter Publishing Company—involuntarily bankrupt.

* * * * * * *

The account of the 1929 bankruptcy that Gernsback gave to Sam Moskowitz in the 1950s "explained" that it was the result of a wicked plot by a jealous rival, and claimed that the creditors all received payment in full. Some other commentators ambitious to patch together a genre history assumed that it must have been the result of the famous Wall Street crash, although it happened several months beforehand. A summary of the *New York Times* account of the incident by Tom Perry, published as a letter in *Amazing* in July 1977, told a very different story, according to which the businesses were insolvent and Gernsback had to fight hard against charges that he had diverted assets from the threatened companies. These assets included the subscription lists which were almost certainly—criminally, if so—used by Gernsback to attract subscribers to the new magazines he launched after the petition for bankruptcy was filed.

Moskowitz—never a man to take contradiction kindly—responded furiously to Perry's initial letter, but his defense of Gernsback's honor in the October 1977 issue of *Amazing* was dramatically upstaged in the May 1978 issue, which reported the results of Perry's further researches. Perry revealed that it was the huge losses of the jewel in the Gernsback brothers' crown—the broadcasting station WRNY—that had run their entire enterprise on to the rocks, causing them to divert money from Experimenter, which had left the magazines' printing bills unpaid. It was the printers who had entered the petition for bankruptcy, and the Gernsbacks had responded by immediately abandoning Experimenter to its fate and setting up a new publishing company unburdened by any debt. Perry suggested that their probable intention was to continue *Amazing Stories*—which was by then the most profitable title in the stable—under the new imprint, and that they must have been very surprised when a buyer was found for the derelict company, who was willing to discharge most of its debts and keep the magazines going.

Perry also observed that Hugo and Sidney had filed their own demands against the company, claiming several thousand dollars apiece for unpaid salaries in the weeks before the bankruptcy. He noted that the other creditors objected strenuously to the Gernsbacks paying themselves a thousand dollars a week for running an insolvent company, although he does not speculate as to what Hugo's subsequent contributors—who were, according to one of them, recompensed by word-rates of "microscopic fractions of a cent, payable on lawsuit"—might have thought of it. At the end of his article, however, Perry indulged in a little speculation himself, pointing out that that if things had not worked out as they did, the pulp science fiction genre might have died almost as soon as it was born, whereas the continued competition between *Amazing* and *Wonder Stories* actually served to inspire other imitators, most notable among them *Astounding Stories of Super-Science*.

* * * * * * *

By the beginning of 1929 *Amazing* had virtually given up using reprints. It had already begun picking up stories submitted by fans—Jack Williamson made his debut in the December 1928 issue—but Hugo Gernsback's involvement in the acquisition of material had probably been limited to issuing a contract for a batch of unwritten stories from David H. Keller, whom he had met socially. When his "new" *Amazing Stories* had to be retitled *Science Wonder Stories*—subsequently combined with its short-lived companion *Air Wonder Stories* as *Wonder Stories*—he again hired a managing editor (David Lasser, replaced in 1933 by Charles Hornig) to do the actual work, although he still handed out contracts for unseen work to writers like Frank K. Kelly.

One can only speculate as to why writers like Charles Wolfe and Clement Fézandié, who had been prolific contributors to Gernsback's early magazines, abandoned the field—although Fézandié lived another thirty years—and why Ray Cummings never wrote for either of Gernsback's sf magazines, although he was perfectly happy to write for *Astounding*. Whatever the reason, Sloane's *Amazing* and Lasser's *Wonder Stories* spent the early 1930s cultivating a new generation of writers, and taking aboard writers like Edward E. Smith, "John Taine" (Eric Temple Bell), and Stanton A. Coblentz, who had previously found no market for their extravagant imaginative fiction.

Having been born out of the pulp magazine publishers' experiment in brand warfare, *Amazing* and *Wonder* suffered its inevitable consequences. In order to defend their rack space, all the publishers had to pump out more and more titles, with the inevitable result that all of them began to lose money hand over fist—but nobody dared let up first, lest he be squeezed out. By the mid-1930s, however, magazine publishing suffered an economic holocaust. Corporate raiders moved in to pick up the pieces of *Amazing* and *Wonder*, both of which were delivered into the hands of editors who now knew that the core of the science fiction market consisted of teenage boys avid for action-adventure. They became, in essence, pulp equivalents of the comic-books that were just beginning their own triumphal march to economic glory.

Science fiction historians, for whom the evolution of *Astounding Stories of Super-Science* into John W. Campbell Jr.'s *Astounding Science Fiction* was the central plot of the story, have tended to represent the economic decay of *Amazing* and *Wonder* as a gradual loss of noble ambition, but it is not at all clear that the noble ambition was ever there. It is certainly true that the editorial with which Gernsback launched the first issue of *Amazing* was full of braggadocio, loudly advertising the potential of the new genre of "scientifiction", but it really was an advertisement, bearing little or no relation to the path actually followed by Gernsback's magazines. He promised that they would be instructive and prophetic, but the actual editorial policies made only token efforts to maintain any such pretence. Unlike *Astounding*, whose first incarnation offered formularistic pulp melodrama in a futuristic setting, *Amazing* and *Wonder* never had any real direction at all; they were neither fish nor fowl, although their creator was eventually to feed Sam Moskowitz a liberal helping of good red herring.

* * * * * * *

Even before the 1929 bankruptcy, Gernsback had started another publishing sideline in association with the one writer he had personally recruited to *Amazing*, David H. Keller. Keller was a Freudian psychiatrist who had a deep and abiding interest in the psychology and sociology of sex. Alongside his fiction, Gernsback issued a ten-volume series of sex education pamphlets, each of which sold for a good deal more than an issue of *Amazing*. When *Wonder Stories* failed to make the best of the flying start it received by virtue of its pirated subscription list, Gernsback was quick to found a digest magazine called *Sexology* in 1933, which continued to thrive long after the fire-sale of Gernsback's fiction magazines. For the next twenty years, Gernsback showed very little interest in science fiction—until he met the worshipful Sam Moskowitz, and was told that he was the father of a precious orphan.

Moskowitz persuaded the aging Gernsback, who was still publishing *Radio-Electronics Magazine* alongside *Sexology*, to get back into science fiction. Moskowitz presumably pointed out that the genre was performing so well in a troubled marketplace that new titles were appearing all the time. Gernsback launched the glossy *Science-Fiction Plus* in 1953 with Moskowitz as "managing editor". To its first issue, Gernsback contributed a boastful editorial in which he complained that he ought to have been allowed to take out patents on all the devices "invented" in *Ralph 124C41+* and a "novelette" that was actually a pseudo-journalistic exercise in futurology about the exploration of Mars.

Gernsback's subsequent editorials similarly combined extravagant self-congratulation with plaintive whining about the refusal of critics to take science fiction seriously as a species of prophecy. If he ever read any of the fiction that Moskowitz bought for the magazine—which was not without interest, but had no value whatsoever as serious technological scientific speculation—he might have understood why that was. What he did quickly realize, however, was that the recent "boom" in magazine science fiction was the result of utter desperation on the part of publishers who were watching their entire marketplace disappear in the face of paperback competition, and he killed the loss-making magazine after seven issues. His last editorial complained bitterly about the tendency of modern science fiction to "gravitate more and more into the realm of the esoteric and sophisticated literature", insisting that science fiction ought to be written "into simple language" for the benefit of children.

Gernsback did make some further efforts to practice what he preached. In the early fifties he wrote a quasi-journalistic novel about the invasion of Earth by alien Xenos. This proved unpublishable, although a version from which Sam Moskowitz claimed to have removed all the extraneous non-fiction material—thus reducing its length by half—was published in 1971, four years after Gernsback's death, as *Ultimate World*. It is an exceedingly bad book by any standards. In addition to this lost endeavor, Gernsback published a series of brief "Christmas annuals" entitled *Forecast*, which reprinted a few of his last endeavors in fiction and futurology from *Radio-Electronics* and *Sexology*, while constantly harking back to the supposed triumphs of his early career. The final edition of *Forecast* (Christmas 1959) featured a lead article on spaceliners, a feature on "The Odorchestra" (an apparatus first proposed in one of Baron Muenchhausen's scientific adventures, somewhat resembling a Wurlitzer organ, whose purpose would be to add a scent-track to movies) and "Jeanne", which advertised itself as a "bizarre romance". This was a story about a transvestite and would-be pioneer of transsexualism, strongly reminiscent in its rhetoric of the Ed Wood movie *Glen or Glenda* (1953).

* * * * * * *

There is no doubt that Hugo Gernsback was a remarkable man. It would be difficult to imagine anyone more likely to respond to Sam Moskowitz's honest and generous hero-worship, and the response Gernsback made is entirely typical of him. Invited to pontificate on the subject of the genre whose father he had been appointed, he opined that it was mostly rubbish, ruined by literary affectation. Of the first anthology of Hugo winners, he said that only one of the nine stories it contained was science fiction (he did not say which one but he probably meant Daniel Keyes' "Flowers for Algernon"), the remainder being fantasy.

Sam Moskowitz was right to identify Gernsback as the father of pulp science fiction, on the grounds that he founded *Amazing Stories* and *Wonder Stories*, and it is understandable that Moskowitz's deep and abiding love of the genre prevented him from noticing that the procreative act in question was more akin to a casual visit to a prostitute than to any kind of responsible parenthood. Countless science fiction fans have heard Moskowitz, while speaking at conventions, recall his meetings with Gernsback with great affection and even greater reverence; it would have taken a brave and callously inconsiderate heckler to point out to him that the father of genre science fiction always seems to have regarded his offspring—and treated it—as a contemptible bastard whose worthlessness was ameliorated solely by the slight evidence its existence provided of his own prophetic genius.

If, as we are perfectly entitled to suspect, the fundamental truth of the matter lies in economic history, then the creation of pulp science fiction was a chapter of accidents. When pulp brand warfare briefly created an economic climate into which science fiction might be launched, Hugo Gernsback did not respond by hiving off the kind of "scientifiction" that he was featuring regularly in *Science and Invention*. What he did instead was in one sense more ambitious, but in another rather cowardly—he went for what looked like a much safer option, cashing in on work that had already proved its popularity. The sudden appearance of a legion of fanatical lovers of the genre, many of whom were begging to supply him with stories for little or no payment, probably astonished him—but it certainly presented him with a chance of saving his neck when WRNY's catastrophic failure looked like dragging him down. It seems highly probable that he intended to carry off as many of Experimenter's assets as he could get away with—including *Amazing Stories*—and never expected to find himself in competition with it. When that competition proved too strong he was quick to bale out—but by that time, the baby was born and the genre label had been swept up into the maelstrom of brand warfare.

Had its care been left to Gernsback, genre science fiction would have died in the mid-thirties. The kinds of science fiction that were still being published then—which bore not the slightest resemblance to the scientifiction of *Science and Invention* or the rather different scientifiction of the original *Amazing Stories*—could easily have been diverted, along with other kinds of exotic costume drama, entirely into the world of comic books. The fact that sf clung on to its foothold in the pulps had nothing to do with Hugo Gernsback and everything to do with people like Sam Moskowitz: the fans who had found far more within the fledgling genre than anyone had yet put into it, and were avid to make up the deficiency.

The adoptive fathers of science fiction were men like Donald A. Wollheim, who edited pulp science fiction magazines without a salary or an editorial budget, because that was his vocation, and John W. Campbell Jr., who believed—unlike Hugo Gernsback—that the genre had authentic potential as a medium of scientific speculation, and as a means of investigating the sweeping social changes that scientific and technological progress would inevitably precipitate. It is they who deserve the credit for its nurture, and for its real achievements.

But then, what did the original Oscar ever do for the movies?

JOHN W. CAMPBELL, JR.

Chroniclers of the proto-autistic condition Asperger's Syndrome have observed that a disproportionate number of sufferers have fathers who were engineers. Currently-fashionable opinion alleges that Asperger's Syndrome bridges a wide gap between "full-blown" autism and normal male behavior on a spectrum of mental disconnection, describing the mind-set of those individuals (almost all of whom are allegedly male) who are not so severely afflicted that they cannot relate to other people at all, but are nevertheless prone to obsessions that take priority over social interactions: hobbies, collections and so on. Asperger's Syndrome apparently assists the brain to be much better at handling physical data and abstract ideas than interpreting human behavior, and bringing such data and ideas into obsessive focus—in cases where it produces no acute symptoms it is, in effect, God's gift to would-be mathematicians, scientists and lawyers.

As with the less problematic manifestations of Adler's inferiority complex, a mild case of Asperger's Syndrome might be reckoned by some to be a more desirable state of being than mere normality. Ordinary people sometimes find it difficult to cultivate the narrow focus and relentless preoccupation that are required for outstanding success in a specialized field; many are too easily distracted by the demands of family and fun. Anyone who aspires to be a mover and shaker in a specific endeavor, especially one requiring relentless data collection or mental abstraction, requires a strong sense of vocation. It is at least arguable that no real man—in an intellectual rather than a brutal sense—would want to be without a slight touch of Asperger's Syndrome, even if he had to bear the cost of finding other people's emotional states difficult to read or respond to.

John W. Campbell, Senior—whose own father had been a lawyer—was an engineer working for Bell Telephone in New Jersey when his similarly-named son was born in 1910. Sam Moskowitz records in the essay on Campbell in *Seekers of Tomorrow* that the young John Junior "had virtually no friends", and that "his relationship with his parents was emotionally difficult" because "his father carried impersonality and theoretical objectivity in family matters to the brink of fetish" and "almost never used the pronoun I". His mother, by contrast, seemed to young John to be "flighty, moody, and...unpredictable from moment to moment" and he was "baffled and frustrated" by her "changeability". She also had a twin sister who lived with the family, who seemed to the young boy to be extraordinarily hostile to him. It is, of course, direly dangerous to offer diagnoses on the basis of such distant reportage, but it is probably safe to say—taking into account later developments as well—that there were few people who were in their teens during the heyday of pulp fiction who were better qualified than John W. Campbell Jr. to become the most obsessive science fiction fan in the world.

In a previous article in this series I observed—somewhat controversially, it seems—that Hugo Gernsback's credentials as "the father of science fiction" were acquired by virtue of a relatively casual act of procreation, and that he subsequently neglected the fledgling genre. Had the infant been left to fend for itself, it would have turned into an exact replica of all the other wayward kids on the same slummy block. We know this perfectly well because we know exactly what happened to the two ex-Gernsback magazines, *Amazing Stories* and *Wonder Stories*, when the former fell into the care of Ray Palmer and the latter became *Thrilling Wonder Stories*, both featuring garish pulp adventure fiction aimed at unsophisticated teenagers. Their foster-parents were not to blame; Palmer and Leo Margulies were following the dictates of logic and nature—but their newer neighbor, *Astounding Stories of Super-Science*, did not go the same way. After a slightly shaky start, it was adopted by a father who was fully prepared, and fully equipped, to lavish far more consistent attention upon it than had ever been lavished upon him.

Hugo Gernsback might have been the bibliographical father of science fiction, but John W. Campbell Jr. was the man who fostered, raised it and educated it in his own image, taking the infant *Astounding Stories of Super-Science* and transforming it, by slow degrees, into *Analog*: the magazine for obsessive but speculatively-inclined engineers.

* * * * * * *

After serving four years as a high-school misfit, John Campbell Jr. studied at the Massachusetts Institute of Technology. He was already a regular reader of *Amazing Stories* and his imagination was greatly inspired by Edward E. Smith's *The Skylark of Space*, which became a key model for his own early writings.

The first story Campbell that submitted to *Amazing* was accepted, but the typescript was lost. The second—the first of five stories he published in 1930—was "When the Atoms Failed", a story in which the future use of atomic power is superseded by a technology of matter-destruction, whose practicability is proved by an electrical calculating machine. The bulk of the story consists of a lecture delivered by the protagonist to an admiring but scientifically naïve friend. A sequel, "The Metal Horde", swiftly followed, similarly employing an alien invasion as the necessity that mothers the protagonist's further inventions. "The Voice of the Void", set ten billion years in the future, uses the cooling of the sun as the spur that drives humankind to perfect faster-than-light travel, although the species' subsequent colonial endeavors bring it into conflict with sentient but immaterial "pools of force" nourished by atomic energy. Unlike the earlier stories, this was an exercise in exposition, whose subject-matter and manner both suggest that, if Campbell had not yet read Olaf Stapledon's recently-published *Last and First Men*, then he had probably read its blueprint, J. B. S. Haldane's fictionalized essay "The Last Judgment".

Campbell did not reprint any of these three stories in his subsequent collections—although his other 1930 publications, the more orthodox space operas "Piracy Preferred" and "Solarite", were reprinted along with a further sequel in *The Black Star Passes*—but between them they laid the groundwork for the greater part of his subsequent work. Although the space opera series begun with "Piracy Preferred" continued—escalating its scale with each new phase—in *Islands of Space* (1931) and *Invaders from the Infinite* (1932), it was his shorter stories that became and remained his primary laboratory of thought.

Campbell's dependence on his writing income increased when he married Dona Stuart in 1931, shortly after being thrown out of MIT without a degree. Some of the stories he turned out in the next year or so, while completing his degree at Duke University, are utterly trivial, but ideative threads already anchored in "When the Atoms Failed" and "The Voice of the Void" were extended to a logical limit of sorts in "The Last Evolution" (1932), a quasi-Stapledonian story in which mankind's heirs give an account of post-human evolution. Here, the pressure of alien assault results in the devastation of Earth's ecosphere, leaving the war to be continued by intelligent machines far less frail than their organic makers—but these "beings of Metal" are superseded in their turn under the same evolutionary pressure, yielding to superior "beings of Force" which use "the ultimate energy of annihilating matter" to defeat the Outsiders. One of the machines, Roal, delivers a curious eulogy for mankind, and for organic life itself, suggesting that the end of life might have been "ordained" and "right" because Man, like all living things, was "a parasite" and "a makeshift" destined to be replaced by machines capable of truly independent existence and of directing their own evolution towards the production of the ultimate "beings of Force".

The idea that immaterial entities of "pure force" or "pure thought" might be the end-point of all evolution was not original to Campbell—his hero, "Doc" Smith, had suggested it in *Skylark Three* (1930) and George Bernard Shaw had earlier employed it in the final act of *Back to Methuselah*—but Campbell formulated his own idea of the likely path and pressure of that evolution. The only element of his later obsessions that had yet to be given a foundation within his work was his fascination with "psi-powers"—but his displacement from MIT to Duke sent him to the arena of J. B. Rhine's pioneering endeavors in experimental parapsychology, two years before Rhine published *Extra-Sensory Perception*.

* * * * * * *

Campbell told Sam Moskowitz that his short fiction changed direction sharply after 1932 because he wanted to capture something of the tone of the elegiac opening chapter of a novel called *The Red Gods Call* by C. E. Scoggins. "Twilight" is a quasi-Stapledonian tale that differs from "The Voice of the Void" only in attempting a quasi-lyrical style, which is actually closer to Donald Wandrei's attempts to write pastiches of Clark Ashton Smith than to Scoggins' work. It is also close to the spirit of such British scientific romances as E. M. Forster's "The Machine Stops" and S. Fowler Wright's *The New Gods Lead*, imagining a degenerate future mankind enfeebled by dependence on the bounty of machines.

"Twilight" was rejected by all the sf magazines extant at the beginning of 1933, but it sold to F. Orlin Tremaine, who took over *Astounding* from Harry Bates later that year. It appeared there in 1934 under the pseudonym Don A. Stuart (adapted, of course, from the name of Campbell's wife). Campbell also sold his new space opera, *The Mightiest Machine*, to Tremaine, but Tremaine rejected its sequels, and Don A. Stuart then became Campbell's principal literary identity. Although he published more action-adventure stories under his own name in *Amazing* and *Thrilling Wonder*, the significant further evolution of his work took place under the pseudonym.

By the time he wrote "Night" (1935), in which the machines faithfully maintaining mankind's degenerate descendants have taken up the torch of evolutionary progress, exactly as they had in "The Last Evolution", Campbell had written half a dozen other Stuart stories. Two dealt with the theme of atomic power and one with eugenics, but the most significant comprised a trilogy reprinted in the collection *Cloak of Aesir* (1952) as "The Story of the Machine" (1935). Earth is here visited by a sentient machine that takes pseudo-parental control over humankind but subsequently abandons its charges, having realized that its protection is initiating the kind of degeneracy featured in "Twilight". This abandonment leaves mankind at the mercy of more brutal alien masters, but that enslavement turns out to be a blessing in disguise, restoring the selective pressure necessary to reinvigorate the race.

The final foundation-stone was incorporated into Campbell's canon by "Forgetfulness" (1937), a parable in which mankind's star-strewn descendants rediscover Earth, but find its cities deserted and their former inhabitants seemingly degenerate. These "last men" have, however, cultivated powers of the mind that have allowed them to transcend their dependency on machines, sidestepping the patterns of "The Last Evolution" and "Night" to take a short cut—or a giant leap—toward their ultimate destiny. This was followed by "Out of Night" (1937), which compounded the two alien invasions of "The Story of the Machine" into one, offering an account of the liberation of mankind from the benign rule of the explicitly maternal Sarn by a symbolic shadow of self-determination.

While he was completing the framework in which his vision of man's place in the cosmos—and the spectrum of evolutionary possibilities which lay before him—was securely set, Campbell went through a series of temporary jobs in research and technical writing. He found nothing to suit him until he was offered, in September 1937, what must have seemed to him to be the best job imaginable: assistant editor to F. Orlin Tremaine. Within a matter of months, he had inherited the editorial chair; Tremaine left in May 1938, shortly after Campbell had completed the most famous of all the Don A. Stuart stories, "Who Goes There?"—whose reputation was assured when it became the basis of the film *The Thing*. Here, the alien invader is unremittingly hostile and supremely dangerous, providing the ultimate challenge—and hence, of course, the ultimate test of human worthiness and capacity for progress.

* * * * * * *

Several stories that Campbell wrote in the late 1930s remained unpublished for a long time. "Marooned" and "All" were reprinted with the title story in the posthumous collection *The Space Beyond* (1976). It is not entirely clear why these stories were not published when they were written, but it evidently had much to do with an eccentric Street & Smith prohibition on their editors doubling as fiction writers, either for themselves or for the competition—a prohibition that Campbell reluctantly accepted as the cost of his influence on and effective control of what other (mostly better) writers were doing. He did publish "Cloak of Aesir"—a sequel to "Out of Night"—in 1939, as Don A. Stuart's last gasp, and was later to write "The Elder Gods" for *Unknown* when a gap was in urgent need of filling, but he respected the ban.

"Marooned" was originally signed Karl van Campen, and was a sequel to an earlier story written under that name, "The Irrelevant", carrying forward a controversial argument regarding the inviolability of the law of conservation of energy. "The Space Beyond" was yet another space opera involving atomic power. Although both stories seemed remarkably crude by 1976, they would have been perfectly acceptable in 1938. It now seems beyond doubt that the Galaxy novel *Empire* (1951)—which carried Clifford Simak's byline although Simak never included it in lists of his own works—was also a Campbell space opera left over from the 1930s. The remainder of Campbell's acknowledged output consists of the short novel *The Moon Is Hell*, issued by Fantasy Press in 1951 not long after the same publisher had issued the previously-unpublished sequels to *The Mightiest Machine* as *The Incredible Planet*, and a story written for Raymond Healy's 1954 anthology, *9 Tales of Space and Time*. The fate of "All"—a tale in which a future totalitarian state imposed upon the Earth by Chinese conquerors is toppled by ingenious scientists disguised as priests and prophets of a new religion—indicated the manner in which his creative ingenuity would subsequently be employed; he gave it to Robert A. Heinlein and asked him to write it anew. It became *Sixth Column*, aka *The Day After Tomorrow*.

For the next thirty years, Campbell would feed his story ideas to his regular writers, demanding that they develop them. Among many others, he fed "Nightfall" to Isaac Asimov, "The Lion and the Lamb" to Fritz Leiber, and "To the Stars" to L. Ron Hubbard; Mack Reynolds has commented that taking on the duty of writing Campbell's stories for him was virtually compulsory in the 1950s and 1960s if the magazine were to serve as one's primary market (as it was for Randall Garrett, Christopher Anvil, and James H. Schmitz, as well as Reynolds). Campbell also felt free to demand that stories submitted to him be brought into line with his own ideas about their development; he surely ought to be reckoned a collaborator in the conclusions of such stories as Theodore Sturgeon's "Microcosmic God", Tom Godwin's "The Cold Equations", Jack Williamson's "...And Searching Mind", and Mark Clifton and Frank Riley's *They'd Rather be Right*. To judge by the remainder of Frank Herbert's output, Campbell must also deserve a great deal of credit for helping to hammer *Dune* into proper shape.

No other editor in the sf field has ever taken such an active interest in shaping the work he published. In frank contradiction to the approved methodology of magazine editorship in the 1930s—which held that one should employ seasoned professionals to pander as cleverly as possible to existing tastes—Campbell set out to build a team of new writers and to cultivate a new audience. Within three years of inheriting Tremaine's chair he had formulated that team, including Robert A. Heinlein, Clifford D. Simak, L. Sprague de Camp, A. E. van Vogt, Theodore Sturgeon, Eric Frank Russell, and Lester del Rey. When his employers encouraged him to use the seasoned hacks Arthur J. Burks and L. Ron Hubbard, he tried as hard as he could to re-educate them in the art of constructive speculative thinking—and, in the latter case, succeeded (far too well, alas). When America's entry into World War II depleted his resources, he filled the gap by encouraging Henry Kuttner and C. L. Moore to develop new identities, recruited George O. Smith, and persuaded Fritz Leiber—a natural fantasist if ever there was one—to turn his hand to serious sf.

Campbell had very definite ideas about what science fiction ought to become, and as soon as he took sole charge of *Astounding* he set out in his editorial writings to persuade the audience to follow him in his crusade. He was eventually to die in the job in 1971, after thirty-three years of full-time parenthood. His obsession with science fiction was subjected to only one slight divergence, when he founded *Unknown*, a fantasy magazine that permitted his writers to extrapolate—usually in a farcical spirit—premises far more fantastic than those licensed by the scientific world-view. It was fun, and had it endured, it might have killed the science fiction genre by demonstrating, long before the US paperback editions of *The Lord of the Rings* made the fact clear, that modern readers were perfectly happy to read fantasy, and that it had a far wider constituency of potential readers than sf. Fortunately for lovers of sf, the war forced a choice to be made in 1942, and Campbell was the man who had to make it; in those circumstances, no other outcome was possible.

* * * * * * *

Although the science fiction genre was never entirely submissive to Campbell's image of it, and began to diversify in directions of which he did not approve after 1950, it did so because the best of his rivals gave writers greater freedom than he was prepared to offer; no one else ever successfully adopted the kind of imperious role to which Campbell appointed himself, although feeble echoes of it can be detected in the careers of Donald A. Wollheim and Michael Moorcock. The science fiction genre grew away from the influence of Campbell's parentage—as all children eventually grow away from the influence of their early environment—and developed all kinds of spontaneous traits, but he was the one man who left his educative stamp indelibly upon its spectrum and its scope.

When he was invited to provide a foreword for Groff Conklin's pioneering hardcover anthology *The Best of Science Fiction* (1946), Campbell summarized his notion of what science fiction could and ought to do. He took aboard the Gernsbackian notion that sf could be prophetic—although he took care to insist that all its predictions were hypothetical and contingent—and he freely acknowledged that there was a thriving species of "adventure science fiction, wherein the action and the plot are the main point", but his own emphasis was on the way that hypotheses were developed: "The modern science fiction writer doesn't merely say 'In about ten years we will have atomic weapons.' He goes further: his primary interest is in what those weapons will do to political, economic and cultural structures of society."

This was the heart of the Campbellian enterprise: science fiction was, for him, a kind of "analytical laboratory", which ought to be as scrupulous as possible in trying to anticipate the myriad ways in which technological development would permit, encourage and force social change. In the process, he pointed out in that same foreword, sf stories could not help but touch on deep philosophical questions regarding man's place in nature and his role in cosmic history. He had already worked out what the core questions were, and although he would henceforth address them obliquely, he never lost sight of them. There is a sense in which the entirety of Campbellian science fiction can be seen as a series of footnotes to "The Last Evolution" and "Forgetfulness".

It is easy enough, looking back at the history of magazine science fiction from 1938 to 1970, to conclude that its central theme was the conquest of space. Donald A. Wollheim—another man who devoted his life to science fiction—observed in *The Universe Mak-*

ers that there had emerged within the genre a broad consensus regarding the likely future shape of human history, whose significant benchmarks extended from the first moon landings to the birth, growth and eventual decline of a galactic empire. It is, indeed, the case that the galactic empire became such a convenient framework for planetary and interplanetary romances—ranging from gaudily exotic adventure stories to extraordinarily elaborate *contes philosophiques*—that hundreds of writers were happy to take it for granted (thus establishing Isaac Asimov's pioneering *Foundation* series as the core project of Campbell's revamped *Astounding Science Fiction* and of the genre) but that future history, and its attendant myth of conquest, was always a means rather than an end. The fundamental question that Campbell bequeathed to the genre he adopted was whether humankind's relationship with technology was fated to lead the species into terminal decadence.

Campbell concluded, almost as soon as he first set pen to paper, that there was a very strong likelihood that humankind would one day be superseded by intelligent machines, whose remotest ancestors were the electric "integraphs" employed at MIT in the late 1920s. He was prepared to wonder whether that would be any bad thing, if the machines themselves were to evolve, in the end, into godlike entities of "pure force"—but he was also prepared to wonder whether there might be a way of cutting out the middleman, so that humankind might find a more direct route to quasi-godhood. That seemed to him to be the preferable alternative, but he was prepared to give supposedly dispassionate consideration to any means that might hasten the ultimate end.

Campbell's attitude to alien beings was, from the very beginning, deeply ambivalent; whereas most of his contemporaries were avid to befriend the nice aliens and annihilate the nasty ones, Campbell wondered whether the ones which sought to enslave or destroy us might actually be far more use to us in the long run than those which were sincerely benign. In Campbell's view, mankind could not possibly hope to win the great game of evolutionary progress without honing his skills against top class opposition. Some have called this "human chauvinism", and a few have thought it incipiently fascist, but Campbell—whose idea of the big picture had been formulated in "The Voice of the Void" and "The Last Evolution"—always thought that his opponents were too narrow-minded.

We can now see, of course, that the fundamental nexus of Campbellian ideas is seriously misguided, if not downright silly. Even if the idea of sentient creatures of "pure force" were imagined to retain some faint shadow of credibility, the idea that humankind might—under the right evolutionary spur—enjoy an evolutionary leap to a magically-sustained post-technological society is patently ridiculous. The fact that we can no longer maintain any serious belief in the galactic empire is merely corollary to these deeper absurdities.

The termites of reason have, by now, eaten out the entire structure of ideas supporting the house of Campbellian sf—but that does not necessarily make his quest any less heroic, or his achievements any less titanic. The one enduring legacy of his work that has not lost its value, and never will, is his insistence—embodied in the colophon of *Analog*—that the methodology of science fiction is analogous to the methodology of science, employing rational extrapolation to establish thought-experiments as thoroughly and as cleverly worked out as the writer can contrive.

To do that properly, of course, requires the kind of tight focus and obsessive analysis that Asperger's Syndrome produces—but only those unlucky enough not to be possessed of that precious gift are likely to be resentful of the fact. Some lovers of the genre may regret that science fiction fans have acquired a reputation and an image that link them irredeemably to train-spotters and computer nerds, but there is no doubt at all that, out of all the literary genres available, science fiction—and Campbellian "hard" science fiction most of all—is the one that is most closely adapted to the needs and skills of dedicated engineers and their precocious children.

EDWARD E. "DOC" SMITH

Edward E. Smith, Ph.D., was the man who invented "space opera", although he preferred the label "epics of space". Many writers before him had written tales of space travel—most of them journeys to the moon or Mars—and a few of their heroes had gone further afield than the solar system, but most imaginary voyagers who had embarked upon interstellar odysseys had done so in the spirit of the *voyages extatiques* penned by the French astronomer Camille Flammarion, rapt with wonder at the immensity and magnificence of the universe. One very obscure British scientific romance—Robert William Cole's *The Struggle for Empire* (1900)—had looked forward to a day when the all-conquering British Empire might extend its colonial wars as far as Sirius, but no one had ventured to suggest that the entire sidereal system might one day serve as a gigantic playground for pioneers until Smith wrote *The Skylark of Space*.

Smith completed the text of *The Skylark of Space* in 1920, when he was thirty years old, having started it five years earlier in collaboration with Lee Garby, the wife of a neighbor. He submitted it to numerous book publishers and pulp magazines, but it was consistently rejected until the specialist science fiction pulps came into being in the late twenties. Smith became one of a precious handful of writers who had already produced work that was too bizarre to find a home elsewhere, but could immediately be slotted into place within the nascent genre, helping to define its field. Stanton A. Coblentz and "John Taine" (Eric Temple Bell) were other such writers but neither was to provide such an important precedent as "Doc" Smith. Although Taine's *The Time Stream*—which was written a decade earlier than its publication in 1931—was equally daring, after its own particular fashion, it did not have the same potential to make an explosive impact on a reader's imagination as *The Skylark of Space*.

It was probably *Amazing*'s then editor, T. O'Conor Sloane, who insisted that Smith should add his doctorate to his byline. The editors of the early sf magazines were very anxious to give the impression that they were not merely marketing one more brand of pulp fiction, and they made the most of whatever scientific credentials their writers had. The fact that Smith was a food scientist specializing in doughnut mixes was to cause much sarcastic comment in years to come, but he was not guilty of any real dissimulation in parading his qualification; he never made any strenuous attempt to pretend that *The Skylark of Space* was a realistic novel of the future.

By the time *The Skylark of Space* actually appeared in print, in the August-October 1928 issues of *Amazing Stories*, Smith's invention had been partly duplicated by Edmond Hamilton, the first of whose tales of the Interstellar Patrol began simultaneous serialization in the August 1928 issue of *Weird Tales*. Hamilton's series, however, consisted of tales of a distant future inhabited by men with bizarre names and superhuman proclivities. While the hectic action/adventure stories were certainly not rhapsodic *voyages extatiques*, they were decisively distanced from the world of the reader. Smith's story began in that world; its opening paragraph dispatched a copper bath coated with a previously-unknown metal into the interstellar wilderness, hurtling through space with breathtakingly casual panache, and then sent supposedly ordinary people off in pursuit of it. Readers could identify with Smith's Richard Seaton with a ready ease that could not be duplicated in contemplating the exploits of the Interstellar Patrol—and the importance of that readiness of identification, especially for young readers, should not be underestimated.

* * * * * * *

The Skylark series proper consists of three volumes, the original serial being followed by *Skylark Three* (*Amazing* August-October 1930), and *Skylark of Valeron* (*Astounding* August 1934-February 1935). A fourth novel, *Skylark DuQuesne*, was serialized in *If* in 1965, but Smith was in his seventies by then and science fiction—including space opera—had become far more sophisticated; the addendum to the series had nothing to recommend it but nostalgia-appeal.

It is difficult for today's readers, who are fully accustomed to the use of galactic empires as narrative stages, to appreciate the impact that the opening paragraph of *The Skylark of Space* had on its contemporary readers. By the same token, young people who find no difficulty at all in orientating themselves with the plots of *Star Trek* and *Babylon-5* are bound to find the clean-cut Seaton, his pal

Martin Crane, and their respective girl-friends a trifle unconvincing as heroes shaped for such a stage. The villains of the Skylark series—rich businessmen with political ambitions, soon to be aided, and eventually replaced, by wave after wave of ugly aliens—have not been so rapidly superseded by the evolution of space operatic cliché, but the author's blithe assumption that genocide is the appropriate solution to most diplomatic problems ("Humanity *über alles—homo sapiens* against all the vermin of the universe!" Seaton cries, as he sets out to save the humans of Valeron from the depredations of chlorine-breathing amoebas) is bound to seem crass as well as crude in a post-Hitler era. In its original incarnation, however, the series was possessed of a remarkable and unprecedented exuberance that transported many of its readers into imaginative *terra incognita*.

The Skylark series is a straightforward and unashamed power-fantasy, which took that underrated art-form to a new extreme. Seaton continually trades in his starships for bigger and better ones with much-increased firepower (usually described in terms of the mastery of new "orders" of radiation). Although his personality remains stubbornly boyish, his mind becomes a sponge for the accumulated wisdom of whole races, increasing his personal capabilities to the point at which he can take on disembodied beings of "pure intelligence"—a conventional representation of the ultimate end of evolution—and beat them at their own game. At the end of the third volume, he bottles up these inconvenient adult-substitutes with "Blackie" DuQuesne in a prison of pure force, exiling them to the very edge of the universe (where they remained, incapable of disrupting the heroes' good clean fun, until they were required to provide leverage for the plot of the belated fourth volume).

It is the subjugation of all the series' science-fictional ideas to the cause of juvenile power-fantasy that establishes *The Skylark of Space* and its sequels as the true progenitors of space opera. Edmond Hamilton's space operas are just as wild in their inventions, but they retain a shadowy respect for scientific method and a subtle undercurrent of adult cynicism—both of which were to be dutifully elaborated in subsequent contributions to the subgenre by John W. Campbell Jr. and Jack Williamson. None of these later writers were bashful in their employment of marvelous super-science, but none of them ever showed the same level of conscienceless disrespect as Smith did in the Skylark series. Despite the Ph.D. that his editors continued to append his byline, Smith did not pay the slightest lip-service to the limits of actual possibility while he was chronicling the continuing adventures of Richard Seaton; as befit their collective title, in the Skylark series he deployed his pseudoscientific jargon as a straightforward mask for magic and miracles.

Smith was not incapable of writing space operas of a slightly more restrained kind, nor was he unwilling to do so. *The Spacehounds of I.P.C.* (1931), which was serialized in *Amazing* after *Skylark Three*, uses its pseudoscientific notions in a manner much more reminiscent of John Campbell, who had made his debut a year earlier. *Triplanetary* (1934)—which Smith wrote for the higher-paying *Astounding*, then edited by Harry Bates, but had to divert to *Amazing* when the Clayton magazine chain collapsed—also plays with its ideas in a more scrupulous and respectful fashion. Significantly, neither novel extends its action beyond the inner solar system, and their reception by readers was sufficiently lukewarm to ensure that Smith then went back to doing what he did best. When *Astounding* began publication again, under the aegis of F. Orlin Tremaine, he completed the Skylark trilogy in the most grandiose fashion he could contrive, and then he went on to plan a new series, whose entire *raison d'être* was that it would be more grandiose still: the Lensman series.

* * * * * * *

When it was reprinted in 1950-54 as a set of books, the Lensman series was expanded to six volumes, and some later reprints added *The Vortex-Blaster* (1941-42; fix-up 1960) as a seventh, on the woefully inadequate grounds that it was set in the same universe. The book series begins with an extensively-revised *Triplanetary*, and continues with a new volume, *First Lensman* (1950), which connects the revamped *Triplanetary* to the four volumes of which the series had initially consisted. These four volumes are based on the magazine serials *Galactic Patrol* (*Astounding Stories*, September 1937-February 1938); *Gray Lensman* (*Astounding Science Fiction*, October 1939-January 1940); *Second-Stage Lensman* (*Astounding Science Fiction*, November 1941-February 1942), and *Children of the Lens* (*Astounding Science Fiction*, November 1947-February 1948).

The first of these six volumes begins with the revelation that a cataclysmic coalescence of two galaxies in the distant past precipitated a conflict between the humanoid Arisians and the monstrous Eddorians, who began a long war for control of the many new planets spawned by the event. The Arisians planned to build a galaxy-wide civilization, while the Eddorians sought to subjugate all worlds to their totalitarian rule. An Arisian group-mind named Mentor initiated and supervised a special breeding-program intended to produce beings capable of battling the Eddorians, using the human inhabitants of Earth as raw material.

After brief interludes set in Atlantis, Rome and the arenas of three World Wars, the book version of *Triplanetary* describes the Eddore-inspired assault led by the Adepts of Jupiter against the human-dominated inner planets of the solar system, causing them to unite—and, after their victory, to set in train plans for human expansion into the galaxy. In *First Lensman*, humans make contact with Arisia, where Mentor arranges that Virgil Samms, the founder of the Galactic Patrol, comes into possession of the Lens: a device that serves as a universal translator. Each individual lens is a semi-living entity attuned to a single wearer; it defies all attempts at analysis or duplication. Armed with lenses, the elite members of the Galactic Patrol fight against the various criminal activities inspired and organized by Eddore's agents.

The four volumes that comprise the main part of the series tell the story of Kimball Kinnison and Clarrissa MacDougall (MacDougall was the maiden name of Smith's own wife). This couple is the penultimate product of Arisia's breeding program, whose union eventually brings forth the children destined to destroy Eddore. *Galactic Patrol* describes how the newly-graduated Kinnison fights the pirates of Boskone, winning a spectacular victory against enormous odds. In *Gray Lensman*, gifted with new mental powers by advanced Arisian training, Kinnison carries the fight to the Boskonians, eventually penetrating the defences of their home planet Jarnevon.

In *Second-Stage Lensman*, Kinnison, having discovered that a much deeper conspiracy lies behind the power of Boskone, traces that activity back to the planets Lyrane II and Lonabar. Clarrissa MacDougall becomes the first female wearer of the Lens in order to work with the matriarchal Lyranians, and discovers the role played in their affairs by the Eich and the Thralians, whose interstellar empire is ruled by Alcon. Kinnison manages to assassinate Alcon, but his initial attempts to take control of the Thralian empire are thwarted when Prime Minister Fossten—the power behind Alcon's throne—reveals that he has powers as great as an Arisian's. Even so, Kinnison destroys this further adversary—without realizing that Fossten is, in fact, Gharlane of Eddore, Mentor's chief adversary since the dawn of their conflict.

In *Children of the Lens* the children of Kimball Kinnison and Clarrissa MacDougall—their son Christopher and four daughters, all partnered with second-stage lensmen—carry on the fight against the masters of Boskone. After suffering various setbacks, they go to

Arisia to undergo the third stage of their training, which they are uniquely fitted to receive. They supervise the defense of Arisia against the Ploorans, the last of Eddore's pawns, and then combine the collective mental power of the Patrol and Arisia for an assault on Eddore itself, where their father is now being held prisoner. When this battle is won, the Kinnison children become the new Guardians of Civilization, while the Arisians pass on to a further phase of existence beyond the limits of time and space.

* * * * * * *

When the four magazine serials that comprised the original Lensman series were first published, it was not until the conclusion of the fourth and last part of the main series that its readers found out—along with the characters—that the Kinnisons' adventures had all been part of a greater scheme. For this reason, readers who first encounter the series in book form obtain a view of its contents and development very different from—and arguably much inferior to—that of its original readers.

The manner in which the pulp serials worked through an ever-escalating series of contexts represented a gradual but inexorable expansion of consciousness from the narrow confines of the inner solar system to the furthest horizons then imaginable. It was this steady but spectacular expansion of perspective that gave the serials their central role within the developing mythos of pulp science fiction, and established them as the key exemplars of classic space opera. The book versions, which establish the largest scale of action within the prologue, distance the reader in much the same fashion as Hamilton's tales of the Interstellar patrol. As in the Skylark series, however, the "science" within the Lensman series is merely a mask for miracles, the lenses being magical devices whose function is simply to provide empowerment in measured stages.

In spite of its grandiose claim to constitute "The History of Civilization" (the original book publisher once issued a boxed set bearing that collective title) the main sequence of the Lensman series is a straightforward allegory of maturation. It is clearly a product of the era in which fear of organized crime first gave prolific birth to the mythology of the all-powerful mafia, and it is also an embodiment of the American Dream of universal conquest by means of super-weapons—which is described in detail by H. Bruce Franklin in *War Stars* (1988)—but this is incidental to its real narrative thrust. The four-volume novel is, essentially, a "boy's book" which does no more and no less than all boys' books do, mapping out a route from present powerlessness to future power and offering elaborate counsel as to the wisdom of using that inevitable inheritance constructively.

Shorn of its fanciful embellishments, the plot of the main sequence describes how young Kimball Kinnison graduates from school, is gifted with the responsibilities and prerogatives of a new adult, gets a girl and falls in love, learns to refine his powers and privileges, brings up his kids while his own kindly "parents" helpfully look on, and eventually passes the torch of responsibility on to them, while his erstwhile Mentor follows the path of destiny into the mysterious world beyond life. As in the myriad allegories of maturation that nowadays constitute the bulk of genre fantasy, the business of learning to juggle authority and responsibility is plagued by many demons, whose evil is represented as a generalized and deep-seated force, from whose fountainhead such phenomena as smuggling, piracy and war all spring.

Like all fantasies of this ilk, the Lensman series is stridently and conservatively moralistic, aiming to inculcate in its young readers not merely a reasoned hatred of evil but a reflexive emotional repulsion. It is not ashamed to use such elementary strategies as labeling its villains with expressions of disgust: Eich!, Ploor! etc. It is, in fact, addressed very frankly to the immature, and ought not to be judged by the standards of adult literature.

When he had finished the Lensman series, with an extravagant flurry of collapsing galactic empires, there was no further stage for Smith to explore. Indeed, the last of the four serials—which appeared six years after the third, delayed in the writing by Smith's war-time stint in a munitions factory—was neither promoted nor received with the same enthusiasm as its predecessors. Between 1942 and 1948 Astounding had undergone a sea-change, partly due to John W. Campbell Jr.'s crusade to make genre sf more responsible to known science, and partly due to the endorsement lent to that crusade by the advent of the Atomic Age, whose dilemmas and prospects sf had anticipated more cleverly than anyone had expected.

Smith spent the next few years revising and consolidating the book version of the Lensman series, and he also revised his other pulp novels for book publication. Ten years passed before he began a substantial new venture, and when he did so he made every effort to accommodate it to the new context, but he could not do it. Perhaps he was simply too old to learn new tricks; whatever the reason, *The Galaxy Primes*, serialized in *Amazing* in 1959, is devoid of any real narrative drive and gives the impression of being an inept pastiche of A. E. van Vogt. Smith wrote one more story for *Astounding*, "Subspace Survivors" (1960), but Campbell rejected its sequel, which was eventually issued in tandem with it in the book *Subspace Explorers* (1965). It is not at all surprising that, after revising a novel left behind by one of his admiring fans, E. Everett Evans, Smith then decided—in spite of the fact that he had almost lost the use of his eyes to cataracts—to revert to the first imaginative territory he had pioneered by writing *Skylark DuQuesne*. Its serial version appeared in print mere weeks before his death.

* * * * * * *

It astonished many readers and critics—who regarded Smith as a virtual dinosaur and his last literary products as a set of embarrassing failures—that the books of Lensman series enjoyed a spectacular renewal of their popularity when they were re-released in paperback editions in the late 1960s. Indeed, they proved so very successful that the 1970s saw a concerted attempt to generate the same kind of boom in second-hand Smithiana that had previously been engineered in connection with the works of Robert E. Howard. A fragment that had appeared in *If* in 1964 as "The Imperial Stars" was completed by Stephen R. Goldin, and became the first of a ten-volume series. Two short stories from 1953-4 starring "Lord Tedric" became the basis for a four-volume series by Gordon Eklund. New titles were added to the Lensman series by William B. Ellern and long-time fan David A. Kyle. Lloyd Arthur Eshbach—who had published the book versions of most of Smith's novels—supplied a sequel to *Subspace Explorers*.

None of this material is of any real interest, nor was any of it successful, even though the presence of Smith's name on the covers guaranteed sales for a while. When the books in question began to pile up in second-hand outlets, unsaleable at any price, the whole enterprise came to seem rather absurd. If one considers the four Kimball Kinnison stories in isolation, however—or in association with the first three Skylark novels—it is not so very surprising that a new generation of teenage readers was able to find them exciting and inspiring, in spite of the fact that their form had been unwisely altered and their imaginative apparatus had become horribly dated. It is no coincidence that the same era saw the phenomenal success of paperback editions of J. R. R. Tolkien's *Lord of the Rings* and the spectacular rebirth of fantasy as a paperback genre. The imaginative apparatus of Tolkienesque fantasy was even more outdated than that of Smith's space operas—but that was, in a sense, the whole point of the exercise.

The function of fairyland and all its literary analogues is that they provide an arena where an adult teller of a tale can meet a naïve reader on equal terms, unconfused by the fact that the teller's experience of the world is far more varied and refined than his hearer's. That was what Smith made of the universe of stars: an arena of adventure, where the limitations of scientific plausibility had no relevance at all. Any tale set in the real world is bound to be experienced very differently by an adult and a child, because they bring such different stocks of knowledge to the understanding of it, but a tale set in Middle-Earth or the Galactic Empire is neutral ground; all that is or can be known about it is the text.

It is for this reason that the Lensman series was—and, to some extent, still is—so wonderfully available to unsophisticated readers. Within this context, we can easily appreciate that the series is indeed a rather special work, for the imagination whose triumphs it celebrates is one that looks forwards rather than backwards, and outwards rather than inwards. Adult literature, which is inevitably devoted to self-conscious introspection and to historical understanding, can find little room for such endeavors as the Lensman series, but children will always be able to accommodate them.

Modern space opera has, of course, evolved to become much more sophisticated than its remotest ancestors. The politics of the galactic empire was extensively recomplicated and refined by writers like Isaac Asimov and Poul Anderson, and their influence has fed through to the TV shows that are now the principal format of the subgenre. It is arguable, however, that the similarities are more important than the differences. Modern space opera still consists largely of allegories of maturation, and its most popular forms still employ pseudoscientific jargon as a mask to conceal all the hoariest clichés of magical fantasy. Richard Seaton's problematic battles with godlike beings of "pure intelligence" are still replayed, time and time again, and avatars of Blackie DuQuesne continue to play their mediating role in such struggles.

There is nowadays a kind of space opera that can qualify as adult literature, which has made the vast stage of the Galactic Empire available for thought-experiments of considerable subtlety and evident incisiveness—an opportunity that has been taken up by such thoroughly adult writers as Ursula K. Le Guin and Iain M. Banks— but the obvious merits of that kind of space opera should not entirely blind us to the merits of the other: the space opera that provided a thoroughly modern alternative to fairyland. The work that he did toward that end fully entitles Edward E. Smith, Ph.D. to be considered one of the most notable creators of science fiction.

ROBERT A. HEINLEIN

Robert Anson Heinlein was born on 7 July 1907 in Butler, Missouri; he was the third of seven children. He attended Central High School in Kansas City and spent a year at the University of Missouri, Columbia before completing his education at the United States Naval Academy at Annapolis, following in the footsteps of his older brother. He graduated and was commissioned in 1929, serving aboard the aircraft-carrier *Lexington* before becoming gunnery officer on the destroyer *Roper*. He suffered continually from sea-sickness and eventually contracted tuberculosis, which caused him to be retired from active duty in 1934 on a small pension. He settled in California and spent some time casting around for a new vocation, later allowing it to be put on record that he tried silver mining, politics, and selling real estate; in the course of these adventures he married Leslyn MacDonald (his second wife; he had been briefly married previously while in the Navy).

Heinlein was subsequently secretive about this phase of his life. When Sam Moskowitz asked him for details while researching an article to be incorporated into *Seekers of Tomorrow*, Heinlein sent a long and detailed letter, but then forbade Moskowitz to make its contents public until he was dead (after he died, his widow Virginia rescinded that permission and demanded the return of the letter). When Alexei Panshin began researching his adulatory study *Heinlein in Dimension*, Heinlein refused to co-operate and forbade his friends to give out any information—and when Panshin eventually tried to introduce himself to his hero, Heinlein angrily refused to speak to him, citing invasions of privacy that Panshin understandably thought imaginary. It was left to Tom Perry, in an article published in 1993, to reveal that Heinlein's short-lived career in politics had involved him with Upton Sinclair's *EPIC News*, a weekly propaganda-sheet promoting Sinclair's campaign to become governor of California, using the key slogan, "End Poverty in California."

In 1938 Heinlein ran in a primary seeking the Democratic nomination to contest a State Assembly seat. Although he was unopposed by any other Democrat, the seat's Republican incumbent, Charles W. Lyon, stood against him and won; by securing victory in both Democratic and Republican primaries Lyon made it unnecessary actually to hold an election. Perry speculates that Heinlein became determined to keep this quiet because of the vulnerability he felt during the McCarthy witch-hunt, when he was attempting to make a career in Hollywood as well as writing juvenile sf novels. Perry suggests that Heinlein would have been perfectly prepared by then to declare that he no longer had any sympathy whatsoever, even for the elements of Sinclair's platform that had once interested him—let alone those which had led Sinclair to call himself a socialist before deciding that the Democrat label was more convenient—but that he would not have been willing to pay the price of forgiveness that McCarthy's lackeys invariably demanded of repentant leftists: to name the friends he had made while he was involved with Sinclair's movement.

Heinlein's abortive campaign left him with a mortgage on his house, which overstretched the resources of his navy pension, and it was his determination to pay it off that led him to try his hand at writing science fiction. He had long been a fan of the sf pulps, although it seems to have been a slightly guilty pleasure; he subscribed to the view, common among intellectuals, that the literary standard of pulp fiction was contemptible. A competition advertised by *Thrilling Wonder Stories* inspired him to write "Life-Line", but he submitted it to the far more reputable *Collier's*; when it was rejected, he sent it to the highest-paying sf pulp, *Astounding Science Fiction*. When John W. Campbell Jr. bought it, he promptly wrote another story, which Campbell also bought, and then several more—and when Campbell rejected those, he entered into fervent correspondence with the editor in order to ascertain exactly what he wanted.

The letters reproduced in the aptly-named *Grumbles from the Grave* make it clear that Heinlein's attitude to his early work was very defensive. He insisted that his only objective was to pay off his mortgage, and when he kept going thereafter he told Campbell that he would stop writing as soon as another story was rejected. He considered the stories that Campbell thought unworthy to have been fatally stigmatized, and attached pseudonymous bylines to them even when it was Campbell who ultimately bought revised versions. Although he did allow himself to be tempted back to work after

Campbell had the temerity to reject another one of his submissions, he did so after an ostentatious pause and some posturing.

Even though they are carefully selected and edited, the early letters in *Grumbles from the Grave* reveal that Heinlein was extremely touchy, and prone to aggressive over-reaction to criticism. He continually referred even to the work he sold to Campbell as "hack"—although Virginia Heinlein's commentary observes that he "strenuously objected" to any editorial amendments—and he took care to tell Campbell that, if and when the day came that he got around to doing some serious writing, it would be very different. Even when he came up with an idea that initially fired his enthusiasm—for the novel *Beyond this Horizon*—he lost that commitment so rapidly that, when he sent the first installment to Campbell, his covering letter said: "Confidentially, it stinks". He became fetishistic about selling all his work, no matter how he affected to despise it, but he seems to have regarded praise from Campbell or *Astounding*'s readers as a double-edged sword: unwelcome confirmation that he had an innate talent for the production of trash.

Heinlein also complained of the terrible difficulty of grinding out *Beyond This Horizon*, adding a macabre quip to one accompanying letter about bloodstains on the page. When one of the many characters who function as his mouthpieces in his later work asks a potential spouse whether she really knows what being married to a writer involves, Heinlein presumably had his own case (and perhaps the fate of his own second marriage) in mind:

> "Writing is antisocial. It's as solitary as masturbation. Disturb a writer when he is the throes of creation and he is likely to turn and bite right to the bone...and not even know that he's doing it. As writers' wives and husbands often learn to their horror.
>
> "And there is no way—attend me carefully, Gwen!—there is no way that writers can be tamed and rendered civilized. Or even cured. In a household with more than one person, of which one is a writer, the only solution known to science is to provide the patient with an isolation room, where he can endure the acute stages in private, and where food can be poked in to him with a stick. Because, if you disturb the patient at such times, he may break into tears and become violent." (*The Cat Who Walks Through Walls*, pp. 43-44)

In spite of such penalties, Heinlein did eventually find in sf writing the vocation that had eluded him since his release from the navy—but he liked to pretend, perhaps because it was true, that it was a vocation into which he had had to be dragged, kicking and screaming. There is no evidence that his enormous popularity ever allowed him firmly and finally to set aside the feeling that his entire literary career had been a craven and humiliating capitulation with ignominy.

* * * * * * *

In "Life-Line" (1939) an experimental scientist shows off a machine for predicting the future to skeptical and scornful Academicians, the twist in the story's tail being that his own death provides the crucial proof of its accuracy. The second Heinlein story Campbell bought, "Misfit" (1939), is a brief "ugly duckling" tale about a young member of a spaceship-crew whose mathematical genius allows him to fill in when the ship's "calculator" fails. The first story that Campbell rejected was "Let There be Light", which appeared in *Super Science Stories*, edited by Campbell's protégé and fledgling rival, Frederik Pohl, bylined Lyle Monroe; it is unclear whether it was rejected because of some mildly risqué dialogue or because its plot—involving attempts by established business to suppress cheap and efficient solar power technology—was too weak.

Heinlein's next efforts were the novellas "Elsewhen" and "Lost Legacy", which blatantly exhibited the pitfalls into which writers easily fall when they make up their plots as they go along. In the former, a professor of speculative metaphysics uses hypnosis to displace his students into alternative worlds reflective of their personalities; the idea was subsequently used to far greater effect in Philip K. Dick's *Eye in the Sky*, but Heinlein's version has no dramatic tension or narrative shape. The second involves a party of parapsychologists who join the war being waged by the world's secret masters against all "antagonists of human liberty [and] human dignity"; it is disorganized and rudderless as well as featuring occult elements that Campbell would not allow into *Astounding*'s pages.

Frederik Pohl bought "Lost Legacy", which he published as "Lost Legion" (1941), and three further Campbell rejects. All of them appeared under the Monroe byline, one of them having been written in collaboration with Elma Wentz, to whom Heinlein had given the story for revision. He had met Mrs. Wentz while working on *EPIC News*, and presumably offered encouragement to her husband Roby, who subsequently sold four stories to Campbell; another

EPIC acquaintance, Cleve Cartmill, also joined the Campbell stable in 1941. Campbell published a revised version of "Elsewhen" as "Elsewhere", although Heinlein insisted that he publish it under the byline Caleb Saunders. Heinlein reverted to his own titles when he condescended to reprint the stories in *Assignment in Eternity*.

The work that cemented Heinlein's relationship with Campbell was another novella, which Campbell retitled "If This Goes On—" (1940). This transformed Heinlein's memories of growing up in the Bible Belt into a vivid cautionary tale of a future America ruled with totalitarian rigor by a Prophet Incarnate. Because it had to wait its turn to be serialized, however, it was preceded into print by "Requiem", a brief Hemingwayesque tale gushing with understated sentimentality, in which the man whose entrepreneurial efforts first made space travel economically viable evades well-meant efforts to stop him making a fatal voyage to the moon.

The other three stories that Heinlein published in *Astounding* before the end of 1940 were the novelettes "The Roads Must Roll", "Blowups Happen", and "Coventry", none of which was long enough to lose its clear narrative focus, although each was liberally supplied with the kind of telling detail that Heinlein employed—more cleverly than any previous pulp sf writer had contrived—to make his near-future scenarios convincing. The first deals with a near-future labor dispute. The second describes social and psychological tensions in and around a nuclear power plant. The third describes life in a reservation to which dissidents from a formal social contract called the Covenant are banished, whose inhabitants stubbornly reproduce all the ills and enmities that the new contract has negotiated out of existence. Although the third is a stylized political fantasy of a familiar kind, the first two were markedly different from the common run of pulp sf stories. Instead of making their technological innovations—moving roadways and atomic power—central elements of narrative attention, the tales simply take them for granted, focusing instead on the social and psychological corollaries of their integration into the pattern of everyday life. It was this *modus operandi* that delighted Campbell and his readers, marking a significant progressive step in the evolution of magazine science fiction.

In retrospect, it is obvious that Heinlein's aborted career in politics had far more influence on his early exploits in science fiction than merely leaving debts to be cleared. His thinking about the future was framed and motivated by practical political concerns—and the hypothetical solutions he came up with all lay outside the spectrum of orthodox party politics. Instead, they embraced an innovative radical pragmatism that was markedly different from the schemes pulp sf had inherited from such works as Edward Bellamy's best-selling *Looking Backward, 2000-1887*, which blithely skipped over the question of how to get from here to there. Even more influential than his nuts-and-bolts approach to social design, however, was the tone of voice that Heinlein brought to these narratives, which addressed the reader with a peculiar combination of relaxed informality and inflammatory urgency. It is now easy to see how the rhetoric of his fiction took over where the discussions in which he participated in connection with *EPIC News*, and the canvassing he did in pursuit of his own campaign, left off.

Heinlein's radical pragmatism and his interest in practical politics are even more blatant in the other Heinlein story that Campbell published in 1940: the fantasy "The Devil Makes the Law" (better known as as "Magic, Inc"), which appeared in *Astounding*'s fantasy companion *Unknown*. This is a tale of political dirty tricks and economic chicanery in a world where magic works—and has therefore been subject to patchwork legal restriction and inefficient political licensing. It was, however, the five *Astounding* stories that established Heinlein's reputation within the field and broke the mold of pulp sf. Campbell used them as paradigm examples of what he wanted science fiction to become, and that is the purpose they have served ever since in analytical histories of the field.

In order to facilitate the sprinkling of his stories with telling details, Heinlein linked them together with a common historical background, which he began to map out in some detail. He had borrowed the idea from Sinclair Lewis, recognizing that Lewis's habit of maintaining files on his settings and characters would be particularly useful to him. Science fiction stories are not usually able to take advantage of the brief scene-setting cues used to establish and dress narrative stages in fiction set in the known world, but Heinlein knew that *Astounding*'s loyal followers would be able to pick up on details referring back to tales they had recently read. When Campbell found out about Heinlein's historical chart, he wanted to publish it, and proposed that Heinlein should reserve his own name for stories set within the scheme. Heinlein readily agreed, putting the byline Anson MacDonald on *Sixth Column* (1941), which he based on the plot of an unsold novella of Campbell's (which ultimately saw print posthumously as "All").

By the end of 1940, Heinlein had paid off his mortgage, but his relationship with Campbell continued smoothly for a few months longer. Heinlein's 1941 publications de-emphasized the element of political speculation in his work, although his radical pragmatism produced the plots of such casually excessive Anson MacDonald stories as "Solution Unsatisfactory" and "We Also Walk Dogs—". He broadened his imaginative scope considerably, producing playful but remarkable extrapolations of neurotic insecurity in the fantasies "They", "—And He Built a Crooked House", and "By His Bootstraps", and taking his future history beyond the limitations of Earth on to the much vaster stage hinted at in "Misfit". The Venus-set "Logic of Empire" was rapidly followed by two classic tales of a generation starship, "Universe" and "Common Sense", which bracketed the episodic space odyssey *Methuselah's Children*.

As 1941 came to an end, however, the USA became embroiled in World War II. Heinlein immediately sought recall to duty. Campbell had four stories in hand for 1942 publication—the fantasies "Waldo" and "The Unpleasant Profession of Jonathan Hoag" (to which the byline John Riverside was initially attached), the quasi-Utopian *Beyond This Horizon*, and "Goldfish Bowl" (the revised version of "Creation Took Eight Days", whose initial rejection had caused Heinlein to stand on his dignity)—but none of these stories had the intensity or immediacy of those Heinlein had published in 1940. Even *Beyond This Horizon*, which had been conceived as a "fully mature, adult, dramatic" work, had turned in its execution into a "hunk of hack" with which the author was profoundly dissatisfied, and he described "By His Bootstraps"—which was widely regarded as the classic time-loop story until Heinlein replaced it with "All You Zombies—" (1959)—as "cotton candy".

It seems probable that even if war had not broken out, Heinlein would probably have given up on pulp fiction. *Astounding*'s readers had liked the gimmick stories and space operas of 1941 even better than their predecessors, and some critics were later to proclaim that *Beyond This Horizon* was a masterpiece of pulp sf, but Heinlein's letters lamenting its painfully slow progress suggest that he had reached the end of his tether. Although the navy still considered him unfit for active service, he found a position at the Naval Air Experimental Station in Philadelphia, and he threw himself into his work there. It was in Philadelphia that he met Virginia Gerstenfeld, who was to become his third wife in 1948; she was serving as a WAVE. She recalls in her annotations to *Grumbles from the Grave* that she first became involved with his work as a writer when she volunteered to rearrange his story-files when he had difficulty finding some tear-sheets that he needed for a proposed anthology— presumably one of the big hardcover anthologies that began to lift science fiction out iof the pulp medium. The routine reprinting of his stories in such volumes made it clear that, although Heinlein had effectively given up on science fiction, the field had not yet given up on him.

* * * * * * *

When Heinlein returned to writing after World War II had ended, it was to write a tract provisionally titled *How to Be a Politician*, which did not sell (it eventually appeared posthumously, as *Take Back Your Government*, during Ross Perot's presidential campaign of 1992). When he did begin to write sf again, after his divorce from Leslyn in 1947, he approached his work very differently. He ignored John Campbell and obtained a literary agent; although he began to produce work aimed at a variety of different markets, he avoided the pulps, using them only as a market of last resort for stories he could not sell elsewhere.

Heinlein began to sell sf stories set in the nearer reaches of his old future history to *The Saturday Evening Post*, beginning with "The Green Hills of Earth" (1947)—a story whose overweening sentimentality put "Requiem" in the shade—but he also dabbled in other genres. "They Do It with Mirrors" (1947) appeared in *Popular Detective*, "Poor Daddy" (1949) in *Calling All Girls*, and "Cliff and the Calories" (1950) in *Senior Prom*. It was, however, science fiction that provided his other breakthrough, when he began to write near future romances for children. Juvenile fiction was the only sector of the market which then offered the possibility of selling science fiction books to mass-market publishers.

Rocket Ship Galileo (1947), the first of the juvenile novels that Heinlein produced annually for Scribner's until 1958, also provided a rough basis for the script he wrote for the George Pal film *Destination Moon* (1950), while the second, *Space Cadet* (1948), inspired the pioneering TV show *Tom Corbett—Space Cadet*. Heinlein published his new sf in periodicals like *Argosy*, *Blue Book*, *Town and Country*, *Boys' Life*, and *The American Legion Magazine*, and tried with all his might to start a career from scratch in arenas that had never sullied their pages with futuristic fiction before. Heinlein was one of the first writers to propose that the pulp-tainted label "science fiction" ought to be replaced on work of merit by the more upmarket label "speculative fiction".

Heinlein's determination to be rid of the stigma of having been a pulp writer was, however, compromised by the fact that the sf community organized around the pulp genre did not want to be rid of him—and was, indeed, intent on celebrating and restoring the heroic status he had briefly attained in 1940-41. John Campbell asked

Heinlein, as a favor, to write "Gulf" (1949) in order that he might respond to one of his readers who had sent in a letter of comment reviewing an imaginary "ideal issue" of the magazine. Heinlein obliged, but subsequently dumped the direly slapdash novella in *Assignment in Eternity*, along with such despised hackwork as "Elsewhen" and "Lost Legacy".

Some fan critics have considered Heinlein's post-war attitude to Campbell and the sf magazines in general to have been a trifle ungrateful, but it should be emphasized that his attitude to the pulps was commonplace even among pulp writers. Almost as soon as he began publishing in *Astounding* Heinlein began socializing with other sf writers, and he continued to do so with pleasure and enthusiasm. He must have participated in hundreds of conversations lamenting the fact that the genre was stuck in a "pulp ghetto", and he sympathized with the ambitions of everyone who wanted to move into better markets. What distinguished him from many of the friends he made in the sf community was not his attitude to the magazines, but the relentlessness with which he stuck to his guns.

What brought Heinlein back into the genre fold—or at least into its margins—were offers to reprint his pulp work in hardcover book form from the specialist small presses that were then setting up in some profusion. That was an opportunity no hard-headed professional could refuse, so *Beyond This Horizon* appeared from Fantasy Press in 1948 and *Sixth Column* from Gnome Press in 1949. When Shasta wanted to reprint the early stories in the Future History series Heinlein went so far as to write a novella to fill out the first book in the series, which became the title-piece of *The Man Who Sold the Moon* (1950).

By this time, commercial publishers were beginning to show the first signs of interest in pulp reprints, and Doubleday stepped in to buy reprint rights to *Waldo and Magic, Inc.* (1950). Eagerly accepting the opportunity offered by this new market, Heinlein wrote *The Puppet Masters*, which Doubleday published in 1951 along with an anthology he edited, *Tomorrow, the Stars*. Shasta issued two more volumes of the Future History series before going broke—leaving *Methuselah's Children* to be issued by Gnome Press in 1958 and *Orphans of the Sky* ("Universe and "Common Sense") by the UK publisher Gollancz in 1963. The remainder of Heinlein's pulp work was mopped up by Gnome and Fantasy Press, but it was Doubleday, after a pause of some years, that provided a market for two more adult novels, *Double Star* (1956) and *The Door into Summer* (1957).

The sf magazines, meanwhile, continued to maintain the claim that Heinlein really belonged to them by making other offers that no professional could refuse. Their editors bought the serial rights to the novels he wrote for hardcover publishers. Galaxy serialized *The Puppet Masters*, while *The Magazine of Fantasy & Science Fiction* serialized the juvenile *The Star Beast* (1954) as "Star Lummox" and *The Door into Summer*, and John Campbell serialized *Double Star* and *Citizen of the Galaxy* (1957) in *Astounding*. By the mid-1950s, although his hopes of doing more work for film and TV had been dashed, Heinlein was getting paid twice over for almost everything he wrote (or had previously written) at novel length. One consequence of this was that he virtually stopped writing short fiction. Although a few stories that had fallen through the upper strata of the market ended up in sf magazines in 1952-53, and two more appeared in 1957, he rarely deigned to write anything specifically for that market. "All You Zombies—", a solipsistic conceit combining the themes of "They" and "By His Bootstraps", was a one-off.

* * * * * * *

The tone of the work Heinlein that did between 1947 and 1957 is more earnest than that of the last few works he left for publication in 1942, and its use of ideas is more disciplined. There is no trace in it of the reckless indulgence in bizarrerie displayed in "The Unpleasant Profession of Jonathan Hoag", in which a neurotically insecure amnesiac is horrified to be told, after hiring a private detective, that he is in the service of ghouls, nor of the calculated absurdity of "Waldo", which blithely juxtaposes the image of a man who cleverly employs technological devices to compensate for his physical difficulties with "hex doctors" intent on lifting a curse placed on the US power-system.

The stories that Heinlein did for the slick magazines are lowkey accounts of domestic dramas and unfortunate accidents, mostly set on space stations or in a lunar colony. The early juveniles are studiously didactic, in terms of their painstaking Vernian explanations and their careful moralism. Although a little of Heinlein's radical pragmatism crept into *Space Cadet* and *Between Planets* (1951), the early juveniles stick fairly closely to the Boy Scout code and the conventional norms mass-marketed by contemporary TV shows. Unlike his pulp novels and novellas, Heinlein's longer works now gave evidence of being planned in advance, although it seems probable that the semblance was sometimes contrived by means of a stratagem popular among hack sf writers: transplanting plots from mundane novels into a futuristic or alien setting.

The work Heinlein did in the early 1950s was that of a thoroughgoing and careful professional, enterprising only in the fact that it tried to make the substance of science fiction sufficiently ordinary to be taken seriously by general readers. There was, however, a progressive element built into the work from the very beginning. *Red Planet* (1949) set a new standard in juvenile science fiction for both technical sophistication and narrative skill, and the novels that followed it became, by slow degrees, more complicated and more demanding. *Between Planets* introduced an element of space opera, but set it within a political framework that transcended mere action-adventure. The young readers who became assiduous followers of the series found themselves being drawn further and further into realms where other writers of juvenile fiction dared not set foot.

Although many writers from Campbell's stable dabbled in the production of juvenile sf in the 1950s, no other American writer produced work that could hold a candle to Heinlein's, and the one Briton who produced work of a similar sophistication, Arthur C. Clarke, interrupted his own production more than once to concentrate on popular non-fiction. *The Rolling Stones* (1952) began life as a *Boy's Life* serial aimed at a younger audience than *Between Planets*, but the full-length version uses the dynamics of the family who provide its protagonists to enliven a robust exploratory tour of the solar system. *Starman Jones* (1953) ventures on to a galactic stage in presenting a taut tale of hard-won maturation. *The Star Beast* deals with alien intelligence in a far more sophisticated way than any juvenile sf novel before it, and stresses the diplomatic niceties that would inevitably surround problems of interspecific interaction.

The marketing of this work was not unproblematic. *Grumbles from the Grave* reveals that Heinlein often reacted angrily to criticism from Scribner's editor, Alice Dalgleish, who found uncomfortable (but unconvincing) Freudian undercurrents in *Red Planet* and *The Rolling Stones*. Oddly enough, it was *The Star Beast*—a novel of which Miss Dalgleish had approved unreservedly—which soured the relationship permanently. When she would not defend the book against the rather puerile criticisms made in an aggressively negative review in *Library Journal*, Heinlein thought that she had betrayed him, and seems to have considered his subsequent working relationship with her an implicitly adversarial one. Typically, however, his response was not to damp down his progressive ambitions, but to press forward more determinedly, ready to fight any points of contention which might emerge.

Tunnel in the Sky (1955) is deliberately contentious in several ways, and its account of the struggle for survival experienced by a party of schoolchildren accidentally stranded on an alien world includes a strong dose of radical pragmatism. *Time for the Stars* (1956), which cleverly develops Einstein's twin paradox, was not so calculatedly provocative, but *Citizen of the Galaxy* (1957), which adapted Rudyard Kipling's *Kim* to a space opera format, contained a great deal of fervent political advocacy. It is, however, a very fine book, which takes full advantage of the scope that juvenile fiction offers for thoughtful didacticism—something of which the action-orientated magazines were still rather wary.

The first novel of this period that Heinlein had written for adults, *The Puppet Masters*, was just as different from his pulp novels as his juveniles were. It is a taut thriller, closely in tune with contemporary products of the other genre that was then emerging from the pulp ghetto to win a measure of respectability: "hard-boiled" mystery and suspense. It anticipated in its manner and its subtext the classic sf film *Invasion of the Body-Snatchers* (1956), which was based on a 1955 novel by another writer who managed to import science-fictional themes into the slick magazines, Jack Finney. It is not improbable that Finney's book took some inspiration from Heinlein's, and if—as seems likely—Heinlein had had one eye on the movie market while writing his own book, he must have felt that Don Siegel's film had stolen his thunder. It is significant, however, that when he wrote another adult novel, after a gap of some years, he employed a method that had been used by other genre writers, most notably Alfred Bester—who was then regarded as one of the field's brightest stars and was trying hard to follow Heinlein into more rewarding pastures.

Double Star is the best of several science-fictional adaptations of the plot of Anthony Hope's definitive Ruritanian romance *The Prisoner of Zenda*, but unlike Edmond Hamilton's slavishly imitative space opera *The Star Kings* (1947), it is a calculated modernization. Heinlein's version of the plot substitutes a diplomat for the kidnapped king and a down-at-heel actor for the noble masquerader; the prize at stake is not a throne but the privilege of establishing and maintaining a mutually beneficial relationship between humans and Martians. The novel won Heinlein the first of his four Hugo Awards.

The plot of *The Door into Summer* also appears be based on a classic romance that had previously seen science-fictional adaptation; as a new version of Alexandre Dumas' *The Count of Monte Cristo*, however, it cannot stand comparison with Bester's *The Stars My Destination*, and it is far more slapdash in execution than its predecessor. Its disappointed hero's voluntary sojourn in suspended animation is no substitute for Edmond Dantès' unjust imprisonment in the Château d'If, and the complications that subsequently modify his "revenge" on the ex-partner who stole his girl leach all the narrative resilience from the story-line.

The politicking in *Citizen of the Galaxy* caused less trouble than it might have because Alice Dalgleish immediately recognized the novel's quality. She also seems to have liked *Have Space Suit—Will Travel* (1958), although the ludicrously bombastic conclusion of the trial to which its young hero and heroine must submit, Everyman-style, on behalf of all humankind, ought perhaps to have sounded alarm bells. By this time, however, Heinlein seems to have considered himself to be at war with her, and *Starship Troopers* might be seen as a deliberate mobilization of his forces, intended to test her tolerance to destruction—which it did. Heinlein probably would not have felt able to do that if he had not opened up a second front with his novels for Doubleday, but he seems to have formed the impression that he was too valuable a commodity for Scribner's simply to dispose of him, and it might have been the case that he expected to be granted immunity from Miss Dalgleish's further demands. Instead, he was simply shown the door.

* * * * * * *

Starship Troopers remains an extraordinarily controversial book, whose ability to generate strong feelings was reignited by Paul Verhoeven's 1996 film version. Thomas M. Disch wrote a scathing quasi-psychoanalytic account of its supposed sublimation of homoerotic urges, characterizing its hero as a "swaggering leather boy" whose invariable response to sexual arousal is to get into a fight, but Samuel R. Delany called attention to the epiphanic potential of the moment when—no prior clue having been provided—the hero casually mentions that the face he is observing in a mirror is black.

Although the book's plot is essentially a science fiction version of Leon Uris's *Battle Cry* (1953), the relatively small modifications to the pattern of the original made in the interests of shifting it into a future context and on to an interstellar stage caused outrage in some quarters; its account of the training of its starship soldiers has frequently been accused of glorifying war and its attitude to their insectile opponents—particularly the assumption that no possible resolution to the conflict of such biologically-different species is imaginable save the extermination of one by the other—is frequently held up as a key example of neurotic xenophobia. Joe Haldeman's *The Forever War* (1974) is a calculated ideological reply to *Starship Troopers*, which introduces a much grittier realism to the depiction of warfare, and more than one commentator has thought it a telling point that whereas Heinlein, deeply frustrated by his own unfitness for active service, was forced to sit out World War II, Haldeman actually encountered the nastiest aspects of modern warfare in Vietnam. Oddly enough, the relatively mild suggestion that some kind of national service might be required of future Americans as a condition of citizenship—which would not have caused a raised eyebrow anywhere in Europe—was construed by many domestic readers of *Starship Troopers* as monstrous. Heinlein's proposition that people who did not wish to do national service might be exempted provided that they gave up their voting privileges was actually far more liberal than the compulsory systems in force in the majority of nations in the early 1950s.

Starship Troopers won Heinlein his second Hugo, but that could not cancel out the pain of its rejection by Scribner's, which he took as badly as he took all rejection. When he eventually decided to write one final juvenile, for Putnam—the publisher who had taken over *Starship Troopers*—he was determined to violate the last and most sacred taboo of juvenile fiction, and actually titled the text *Podkayne Fries*. When the publisher refused to let him get way with it, however, he consented to let his heroine live, and the book actually appeared as *Podkayne of Mars* (1963). Following the success of *Starship Troopers*, in spite of the doubts entertained by Alice Dalgleish—and, for that matter, John Campbell, who rejected the serial version—Heinlein evidently decided that, if the market's gatekeepers did not appreciate his attempts to broaden its horizons, then he would henceforth refuse to tolerate their preferences, and would write exactly what he liked in whatever way he chose.

The first and most spectacular produce of this new resolve was *Stranger in a Strange Land* (1961), a mammoth guide to Heinlein's elaborately-revamped but still radically pragmatic ideas on politics, law, religion, psychology, and pretty much everything else, compounded out of sarcastically hectoring dialogues, sneeringly heated diatribes, and stagily melodramatic but widely separated action sequences. In order to get it published he had to compromise and prune it from well over 200,000 words to 160,000, but its subsequent success seemed to him—and to his publishers—to be a triumphant vindication of his new attitude. The fact that it won yet another Hugo presumably seemed trivial by comparison with the success it eventually had in finding a much wider audience than any previous genre product except Ray Bradbury's *The Martian Chronicles*, whose fame had taken even longer to accumulate. From the moment the true scale of his success became clear, however,

Heinlein produced nothing but big bad-tempered books in an openly combative style that was equally redolent with overbearing vanity and neurotic anxiety. Those books grew crankier as he grew older and more set in his ways, although they never lost the torrential lucidity with which long years of practice had by now gifted him.

Stranger in a Strange Land proved just as controversial as *Starship Troopers*, and with far better reason. The most notorious charge aimed against it is, however, based on a lie. It is not the case that Charles Manson based the philosophy of his murderous cult upon the book's description of the new religion based by Michael Valentine Smith on the world-view of his Martian educators. Other would be commune-dwellers did try to practice "grokking" for real, but Virginia Heinlein is careful to reproduce in *Grumbles from the Grave* a long letter the author wrote to a fan from one such group, which stresses that, although the book is a parable in fictional form, it was written firstly to earn money, secondly to entertain, and only thirdly to make people think. "I was asking questions," the author declares, firmly. "I was not giving answers." The letter goes on to say that the book on which Heinlein was working at the time, *I Will Fear no Evil* (1970) "is even more loaded with serious, unanswered questions".

It is not entirely surprising, given the extent to which the worldly-wise lawyer Jubal Harshaw lectures the protagonists of *Stranger in a Strange Land*, and the manner of their response, that many readers either felt crushed by the weight of his persuasion or resentful of his assertiveness—but Michael Valentine Smith, the messiah from Mars, is a much more ambiguous character, and the principal narrator is much more ambivalent about him. When the head of steam that Heinlein had built up before starting the novel eventually runs out—and it does not begin to fade until after half way—it is not merely the story-line that begins to ramble, having lost its bearings. The plot does indeed raise far more questions than it answers, and even begins to question many of the answers that had earlier seemed to be established with all apparent conviction.

One of the problems with Heinlein's subsequent novels is that they return again and again to the problems that he set centre-stage in *Stranger in a Strange Land*, hammering out the same answers with the same aggressive insistence, without ever mustering sufficient real conviction to consider them settled. However determined Heinlein became to fear no evil, it seems that he could not escape the worst evil imaginable—not so much the thought that his ideas might be rejected, but the suspicion that they might deserve it.

* * * * * * *

For the last twenty-five years of his life Heinlein was famous as the man who had first remade science fiction, and then led the way out of the pulp ghetto along a hard road that few could follow. His old work remained in print alongside the new, explaining and sustaining that reputation even as his new books—which inevitably sold much faster than their predecessors, even if they failed to find as many readers in total—began to spark violent antagonism in many of their readers. Towards the end, the awfulness of some of his work severely tested the loyalty even of his most diehard fans— but he was by then an institution of worship, criticism of whom was widely regarded as a kind of heresy.

Heinlein followed *Stranger in a Strange Land* with a fantasy novel as self-indulgent as anything he had written since "Waldo", *Glory Road* (1963). Then came the "survivalist" novel, *Farnham's Freehold* (1964), which is, in essence, a science-fictional version of *The Swiss Family Robinson*. Both novels exhibit the same frankness with regard to sex and the politics of sexual attraction as their predecessor, nauseating feminists and bravely exposing idiosyncrasies that might well have led Alice Dalgleish, if she ever read them, to congratulate herself on her acuity in spotting suspect hidden meanings in his early juveniles.

The Moon Is a Harsh Mistress (1966) was regarded by diehard sf fans as a return to top form, and it won a fourth Hugo, perhaps as much for its depiction of a fledgling artificial intelligence as for its ringing account of lunar secession from Earthly tyranny. The political campaign featured n the novel is more realistic than the religious revival in *Stranger in a Strange Land*, and obviously engaged its author far more enthusiastically. Tom Perry suggests that Heinlein may have lost that fateful primary not because of the elements of Sinclair's platform that he adopted but because of the one he disowned: a giveaway policy borrowed from the Social Credit Movement, which was pushed in California by means of the slogan "Ham and Eggs" because it provided a nicer soundbite than the official "Thirty Dollars Every Thursday". If so, the fact that the lunar revolution marches to victory under the banner TANSTAAFL (There Ain't No Such Thing as a Free Lunch) becomes doubly significant.

Alas, having won his election at last—if only vicariously— Heinlein had nothing left to do but repeat himself, and try with increasing violence to kill the doubts that he simply could not shake off. The posthumous fantasy *I Will Fear No Evil* (1970), in which the mind of a crotchety old man becomes a co-tenant of the brain of a young female, is a dreadful book. Its plot is preposterous, its narrative style horribly clotted, and its philosophical pretensions silly. The various sections of the mosaic novel *Time Enough for Love* (1973), which take up the threads of *Methuselah's Children* in presenting an episodic *bildungsroman* of immortal existence, are much sturdier in manner and thought, but the book remains an exercise in wish-fulfilment by a man embarked upon a uniquely pernicious invasion of his own privacy. *'The Number of the Beast'* (1980) is in the same dire vein, but lacks the redeeming virtue of any kind of sturdiness, and concludes with a long and embarrassing essay in absurd self-congratulation.

Heinlein did try to return to the production of solid professional fiction, and made a fair stab at it in the hectic space opera *Friday* (1982). He also tried to do something decisively new in the comic religious fantasy *Job: A Comedy of Justice* (1984), which might have seemed a little less crude had its title not demanded comparison with the work of James Branch Cabell. *The Cat Who Walked Through Walls* (1985) attempts to be a robust action-adventure novel with occasional lectures, but keeps slipping sideways into grotesque idiosyncrasy, and the volume that continued the story it began, *To Sail Beyond the Sunset* (1987), could only achieve a measure of narrative fervor by returning to the method as well as the core subject-matter of *Time Enough for Love*.

Heinlein's most steadfast supporters continued to defend the books he wrote between 1970 and 1980, citing with pride the fact that no one had ever done anything remotely like them before. Many of the critics who wanted to give Heinlein due credit for the awesome achievements of his early *Astounding* stories and the worthy ambitions of his work in the 1950s, on the other hand, feared that the glaring example of his worst work might render laughable any claim that they might make about the incisiveness of his intellect, the power of his imagination or the effectiveness of his literary style. The fact remains, however, that the man who wrote "Blowups Happen", "The Roads Must Roll", *Double Star*, and *Citizen of the Galaxy* was not only responsible for *Starship Troopers* and *Stranger in a Strange Land* as well, but also wrote *I Will Fear No Evil* and *'The Number of the Beast'*—and had he been any less remarkable than he was, he probably would not have been able to write any of them.

According to the testimony of all extant evidence, including that which he provided himself, Heinlein was always a man of contrasts and a man of extremes. He could be stridently aggressive but was also capable of acts of extraordinary generosity. He was famed for his fierce loyalty to his friends, but was perfectly capable of abruptly and rudely removing people from that category (as he apparently did with Arthur C. Clarke in the course of a public altercation provoked by Clarke's skepticism about the merits of Ronald Reagan's Strategic Defense Initiative). It was probably the strength of his desire to be loved and admired that made his writings occasionally seem hateful, and the strength of his desire to avoid error that made his writings occasionally seem ridiculous. He really did do a great many things, as a writer, that nobody had ever done before—and doubts as to whether some of them were worth doing should not obscure the fact that, from the viewpoint of any lover of speculative fiction, more than a few of them undoubtedly were.

JAMES BLISH

James Blish was part of the second generation of genre sf writers: the generation that came to prominence in the years following the end of World War II. Had it not been for the war it would not be so easy to speak in terms of distinct generations, but many would-be writers who might have spent the early forties making steady progress were interrupted by the draft; Blish was one of several who picked up the threads after a lapse of several years, the process of his maturation having been bottled up but by no means stalled in the meantime.

Like many of his fellows in the New York-based fan group who styled themselves the "Futurians", Blish placed a few amateurish stories in magazines edited by other members of the group (Donald A. Wollheim, Robert A. W. Lowndes, and Frederik Pohl) during 1940-42, but then served as a medical laboratory technician in the Army. Although he was discharged from the Army after refusing to obey an order, and then became a conscientious objector, he took advantage of the GI Bill to return to graduate school. He studied zoology for a year and then switched to literature, completing a thesis on Ezra Pound that he never submitted for his MA.

It was during the latter phase of his postgraduate work that Blish resumed writing in earnest, producing poetry and criticism as well as stories that ranged over a wide spectrum of the pulp market—although the great bulk of them were bought by a single editor, Bob Lowndes. Blish and Lowndes shared an apartment for some time in 1945-46, during which time they wrote the sf novel *The Duplicated Man* in collaboration, although Lowndes did not get around to publishing it until 1953. The head start that Blish gained as an sf writer by virtue of his friendship with Lowndes was counterbalanced by a rift in the Futurian clan, which set Blish and Don Wollheim fatally at odds—a hostility that endured for such a long time and cut so deep that Wollheim not only refused to publish Blish for nearly thirty years, but remained reluctant to have any dealings with the literary agency run by Blish's first wife, Virginia Kidd.

When he married Kidd in 1947, Blish was working part-time—alongside Damon Knight and other Futurians—for the Scott Meredith Agency, "evaluating" stories sent in by neophyte writers who paid a fee for such criticism. The advice they gave out specified strict adherence to the Scott Meredith "plot skeleton"—which Blish allegedly extended from four elements to five by the addition of a penultimate crisis (although commonly-quoted versions of the formula usually stick to the original four: a sympathetic protagonist; an urgent problem; complications caused by initial failure to solve the problem; and a solution by means of the protagonist's heroic efforts.)

His experience with the Meredith Agency helped Blish to cultivate a keen awareness of the mechanics of fiction, which became the part and parcel of the critical dissections he was to carry out in reviews and essays published between 1952 and 1962, mostly under the pseudonym William Atheling Jr. Many of these were collected in *The Issue at Hand* (1964), which became—and remains—one of the foundation-stones of science fiction criticism.

****

When many of the pulps that Lowndes edited collapsed in 1948, Blish obtained steadier work editing trade journals in the pharmaceuticals and food science field. With his spare time under pressure he restricted his writing to the sf field and began to produce work that was both adventurous and thoughtful.

Although he also found time to write scripts for the pioneering children's TV show *Captain Video*, the early 1950s were to be a productive period whose extraordinary fruitfulness Blish never managed to recapture. The early stories in his *Cities in Flight* series appeared between 1950 and 1954. The two stories for which he is best-remembered, "Surface Tension" and "A Case of Conscience", appeared in 1952 and 1953—years which also saw the first appearance of "Beanstalk" and the enigmatic "Common Time". There is a sense in which his entire career grew from seeds planted in the first five years of the 1950s.

It was, of course, not unusual for writers of the period when magazines were gradually giving way to paperback books as the primary medium of popular fiction to make up manuscripts for book publication by expanding stories written to the tighter requirements of the pulps, as Blish did when converting the early ESP story "Let the Finder Beware!" (1949) into *Jack of Eagles* (1952). Nor was it unusual for writers to combine sets of shorter stories into episodic novels—the term "fix-up" had been coined by A. E. van Vogt, an inveterate reprocessor of this kind, although Raymond Chandler had earlier termed such clever melding of initially-distinct items "cannibalization". Where Blish was exceptional was that he was never content simply to inflate the wordage of his stories or to stitch up pre-existent materials into passable patchworks. His fascination with the ideas contained in his best stories was always strong enough, and thoughtful enough, to make him want to extend and extrapolate their implications.

The manner in which Blish extrapolated his most precious notions often followed a particular pattern, which might be characterized as "one step sideways, one step back and a big leap forward". The most straightforward example of the pattern can be seen in the way that "Surface Tension" became *The Seedling Stars* (1957). "Surface Tension" is itself an elaboration of the idea contained in the best of Blish's early stories, "Sunken Universe" (1942 as by Arthur Merlyn), which imagined human beings reduced to the same scale as micro-organisms, befriending paramecia and fighting off marauding rotifers. "Surface Tension" provides a much more elaborate account of what such an existential situation might be like, with particular reference to the negligibility of gravity and the awesome power of surface tension—which becomes a barrier to be breached when the tiny humans must build a "space-ship" in which to move from their own stagnating puddle to a fresher one.

Blish always knew that the scientific basis of "Surface Tension" was weak, and that miniaturized humans were not really plausible; he was consequently surprised when the story was hailed as the best thing he had done. Typically, he immediately set out to see if he could repeat the success by producing a "copycat" story with an identical plot-structure: "The Thing in the Attic" (1954). It failed utterly to find the same favor with the readers, who found its account of humans adapted for life in a forest canopy far less engaging, but it did encourage Blish to elaborate a conceptual framework in which human beings could be functionally adapted—by what would nowadays be called genetic engineering—for any kind of environment, however extreme.

Having established that framework, it seemed natural to him to perform two more exercises: one to explore the way in which such a grandiose project might have got off the ground, and one that would take it to its logical conclusion. In this instance the last element, "Watershed" (1955)—in which the creatures adapted for life on a much-changed Earth are ferried to their new home by the "true" humans who are now adaptively fitted only to the artificial environments they have taken into space—was written before the first, "A Time to Survive". It must be noted, though, that if "A Time to Survive" had been written before any of the others, its subsequent extrapolation would probably have been far less ambitious—as was the extrapolation of Blish's other tale of near-future genetic engineering, "Beanstalk", later expanded into *Titan's Daughter* (1961; that being the original publisher's rendition of Blish's *Titans' Daughter*). It was the attempt to support the ludicrously daring "Surface Tension" that required the extremism of what Blish termed "pantropy": the mission of human life to "change everything" and "go everywhere".

The fact that "Surface Tension" became established as a "classic" of sf probably has less to do with its plot structure—or, for that matter, its prophetic character—than its unusually bold celebration of what Peter Nicholls dubbed "the myth of conceptual breakthrough": the identification of a crucial historical moment at which a single discovery or endeavor brings about a dramatic and irrevocable shift in a whole society's conception of the universe. There is a certain irony, therefore, in the fact that *The Seedling Stars*—which grew hindwards out of "Surface Tension"—now warrants reappraisal as a pioneering extravaganza based in a kind of biotechnology that is now in the process of actual development. "A Time to Survive" looks far less exotic now than it did in 1956—but there is surely no higher compliment that one can offer a science fiction writer than to observe that it was not until he had been dead for two decades that the magnitude of his achievement became clear.

* * * * * * *

A much more elaborate superstructure was eventually to be erected on the base provided by "Okie" (1950), a novelette that gained Blish entry to John W. Campbell Jr.'s *Astounding*—a market that many of the Futurians found inhospitable. It looks forward to a day in which a technology of anti-gravity (the "spindizzy") has enabled the cities of an economically-depressed Earth to convert themselves into vast spaceships, taking off into the galaxy in search of profitable employment. David Ketterer's excellent biography of Blish, *Imprisoned in a Tesseract* (1987) observes that "Okie" was preceded by an early draft of the story that was ultimately to become "Earthman, Come Home" (1953), and that it was Campbell's suggestion-laden rejection letter for that first story that provided the fuel for the early extrapolation of the series.

The immediate sequel to "Okie" was "Bindlestiff" (1950), which similarly appropriates an item of Depression slang. The novella "Sargasso of Lost Cities" (1953) and the revised "Earthman, Come Home"—which completed the fixed-up *Earthman, Come Home* (1955)—expanded the "space operatic" aspects of the original stories by introducing ever-more grandiose contests between the cities. More importantly, they also introduced an element of historical repetition, as the 1930s-echoing depression that first forced the cities off earth is duplicated yet again on a galactic scale, forcing the cities to explore even further horizons.

Although science fiction was notionally committed to a "linear" theory of history—in which change, although inconstant, is always progressive—sf writers dabbling in future history had inevitably been tempted by the imaginative crutch of "recurrence" theories, in which the future simply recapitulates the past on a larger scale. Isaac Asimov and A. E. van Vogt had plundered the history of the Roman Empire in constructing histories of the Galactic Empire to come, and the future histories elaborated by Robert A. Heinlein and Poul Anderson also drew heavily on historical analogies. Typically, Blish decided that if he were to do the same, then he would do it in earnest, making the very most of the scheme that he adopted: the onet laid out by Oswald Spengler in *The Decline of the West*.

By the time he got the Okie sequence back to square one in the revised version of "Earthman Come Home" Blish had already written "Bridge" (1952), one of two novellas that were to make a near-future foundation-stone for the whole *Cities in Flight* series in *They Shall Have Stars* (1956). It was, however, the second—"At Death's End" (1954)—that really laid down the intellectual and philosophical groundwork for the whole enterprise.

Blish was already committed to the cause of making genre sf more sophisticated in literary terms, in the hope that it might transcend the limitations imposed by the pulp ghetto and take its place as an important element of twentieth century literature. He had issued a manifesto to this effect in the critical essay published in 1952 that later became the first chapter of *The Issue at Hand*. "Bridge" had attempted such a sophistication in a relatively straightforward but nevertheless "scientized" manner, recruiting the supposed insights of psychological science to the minutely-detailed characterization of its troubled protagonist. "At Death's End" goes a step further, interweaving the characterization of the *dramatis personae* with the characterization of the recapitulative "historical moment" of the story.

In one sense, "At Death's End" plays the relatively modest role within *Cities in Flight* of introducing the "anti-agathic" drugs that were to enable the inhabitants of the spacefaring cities to undertake very long journeys, but, in clothing this simple motif in a multilayered context of significance, it took science fiction to a level of intellectual sophistication that was at least one step beyond anything that Asimov or Heinlein had previously achieved, or were ever to attempt.

They Shall Have Stars did not complete the work of establishing a base for *Earthman, Come Home*. The market for sf books was still very limited in the early 1950s. Although *Earthman, Come Home* had been issued in hardcover by Putnam in the USA and Faber in the UK, *They Shall Have Stars* could not repeat the double coup. Faber—who remained remarkably loyal to the select few sf writers they took on—issued it in Britain, but in the USA it went straight to paperback in an Avon edition that was unceremoniously cut, and retitled *Year 2018!*. Putnam had apparently decided that, so far as hardcover publication was concerned, science fiction could only make money if it were aimed toward juvenile readers. Blish therefore followed Heinlein's example by writing a number of juvenile novels alongside his adult novels, and the next book in the internal chronology of *Cities in Flight* (but the last to be written) was cast in this mould. This was *A Life for the Stars* (1962) which explained and described the exodus of the cities from the surface of the Earth. Ironically, the kind of explanatory material that Avon had rudely excised from *Year 2018!*, on the grounds that it slowed down the plot, proved more tolerable in a juvenile novel, because juvenile novels were expected to be didactic.

While Blish was still filling in the background to *Earthman, Come Home*, however, he had already carried the notion forward to its logical limit. Given the deep pessimism of Spengler's version of eternal recurrence, a futuristic extrapolation of it could have no terminus but one in which the entire galactic civilization would "go west". Blish had not yet started writing juveniles, but there would have been no prospect of aiming such a story at that market; children's fiction makes ample room for the didactic but none at all for the apocalyptic. *The Triumph of Time* therefore followed the ill-fated *They Shall Have Stars* to Avon, with a text carefully designed to remain editorially unscathed; this time it was Faber who substituted a new title, but they were polite enough to let Blish choose his own (*A Clash of Cymbals*). Eight years passed before Avon began to make up for past derelictions by reissuing *They Shall Have Stars* under its original title; in 1970 they issued the whole series in an omnibus edition—but even that did not restore the entirety of Blish's preferred texts.

****

Shortly after publication of "A Case of Conscience" in 1953, the pseudonymous William Atheling Jr. wrote an essay called "Cathedrals in Space" about the various implications of the story: its situation in the problematic borderlands of the sf genre, its actionless but rhetorically scrupulous approach to its central question, and its relation to a sudden flood of religious sf stories which seemed to constitute "instruments of a chiliastic crisis" (Blish preferred "chiliastic" to the more familiar "Millennarian"). The essay observes that "Blish is a professed agnostic" but concludes that this cannot exempt him from the symptoms and concerns of a "chiliastic panic" allegedly afflicting contemporary society.

The plot of the novelette is simple. Human emissaries on Lithia must decide whether the planet is to be opened up to commercial exploitation—a question complicated by the presence of amiable indigenes whose Utopian society would inevitably be disrupted. One of the four, a Jesuit, places the question in a context very different from that of his fellows; he concludes that because the seemingly sinless aliens have no record of a savior, and because their life-cycle makes it obvious that they are the product of evolution rather than Creation, they must be inventions of the Devil laid out as an ideological trap for mankind. As "Atheling" argued, however, the implications contained by the halo of doubt surrounding this simple proposition are potentially profound; following them through was to involve Blish in the most extravagant—and most extended—version of his customary pattern of analysis.

The sidestep part of the pattern was undertaken by expanding the novelette into the similarly-titled novel of 1958, which won a Hugo—thus confirming that the cutting edge of genre sf had shaken off the shackles of the Scott Meredith plot skeleton. In the new second part, the Catholic hierarchy decides that, if Lithia is the Devil's invention, then it must be exorcized—although the possibility is carefully left open that its abrupt destruction might also (or, more probably, instead) have a mundane cause.

The backward step took Blish outside the sf genre altogether, removing the question of whether the search for secular knowledge and technological expertise might itself constitute a sin to its actual historical origins in the thought and work of Roger Bacon. Blish's hypothetical "spiritual biography" of Bacon, *Doctor Mirabilis*

(1964), has many claims to being his best book—it was certainly his own favorite—but it defied the preconceptions of genre historical fiction as casually as it defied the expectations of Blish's ready-made audience, and it did not find a publisher in the USA. Had Blish not been established with Faber it would probably have been deemed unpublishable, in the unfortunately-extensive tradition of stern warnings issued to writers of every stripe that they must respect the real and imaginary configurations of popular demand—but Faber stood by their man. (It should perhaps be noted that Faber no longer operates that way; nor does any other publisher in the English-speaking world.)

Having clarified the roots of his question, Blish then took his customary leap forward, not to a far future, but to an imminent one—the proper locus for a minute analysis of contemporary "chiliastic panic". Unfortunately, Blish began to find the actual process of writing increasingly taxing after the mid-'60s; his novels grew shorter and shorter and gave the impression of having been drawn out with the utmost difficulty. What he initially produced was only half of the concluding element of the sequence he would later term the "After Such Knowledge" trilogy: *Black Easter* (1968). This describes the build-up to the end of the world imagined in terms of Miltonian Christianity, but ends with a brutally abrupt climactic twist revealing that God no longer rules the metempirical universe. Three years passed before *The Day After Judgment* (1971) completed the task by explaining what happened after the irreversible liberation of the forces of evil; no omnibus edition putting the two halves together was published until 1980.

"After Such Knowledge" remains Blish's most ambitious and most crucial contribution to the literary and philosophical sophistication of science fiction. It is an unashamedly esoteric work, which did not readily fit into the genre even at its inception, and which subsequently paid no attention at all to marketing categories and their boundaries. It was, in its way, a pioneering work, which might have set a significant precedent for later endeavors, but in marketing terms it constituted a series of remarkable and probably unrepeatable flukes. Had "A Case of Conscience" not been part of a groundswell of interest in religious themes, it might not have sold to the magazines or recommended itself as a safe bet for expansion. Had the British publishing establishment been Americanized a few years earlier, *Doctor Mirabilis* would not have been published and the concluding diptych would almost certainly have remained unwritten.

* * * * * * *

It was not until 1969 that Blish was finally able—at the third attempt—to give up his day job and become a full-time writer. The recent publication of *Black Easter* was irrelevant to that achievement; his new financial security derived from the fact that he had contracted to produce story versions of the original *Star Trek* scripts, which appeared in a series of collections between 1967 and 1975. Blish also wrote the first original *Star Trek* novel, *Spock Must Die!* (1970). These books were far more widely read than anything else he had produced, and remain the chief claim to such posthumous celebrity as he has contrived to retain.

Now that sf—insofar as it remains a mass-market genre—is TV-based and largely TV-standardized, Blish is fully entitled be named as one of the significant pioneers and foundation-builders of the current state of affairs. Not is it inapt that he attained this status because he regarded the relevant endeavors as elementary hackwork required to buy time for worthwhile enterprises. The prospectus for sf sketched out in *The Issue at Hand* was remarkably prescient, although not quite in the way Blish imagined; sophisticated sf is now on the very brink of becoming part of the literary "mainstream", in the ironically unanticipated sense that what there is of it has to survive as esoteric material supported by academic study. Popular sf has, by contrast, abandoned every last vestige of its ambition to sophistication, accepting instead that TV is the one and only broker of fame and fortune in modern society.

Alas, the time Blish bought with his *Star Trek* adaptations was never spent. He could not recover the fluency of the early 1950s, and found it extremely difficult to write at all. He had undergone an operation for cancer of the tongue in 1964, but the cancer had already spread to his tonsils and it was to fight a nasty war of attrition for ten more years until it finally killed him. He fought back as best he could, but after *The Day After Judgment* he produced only one more work of substance: the awkwardly dense *Midsummer Century* (1972). He did try to expand yet another of his *contes philosophiques* from the early 1950s, "Beep" (1954), into a novel, but he could contrive no more than a flaccid inflation to novella length in *The Quincunx of Time* (1973).

If Blish's other biotechnological explorations, *Titan's Daughter* and *A Torrent of Faces* (1967; written in collaboration with Norman L. Knight), are parceled up with *The Seedling Stars*, then it would not be unfair to say that he produced no novels of much interest outside his three major exercises in patterned analysis. *Fallen Star* (1957), also known as *The Frozen Year*, was an attempt to write a mainstream novel that eventually chickened out and lamely turned itself into sf. *Welcome to Mars!* (1967), also known as "The Hour Before Earthrise", is the second-best of his juveniles—but that only serves to emphasize what a sorry lot the rest of them are. Other novels based on pulpish magazine stories are as weak as might be expected—although *The Night Shapes* (1962), based on a novelette from *Jungle Stories*, exhibits a bizarre spirit of enterprise few others would have thought to attempt. Among Blish's shorter works, however, there are several worthy of further attention.

"There Shall Be No Darkness" (1950) is an interesting attempt at a rationalized supernatural story, providing a sciencefictional "explanation" of vampirism and lycanthropy. "Art-Work" (1956), frequently reprinted as "A Work of Art", is a touching and thoughtful tale of the technological resurrection of composer Richard Strauss. "The Oath" (1960) is a neat moral conundrum of the kind which is often posed by advocates of moral pragmatism in order to expose the limitations of moral absolutism. Half a dozen more might be named, including "Common Time"—which became the basis of a classic exercise in psychoanalytic story-analysis by Damon Knight—and "Mistake Inside" (1948, initially as by Arthur Merlyn), which is subject to equally imaginative depth-plumbing analysis by David Ketterer. It would certainly not be true, however, to say that Blish shared with fellow Futurians Knight and Cyril Kornbluth a facility for excellent short work that he could not extrapolate to novel length.

Blish's true forte was not even the novel, but the constellation of novels: a "constellation" meaning, in this coinage, a group that, although not necessarily linked into a trilogy or a tetralogy, illuminates a single theme from all the vital angles. Blish was not the first sf writer to work in this way, nor was he the last, but he was uniquely methodical and—in the best possible sense of the word—the most eccentric. It would be a great pity if there were to be no future market space for such remarkable and fruitful exercises in idiosyncrasy.

GREGORY BENFORD

Gregory Albert Benford was born, along with his identical twin James, on 30 January 1941 in Mobile, Alabama. The twins' parents had both been schoolteachers but after serving in World War II their father embarked upon an Army career, which resulted in their spending several childhood years in Japan and Germany as well as various locations in the USA. Both brothers completed their schooling in Oklahoma, graduating from the University of Oklahoma in Physics in 1963; each went on to obtain a Ph.D. from the University of California, San Diego, Gregory in 1967 and James in 1969. Although their careers did not begin to diverge markedly until Gregory undertook post-doctoral research—under the directorship of Edward Teller—at the Lawrence Radiation Laboratory in Livermore, California, Gregory was later to declare that he was always primarily a theorist while James had taken up a complementary role as an experimenter.

The theoretically-inclined Benford's speculative bent was also expressed in his activities as a science fiction fan during his teens; he was later to suggest that his recruitment to a career in science had been determined by reading Robert A. Heinlein's juvenile sf novels. He launched the fanzine *Void* in collaboration with his twin at the age of fourteen and continued it for seven years with various other co-editors, two of whom—Ted White and Terry Carr—also went on to build substantial careers within the genre.

Benford never lost his enthusiasm for collaborative projects, which he carried forward into his work as a professional scientist as a matter of necessity and into his science fiction as a matter of choice. The only other writer in the sf field who has produced fiction in association with as wide a range of collaborators is Harlan Ellison, who expanded his own list considerably as a tactical move in marketing the particular collection *Partners in Wonder* (1971). Benford's spontaneously-recruited collaborators in fiction include his brother James, Lawrence Littenberg, Donald Franson, Gordon Eklund, Marc Laidlaw, William Rotsler, David Brin, Paul A. Carter, Mark O. Martin, and Elisabeth Malartre.

In 1969 Benford took up a professorship at the University of California, Irvine, which he held for the next thirty years. He has also been a visiting professor at Cambridge University in Britain, Torino University and Florence Observatory in Italy, and the Massachusetts Institute of Technology. His principal fields of research have been plasma physics and astrophysics. He has published about 150 scientific papers, has served as an advisor to the Department of Energy, NASA and the White House Council on Space Policy; in 1995 he received the Lord Foundation Award for contributions to science and the public comprehension thereof.

Benford's first professionally-published story, written while he was in graduate school, was "Stand-In" (1965), which won second place in a contest for amateurs organized by *The Magazine of Fantasy & Science Fiction*. The contest's specification—derived from a poem by Doris Pitkin Buck—was to combine the motifs of the Unicorn and the Univac computer. He sold two more lightweight stories to the same magazine in 1966 but he did not begin to publish consistently until 1969, when the novelette that was to become the basis of his first novel, "Deeper than the Darkness", appeared in *Fantasy & Science Fiction*. It was in the same year that Benford began writing regularly for Ted White, the former co-editor of *Void* and assistant editor of *The Magazine of Science Fiction*, who had taken over *Amazing Stories* and *Fantastic Stories*.

For *Amazing* Benford wrote a series of articles on "The Science in SF" in collaboration with David Book; the column was a regular feature from 1969 to 1972, and continued—without any further input from Book—on an occasional basis until 1976, alongside similar articles in the short-lived magazine *Vertex*. The fiction published alongside the early items in the former series included "Sons of Man" (1969), which served as a preliminary sketch for "Threads of Time" (1974), one of the three elements of the mosaic novel *In the Ocean of Night* (1977). Most of this early fiction—published under the signature "Greg Benford"—worked towards twist-in-the-tail endings, whose ingenuity increased as he became more practiced.

Although "Flattop" (1966) contains a scrupulously modest description of the life found on Mars, by an expedition of 1985, few of Benford's fictional finger-exercises were strongly biased towards the "hard" end of the sf spectrum. "Battleground" (1970, with "Jim Benford") and "Star Crossing" (1970 with Donald Franson)—both of which feature exotic conflicts between humans and aliens—come closer than any of his solo pieces. Two of Benford's most earnestly-inclined early stories were the mildly jaundiced political fantasies "The Movement" (1970 but written some years earlier) and "Nobody Lives on Burton Street" (1970; once reprinted as "Nobody Lives Around There"). He was a contributor to Samuel R. Delany and Marilyn Hacker's *avant garde* series of original anthologies *Quark* five years before he published his first story in *Analog*, offering a cynical account of amateur assassins queuing up to kill the world's first technologically-produced immortal, "Inalienable Rite" (1970).

"Deeper Than the Darkness" is, among other things, an anti-Socialist political fantasy, although it is cast in a more obviously—and more adventurously—sciencefictional mode than Benford's other contemporary exercises in social commentary. It describes the first phase of an alien conquest of a China-dominated human race by means of artificially-aided psychological warfare. The novel version published in 1970 took aboard other models of human society but its extended plot took the form of a space opera, which Benford later found embarrassing; when he issued a heavily revised version as *The Stars in Shroud* (1979) he described the earlier novel, a little harshly, as "a stamp-press job from the attic".

Even when Benford decided to take his writing more seriously—a shift correlated with his adoption of the more formal signature "Gregory Benford"—he did not immediately move into the field of hard sf. The articles he wrote for *Amazing* presumably helped to generate story ideas and his criticism of fudges that had become commonplace within the field undoubtedly encouraged him to tighten up his own act, but the first story he wrote about tachyons—a concept to whose development he had made a significant contribution—was the playfully slapdash time-paradox story "3.02 P.M., Oxford (1970). Five years passed before he published an earnest complementary piece, ironically entitled "Cambridge, 1.58 A.M." (1975), which became the seed of *Timescape* (1980). His only other story of the seventies set in a university laboratory was the flippant "But the Secret Sits" (1971).

* * * * * * *

Benford began the most productive of his many literary partnerships in 1971 when he teamed up with Gordon Eklund to write "West Wind, Falling" for the first in the *Universe* series of original anthologies edited by another of his fellow *Void* editors, Terry Carr. The story concerns intergenerational conflicts among the "colonists" of a comet, who have hitched a ride thereon to the further reaches of the solar system but now must decide whether to get off again as the object returns to the inner system. Although the hard-sf motif is a relatively sketchy backcloth this story marked the beginning of Benford's attempts to use his scientific background as cleverly and as scrupulously as he could in the construction of hypothetical environments for his stories.

"In the Ocean of Night" (1972) is a first contact story cast in a classic hard sf mould, combining the scrupulously objective commentary of the novella's opening with the lyricism of the revelation vouchsafed to the story's hero, who rebels against instructions to play safe and nuke the intruder. The same story-patterns recurs, in a more restrained version—the alien spaceship on a collision course with Earth here being safely lifeless—in "Icarus Descending" (1973), which was subsequently rewritten and combined with it *In the Ocean of Night* (1977). Most of Benford's solo work of this period was to be rewritten for further use. "The Scarred Man" (1970), which resurfaced, in a much neater version, as "Man in a Vice" (1974), was probably the first sf story to feature a "computer virus" and a solution thereto, prophetically dubbed a "vaccine". "Inalienable Rite" was rewritten as "Immortal Night" (1985), while "And the Sea Like Mirrors" (1972)—Benford's contribution to Harlan Ellison's anthology *Again, Dangerous Visions*—was rewritten as "Swarmer, Skimmer" (1981) en route to incorporation in the first sequel to *In the Ocean of Night*, *Across the Sea of Suns* (1984).

As with other writers before him—most notably Robert A. Heinlein and Arthur C. Clarke—and recalling its influence on his own intellectual development, Benford decided that "young adult" fiction was a uniquely suitable medium for painstaking hard sf, by virtue of the hospitality it offered to naked didacticism. Although *Jupiter Project* was serialized in *Amazing* in 1972, however, it did not appear in book form until 1975. Benford did not repeat the experiment, but the novel remains significant within the context of his career, in that it established a scenario—whose central element was the Jovian moon Ganymede—which he was to revisit on several occasions. An episode from the novel provided the basis for "Shall we Take a Little Walk?" (1981), which helped bridge its background to that elaborated in *Against Infinity* (1983) and further deployed in "Warstory" (1990; reprinted as "Sleepstory").

In the interim between the serialization and book publication of *Jupiter Project*, Benford achieved his first major breakthrough as a fiction writer when he and Gordon Eklund collected a Nebula Award for the novelette "If the Stars are Gods" (1974), published in the fourth *Universe* anthology. The novelette's account of a first contact focuses on the motives and attitudes of aliens who turn up in the solar system intent on getting to know the sun—which they regard as a sentient godlike being—and the effect they have on the humans who offer ambivalent assistance to their mission. The idea that religion might be a more powerful motive force than intellectual curiosity in impelling interstellar travelers to visit Earth was one that Benford was to return to in the earnestly eerie "Of Space/Time and the River" (1985) and the flippantly sarcastic "Proselytes" (1988). None of these stories gives any clue to Benford's own attitude to religion, but he was interested enough in the subject to formulate some ingenious apologetic arguments in his excellent philosophical romance "The Rose and the Scalpel" (1990), which features a fascinating contest—and eventual alliance—between Joan of Arc and Voltaire.

Benford and Eklund quickly made plans to incorporate "If the Stars are Gods" into a mosaic novel, in which it became the second element of four. Benford cannibalized a novelette of his own, whose original version was eventually revised as "Titan Falling" (1980), to produce a conclusion. The collaborators added the impressive novella "The Anvil of Jove" (1976), which provided the third element, and "Hellas is Florida" (1977), which provided the first, plus a brief link section to bridge the second and third elements. The novel was published in 1977, advertised as a work of "philosophical science fiction" and aptly compared by its cover blurb to Arthur C. Clarke's *Childhood's End*. The complete story adds up to a "spiritual biography" of its hero, who suffers an early disappointment while searching for life on Mars but eventually finds enlightenment through his encounters with alien beings in the further reaches of the solar system.

By the time that *If the Stars Are Gods* appeared, Benford had also completed the mosaic novel based on "Sons of Man"/"Threads of Time", "Icarus Descending" and "In the Ocean of Night". (To add to the bibliographical confusion, the rewritten version of the last-named story was separately published as "A Snark in the Night" in 1977.) The full-length version encapsulated a central theme that was to become highly significant in Benford's subsequent work: the notion of the galaxy as a battlefield in which self-reproducing and continually-evolving machines are engaged in a war that threatens the extermination of all organic life. This was the most inherently melodramatic of several notions that were then being bounced around the sciencefictional arena as possible "solutions" of the so-called Fermi paradox, which asked why, if the galaxy were as full of life-bearing planets as the calculus of probability suggested, no alien race had yet visited the Earth. Because the early phases of Search for Extra-Terrestrial Intelligence had found no evidence of alien intelligence, the question had come to seem increasingly challenging to the ingenuity of science fiction writers.

In the Ocean of Night eventually became the first element of a "trilogy", whose third part was intended to be published as a three-decker novel, although its own third element was eventually split into two volumes. The six-volume series gradually extrapolated Benford's "solution" to the Fermi problem across tens of thousands of years. The Stapledonian proportions thus achieved recalled Arthur C. Clarke's second great endeavor in the field of philosophical science fiction, *The City and the Stars*, and it is hardly surprising that when a publisher hit upon the idea of commissioning a sequel to the earlier version of Clarke's masterpiece, *Against the Fall of Night* (which many American readers preferred to the definitive version for nostalgic reasons), Benford seemed the obvious man to take on the task.

* * * * * * *

The short stories Benford produced in the late 1970s that were not destined to be incorporated into novels were very various in tone and manner, reflecting his taste for carrying out brief literary experiments. His first contribution to *Analog*, supposedly the hard sf writer's Mecca (although Benford published only a handful of stories there during the first thirty years of his career), was an eccentric tribute to the Beatles' front man, "Doing Lennon" (1975). A fraudster reawakened from cryonic suspension claims to be John Lennon, but conceives a more ambitious plan when he discovers that his pretence cuts deeper than he thought. "Beyond Grayworld" (1975), which followed a few months afterwards, redeployed its key plot-twist in a much more typical *Analog* tale of heroic individualism on the far frontier.

"White Creatures" (1975) was the first of several psychological studies in which the minds of scientists are profoundly affected by the humbling enlightenments of astronomy; later works in the same idiosyncratic vein include "Exposures" (1981) and "Mozart on Morphine" (1989). Although many hard sf writers have attempted to capture something of the visionary grandeur of cosmological models, and some—most notably "Philip Latham" (Robert S. Richardson)—have juxtaposed those insights with the everyday lives of research scientists, Benford's work in this vein remains quirkily unique.

"John of the Apocalypse" (1975, with James Benford) is a political fantasy in which the cynical use of drugs and religion as mass-manipulative devices is ironically revealed to be a two-edged sword. "Seascape" (1976), by contrast, imagines religion as an instrument of liberation from manipulation, albeit in a far more remote context. "Where Did You Go Last Year?" (1976, with Gordon Eklund) and "Knowing Her" (1977) are studies of female vanity that carefully avoid misogyny while retaining a sharp critical edge; the more dignified "Cadenza" (1981) works more poignantly along similar lines. "A Hiss of Dragons" (1978, with Marc Laidlaw) is a tale of genetically-engineered dragons and the difficulties involved in their slaying, which prefigures a far more dignified tale of dinosaurs reborn from fossil DNA, "Shakers of the Earth" (1992).

The most impressive story of this middle period is "In Alien Flesh" (1978), which became the title story of Benford's first collection. The collection adds illuminating commentaries to the stories, noting of this one that "rendering the alien is the Holy Grail of sf, because if your attempt can be accurately summarized, you know you've failed". The lumpen leviathans of this story, into whose bodies brave men venture in order to plant sensory equipment, represented one of many approaches Benford made to this particular grail. The contemporary "Starswarmer" (1978) was even more adventurous, fully warranting the further elaboration it received when the featured alien was integrated into the plot of *Tides of Light* (1989).

A wry comment appended to "Time Shards" (1979) in *In Alien Flesh* admits that "the alien" does not have to be very far removed from ourselves; the story features a proto-phonographic recording of medieval speech, whose blithe inaccuracies horrified historians. "Dark Sanctuary" (1979) is another oblique first contact story whose hero—mindful, perhaps, of what befell the heroes of "In the Ocean of Night" and "Icarus Descending"—decides to keep quiet about it. Another enigmatic alien is featured in *Find the Changeling* (1980, with Gordon Eklund), although its mimetic abilities recall those of the aliens in "Star Crossing". As in the earlier novella, those abilities are deployed in a relatively routine action-adventure novel of the kind that Eklund (who had produced far more sophisticated work in the early years of his career) had begun to churn out in some quantity.

Benford obtained another collaborative credit in 1980 for his work on *Shiva Descending*, written with William Rotsler. This was a disaster novel cast in a mold that had demonstrated considerable best-selling capability during the previous decade. It uses the motif of an Earth-impacting asteroid, which Benford had already used in "Icarus Descending" and the brief apocalyptic comedy "How it All Went" (1976), but develops the notion more conventionally, using multiple viewpoints to contemplate the impending threat and its tragic promise. The novel probably came too close on the heels of Larry Niven and Jerry Pournelle's *Lucifer's Hammer* (1977) to attract much attention. Benford presumably achieved a greater commercial success as well as winning far more kudos with *Timescape*, which appeared under his name alone, although the significant input of his sister-in-law Hilary is credited in an acknowledgment and her name is included in the copyright notice.

Timescape was widely, and deservedly, hailed as the best novel about scientists at work yet produced within the sf genre—or, indeed, within modern fiction as a whole. There is, in truth, not a great deal of competition for that title, because images of scientists at work that can be seen to be convincing at every level have perforce to be set in the recent past, the present or the very near future—thus ruling out some ninety-nine percent of science fiction—and writers outside the genre had tended to deal with scientists satirically, after the fashion of Thomas Pynchon's *Gravity's Rainbow* (1973) and Don deLillo's *Ratner's Star* (1976). Kate Wilhelm's excellent *The Clewiston Test* (1976) had, however, set a high standard for the genre only a few years earlier and *Timescape*'s triumph was no mean achievement.

Extrapolating the argument of "The Tachyonic Antitelephone", a research paper co-authored with D[avid]. L. Book and W. A. Newcomb, which had appeared in *Physical Review* in 1970, the novel tells two parallel stories. One is set in 1998, when scientists in a world on the brink of ecocatastrophe are trying to use tachyons to send a warning back in time, the other in 1962, when uncomprehending physicists attempt to figure out what the anomalies caused by the signal might be. The two central characters, Gregory Markham and Gordon Bernstein, are both based on the author, at two different points in his life. (Benford was to use Markham as an *alter ego* again in the posthumous fantasy "Newton's Sleep", in which the Shared World of a series of anthologies launched with *Heroes in Hell* gave him the chance to meet up with Isaac Newton, Ernest Hemingway and Che Guevara.) The manner in which the world is delicately tilted in the direction of salvation is carefully modest, but pays deft and earnest homage to the life-enhancing potential of scientific research.

Timescape won Benford a second Nebula and a John W. Campbell Memorial Award, and established him firmly as a key writer of hard sf—indeed, as a writer whose endeavors would henceforth help to define and delimit that controversy-beleaguered subgenre. When he was invited to write something for the Nebula Awards anthology celebrating that year's produce Benford chose to contribute an article entitled "Why is There So Little Science in Literature?"—and from then until he took over Isaac Asimov's science column in *The Magazine of Fantasy & Science Fiction* in 1992 the bulk of his nonfictional contributions to the field shifted from the popularization of science towards literary criticism. The article concluded with the judgment that "The excesses of SF can be corrected by paying more attention to how science is done, rather than by relying on the hoary old images of the dashing astronaut, the inevitable cranky-but-wise administrator, and the rest of the leaden cast left over from our earlier days".

Even in the early stories in which Benford had appropriated that "leaden cast" he had found difficulty adapting himself to the expectations of genre sf readers, and by the time he wrote *Timescape* he had made a firm decision to go his own way. In the article he contributed to the "Profession of Science Fiction" series in the journal *Foundation*—published in 1981—he wrote: "I know that the sf audience as a whole is more interested in wish fulfillment fantasies than anything else, and that's not my vector. The question is whether I should seek a larger audience, maybe outside sf, which has my interests." The British edition of *Timescape*, issued by Gollancz, did not label it sf, but it is doubtful that the move attracted many readers who would not otherwise have seen the book.

Benford had already begun preliminary investigations of this kind in such stories as "Homemaker" (1977, reprinted as "Snatching the Bot") and "Nooncoming" (1978), both of which were deliberate experiments in style which attempted to formulate science fiction stories according to narrative methods favored by "slick" magazines. Other, more wide-ranging experiments had followed in their train, including "Time Guide" (1979), "Calibrations and Exercises" (1979) and "Slices" (1981). He soon began trying to apply his new dicta to casts of characters left over from his own earlier days, including the dashing astronaut Nigel Walmsley, who had been compounded from several predecessors in the fixing-up of *In the Ocean of Night*, and the cranky-but-wise adults who had provided the supportive cast for the boy adventurers of *Jupiter Project*. In writing another novel set in the latter's Ganymede colony, he turned for inspiration and guidance to William Faulkner, the writer who had perfected the literary voice of the American South (to which the much-traveled Benford still respectfully traced his roots). The first few chapters of *Against Infinity* (1983) transplant the tone and plot of Faulkner's novella "The Bear" into the alien world, preparing for another sustained assault on "the Holy Grail of sf"; the creature that stands in for the bear is, inevitably, a far more enigmatic and portentous being.

The redemption of Nigel Walmsley was accomplished in a not dissimilar fashion in *Across the Sea of Suns* (1984), which was fixed up from "And the Sea Like Mirrors"/"Swarmer, Skimmer", "The Other Side of the River" (1982), and "Lazarus Rising" (1982). While his homeworld is devastated by subtle alien attack, Walmsley is dispatched to the star Ra to investigate mysterious radio signals—which draw, him, inexorably and inevitably, towards the dark grail of alien confrontation. More than half a century older than his previous manifestation, the new Walmsley is far from dashing. Soured as he is by his earlier experiences, afflicted with cancer and torn between two awkwardly-problematic females, the bad news he receives about humanity's unlooked-for involvement in the galaxy-wide war between organic and inorganic intelligences mockingly mirrors his own inward turmoil.

A short story spun off by a momentary inspiration while Benford was writing *Across the Sea of Suns*, "Relativistic Effects" (1982), works even harder to substitute ordinary working folk for dashing astronauts, even though they are party to events which change the fates of stars and civilizations. Further experiments in style were conducted in "The Touch" (1983, reprinted as "Touches"), which examines life in the light of game theory, and "Me/Days" (1984), which tracks the evolution of a machine consciousness. Benford reprinted all these experiments in style in his two collections, while consigning many of his more conventional genre sf stories to oblivion.

* * * * * * *

Benford made a more concerted attempt to invade the territory of popular best-sellers with the long novel *Artifact* (1985). The grey area between sf and the thriller had extended considerably in the 1970s, reflected in the success of such writers as Martin Caidin, Robin Cook, and—most significantly of all—Michael Crichton. Benford's decision to enter this arena was undertaken partly in the spirit of experimentation and partly because he had taken note of a powerful current of technophobia running through the entire "technothriller" subgenre. To some extent the technophobia in question was tacit, reflecting the fact that the borrowed sciencefictional devices had to be used to generate melodramatic threats in order to qualify the stories as thrillers, but writers like Crichton had increasingly taken leave to turn the alarmist tendencies of their work into explicit anti-scientific propaganda.

The lever that serves to move the plot of *Artifact* is a mysterious block of stone uncovered in Greece by American archaeologists, whose extraordinary mass suggests that it contains a captive black hole. The motives of the Greek military man who tries to stop the export of the artifact are given a relatively sympathetic hearing, but the main ideological thrust of the steadily-thickening plot is that the scientific method is the one thing which stands between civilization and catastrophe, and the only means of saving the day when unprecedented apocalyptic problems arise. *Artifact* failed to reach best-selling status, and when Benford tried a second experiment of a similar kind in the even longer *Chiller* (1993)—a tale of a serial killer whose favored prey is scientists working in the field of cryonics—he used the pseudonym Sterling Blake in order that it would not be weighed down by the genre associations of his own name. Unfortunately, it fared no better.

Heart of the Comet (1986), which Benford wrote in collaboration with David Brin, was yet another attempt to reach a wider audience, this time without straying into the margins of the field. The collaborators set out to use the re-entry into the solar system of Halley's comet—and the close inspection thereof by a space probe—as a hook to catch the public imagination. In the event, the comet did not live up to the hopes of those who wanted to see a spectacular tail, and the probe merely confirmed what everyone already knew about the nature of comets, but the novel provided some compensation to those who hungered for more dramatic revelations. Brin had already achieved considerable success in modernizing space opera and bringing that despised subgenre to a new pitch of sophistication, and he and Benford set out to equip their comet with a native ecology that included real Bug-Eyed Monsters. The core of the plot is a painstaking recapitulation of the kind of project featured in "West Wind, Falling", describing the establishment of a colony within the comet's head in order to hitch a ride thereon to the remoter regions of the solar system, and the subsequent alienation of that colony from its point of origin. The sudden blossoming of the object's dormant life-system does, however, provide a useful melodramatic boost to an exercise in classic hard sf.

Benford's experiments in literary method also produced four significant novellas in the late 1980s. His first attempt to transpose the manner and tone of William Faulkner's work into sf had been sufficiently successful to warrant repetition, and he modeled his post-holocaust story "To the Storming Gulf" (1985) even more explicitly on *As I Lay Dying*. The stratagem called forth some sharp criticism from Gary K. Wolfe, who doubted its propriety and wondered publicly about Benford's motives, but Benford produced a reasonable defense (whose substance is appended to the story in *In Alien Flesh*) and the story itself is remarkably effective, although the coda formed by incorporating "Old Woman by the Road" (1978) is slightly awkward. The future war scenario, in which America is devastated after the USSR is provoked by a deceptive third party into launching a nuclear strike, but refrains from retaliation, is an intriguing variation on a familiar theme, which recalls Theodore Sturgeon's "Thunder and Roses". Benford was to recapitulate and deftly recomplicate the themes of other classic stories that he had read and admired in youth, most notably in "Matter's End" (1990), a hard sf variation of the theme of Arthur C. Clarke's "The Nine Billion Names of God", and "Centigrade 233" (1990), a wry inversion of the ultimate heresy defined by Ray Bradbury's *Fahrenheit 451*.

Less successful than "To the Storming Gulf" was "As Big as the Ritz" (1986 abridged; 1987), a Utopian satire modeled on a story by F. Scott Fitzgerald. An astrophysicist takes advantage of his affair with the daughter of the richest man in the solar system to investigate the ultra-socialist Utopia, Brotherworld. The idealistic plutocrat has established Brotherworld on the Hoop, an artificial habitat sustained by the energy-output of matter falling into a black hole, employing genetic as well as social engineering to ensure that its people really are equal in every possible respect. The hero's analysis of this peculiar state is aided by a reference book credited to one Darko Drovneb, whose name strongly suggests that Benford was using the story to explore his own anarcho-libertarian objections to socialist ideals. The social thought-experiment seems to have had no clear result—the story's ending is weak and ambivalent—but the speculations about black holes and their uses bore further fruit in "The Worm in the Well" (1995; reprinted as "Early Bird").

Much more closely allied to the experiment Benford undertook in collaboration with Brin was "Proserpina's Daughter" (1988; reprinted as *Iceborn*), which he wrote in partnership with Paul A. Carter. The story juxtaposes the discoveries made by a lone astronaut on Pluto—which unexpectedly turns out to harbor a complex ecology including sentient life-forms—with political upheavals that threaten to put a stop to the entire space program. Although it echoes "Sons of Man" in this respect, it is a more powerful story, embodying a blithe flamboyance that the ever-more-conscientious Benford had by now virtually squeezed out of his solo work. This reflects the fact that Carter was the only one of Benford's many collaborators who had made a contribution to hard science fiction's "Golden Age", when John W. Campbell Jr. had steered *Astounding* through the troubled 1940s. Benford did follow it up with a pulp sf pastiche of his own in "Alphas" (1989), a thoroughly Campbellian tale of a dashing astronaut who takes a trip through the core of Venus whole investigating the activities of alien miners whose tools are cosmic strings. The Alphas and their exotic mining techniques reappeared in *Tides of Light* and "Doing Alien" (1994).

The fourth item in the quartet of novellas was Benford's sequel to *Against the Fall of Night*, whose collaborative aspect was emphasized by the fact that it was published in an omnibus with its predecessor. Although the young hero of the earlier text reappears as an adult, the central character of the sequel is Cley, an Ur-human whose species has been resurrected with the aid of the Library of Life. Unfortunately, her kind has to bear the brunt of the wrath of the Mad Mind, released from the prison to which Clarke's future history had condemned it. The main virtue of the story lies, however, in its images of remarkable ecologies filling entire solar systems, and its establishment of an ultimate destiny one step beyond that which had been imaginable in Clarke's day, even to a man of Clarke's vision. That potential for transcendence, which made the project worthwhile in spite of a certain dramatic flaccidity, was unavailable when Benford wrote *Foundation's Fear* (1997), which had to be slotted into an exceedingly narrow slice of the historical infilling which Isaac Asimov had already inserted into the cracks of his own much grander scheme. The latter project did, however, offer him the opportunity to offer an oblique commentary on Asimov's crucial contribution to the evolution of sf. Benford's preparatory contemplation of the hypothetical human science of psychohistory encouraged him to develop his own hypothetical "sociohistory", whose scope is mapped in the Africa-set "Immersion" (1996). The imaginative work devoted to "Beyond the Fall of Night" also bore further fruit in the sophisticated space opera "Galaxia" (1997).

The later novellas in this sequence were sidelines to the biggest—and, as it turned out, the most problematic—project that Benford had yet tackled. This was the completion of the series begun with *In the Ocean of Night* by a trilogy, employing a new cast of characters, which took up the story more than 35,000 years after the conclusion of *Across the Sea of Suns*.

* * * * * * *

Great Sky River (1987) begins at the end of the 375th century, and tells the story of the struggle for survival of members of the family Bishop following the destruction of their Citadel, on the planet Snowglade. The destroyers of the Citadel are "mechs" engaged in an apparent program of extermination—although the surviving Bishops, led by Killeen, are themselves partly mechanized by virtue of various inorganic augmentations. The most significant of these augmentations are the information storage facilities which equip them with Aspects: supplementary intelligences retaining the personalities of dead family-members.

The Bishops are pursued by a mech called the Mantis, an "anthology intelligence" whose purpose is not merely to wipe out the Bishops but to record and "digest" them. It is, after its own fashion, an artist, and it regards organic matter as a medium of "sculpture". In the course of its pursuit it becomes sufficiently interested in its prey to open a channel of communication with them—but no sooner is the dialogue begun than a third party intervenes: a "magnetic mind" based in the warped space that surrounds the Eater, the huge black hole at the centre of the galaxy. The magnetic mind relays a message to Killeen, allegedly from his long-lost father, Abraham, instructing him not to attempt to build a new Citadel.

This instruction sends Killeen forth on a quest of the kind that Maxwell Perkins once advised Thomas Wolfe to employ in order to give anchorage and direction to his initially-inchoate novels. In *Tides of Light* the quest takes Killeen's band to Abraham's Star, on the edge of a dust-cloud near the galaxy's centre, while the interested anthology intelligence—which has assisted the escape from Snowglade—keeps clandestine watch on their progress. They find more human refugees, but they also find Cybers: hybrid entities which have taken cyborgization much further than those who still think of themselves as natural beings. The Cybers have ambitions on much the same scale as the mechs, involving the use of cosmic strings as tools to plunder planetary resources, as in "Alphas". The situation is further complicated by the involvement of the alien Starswarmers, who had been introduced in the 1978 novelette.

Tides of Light fills in much of the history overleapt by the gap separating *Across the Sea of Suns* from *Great Sky River*, going so far as to append a "report" compiled by the Mantis in the hope of making the human world-view intelligible to others of its kind. The first subdivision of this chronology of the human species—which is classified parenthetically among the "dreaming vertebrates"—is the Great Times, when humans, despite the mech-assisted devastation of

Earth's ecosphere, built a galactic empire to rival that of mech civilization. Explorers arrived at the centre of the galaxy in several distinct groups, at widely spaced intervals, most of which disappeared. Some of these came in search of a fabled Galactic Library, of which no trace remained. The Great Times were followed by the Chandelier Age, in which human gathered into vast spacefaring cities under he pressure of mech attrition, which culminated in the "Hunker Down", when the Chandeliers had to be abandoned and their former inhabitants took refuge on planetary surfaces, usually in vast Arcologies. Eventually, the Arcologies suffered the same fate as the Chandeliers, proving unsustainable under the pressure of mech aggression, and their survivors lost much of their technology, apparently becoming mere pests in the margins of a universal mech civilization.

After publication of the second volume, progress on the trilogy came to a temporary halt, partly because new discoveries and theories regarding the actual galactic centre—to which Benford's own papers made a significant contribution—were continually being reported. He was also distracted by writing and hosting an eight-part television series for the Japanese National Broadcasting organization NHK, *A Galactic Odyssey*, which attempted to popularize modern physics in the context of an account of the evolution of the galaxy; although popular in Japan it was never aired in the US. (Benford's subsequent TV credits include *Japan 2000* and service as scientific consultant to the NHK Network and *Star Trek: The Next Generation*.)

It is perhaps ironic, given the series' evident inspirational debt to *The City and the Stars*, that one of the other projects which interrupted the trilogy was the belated sequel to "Against the Fall of Night", but the spinoff from Benford's work-in-progress—which determined the recasting of the Mad Mind as a magnetic mind and its insecure prison as a black hole identical to the Eater—worked to the advantage of "Beyond the Fall of Night". When Benford's own series got going again the projected third volume became too unwieldy and was split into two: *Furious Gulf* (1994) and *Sailing Bright Eternity* (1995).

The story told by these volumes takes Killeen and his allies—now including the alien Quath, whose portrayal here brought Benford closer than he had ever come before to sf's Holy Grail—into the Esty, an exotic space-time continuum accessible via "portals" from the ergosphere surrounding the Eater. The Esty is constantly redesigning itself as more infalling matter is added to it but appears to observers as an infinite, chaotically lit and perpetually windblown plain of "timestone", liberally pockmarked with "Lanes". Certain sectors of the Esty stabilized by the "Old Ones" support an ecosphere and comprised the habitable Wedge or Redoubt, which turns out to be the site of the lost Galactic Library. The Wedge's independence from ordinary galactic time has allowed it to accumulate a population drawn from all the eras of humanity's galactic history. Nigel Walmsley is there, ready to greet Killeen's son Toby, take him on a journey of discovery down a river (which preserves sensitive echoes of Mark Twain's mythicized Mississippi) and explain the necessity of Killeen's quest.

In the climax of *Sailing Bright Eternity*, the Mantis-led mechs finally find a way into the Esty, thus precipitating the final crisis in their long war against organic beings—but they too have been forced to reappraise their place in the scheme of things and their relationship with organic species. The chronology laid out in the appendix to the final volume concludes, with a slightly tired flourish, with the "Beginning of [the] mature phase of self-organized forms".

In looking at this series as a whole one has to bear in mind that when the author set out on his imaginary voyage he had no inkling of the terminus it would eventually reach. All extended enterprises within the field of science fiction are, almost by definition, exploratory; the essence of their development is to move further and further into terra incognita, ascending through a whole series of levels of revelation. The best enterprises of this kind are those which arrive somewhere that is not only new and interesting but quite unexpected; Benford's is certainly among the best—and its final achievement is ample justification for the occasional unprofitable detours and patchwork engine-repairs that occurred along the way.

* * * * * * *

The previously-steady flow of Benford's short fiction was muted while he struggled to finish his galactic history series, but he made some compensation by editing a series of anthologies in collaboration with Martin H. Greenberg, all but one featuring exercises in alternative history. He also wrote "World Vast, World Various" (1992) for the Shared World anthology *Murasaki*, edited by Greenberg and Robert Silverberg, in which scientists exploring Murasaki's neighbor-world attempt to apply sociobiological theory to the understanding of the native "chumpclamps".

Benford returned to his own work in a more playful mood, exhibited in such tales as "Not for an Age", a time-tripping story written for an anthology of *Weird Tales from Shakespeare* (1994), but first published in the previous year as "The Dark Backward", and "Kollapse" (1995), a sarcastic satirization of Net-nerds. "A Tapestry of Thought" (1995), in which two machines philosophize about the nature of a captive human, and "High Abyss", which offers a mildly satirical glimpse of life on a cosmic string, partake of a similar spirit. "Paris Conquers All" (1996 with David Brin) proposes that Jules Verne's response to the kind of alien invasion described in H. G. Wells's *The War of the Worlds* would have been more pragmatic than that of the protagonist of the novel. "Zoomers" (1996) and "The Voice" (1997) offer different images of a post-literate future in which new media have extended the human sensorium in remarkable ways; the latter includes a wry reference to "Centigrade 233", acknowledging that its central joke might not have been as funny as it seemed at the time. "High Abyss" appeared in Greg Bear's *New Legends* (1995), for which Benford also wrote "A Desperate Calculus (signed "Sterling Blake"), a calculatedly-controversial political fantasy, and the essay "Old Legends", which discusses—partly from the author's own experience—the interrelationships between American science and American science fiction during the previous 55 years.

Benford's next major project returned from the further reaches of space and time to the tangibility of the present day and the laboratory, although it did not entirely forsake the cosmic perspective of his four-volume trilogy. *Cosm* (1998) describes an experiment in which smashing Uranium atoms together inside a Relativistic Heavy Iron Collider produces a mini-Big Bang and opens a window into a virgin universe, which continues to expand into its own private space. This accident befalls Alicia Butterworth, a professor at the University of California, Irvine, who is comprehensively distanced from the author in being a single black female. Her misfired experiment opens up the glorious possibility of manufacturing universes wholesale and observing the entire course of their lifetimes in a matter of weeks. The plot is a little contrived—in order to stoke up the melodrama the author throws in an entirely gratuitous attempted kidnapping and arranges matters so that the cosm causes a flukish fatality—but the core of the story is its painstaking study of the obsessive psychology of its heroine, her allies and her rivals. In constructing this analysis the novel offers its readers a less charitable picture of the concerns, habits and ethics of scientists than *Timescape*, but one that is every bit as compelling and just as convincing.

It is arguable that works like *Cosm* are what Benford does best—or, at least, that they are the one thing he does conspicuously better than anyone else. What is truly remarkable about his work is, however, its awesome range. He has tried harder than any other contemporary sf writer, and far harder than any other writer of hard sf, to explore all the potentialities that the genre has to offer. The spectrum of his works includes a few enterprises that some critics have considered to be beneath the dignity of a real writer—especially a self-declared amateur who has a taxing and worthwhile day job—but Benford has always seen such exploits as contributing to Shared World anthologies and writing belated sequels to other people's books as intellectual and artistic challenges. In addition to those items already mentioned he and Mark O. Martin contributed a novella, "The Trojan Cat", and a full-length novel, "A Darker Geometry" to the sixth and seventh volumes of *Man-Kzin Wars* (1994 & 1995), based on Larry Niven's scenario. Like any true scientist, Benford has always been willing to try such experiments, just to see how they come out. His amateurism is not the kind that despises money-making, but the kind that can embark upon any enterprise at whim, without any need to fear the consequences of occasional failure.

Given this, it is not surprising that Benford's very best work constitutes an ongoing celebration of curiosity as a motive force and enterprise as an attitude of mind. This can be seen very clearly in *Timescape* and *Cosm*, and in the long series built on the seed of "In the Ocean of Night", but it does not diminish Benford in the slightest to suggest that it shows most nakedly in some of his collaborative pieces, including *If the Stars are Gods*, "Proserpina's Daughter" and their most striking successor: "A Cold, Dry Cradle" (1997, written with Elisabeth Malartre). This heartfelt hard sf story accepts James Lovelock's judgment of the implications of its chemically-neutral atmosphere and the scant findings of the Viking lander, but begs leave to argue that there is still a possibility not merely of finding life on Mars but of finding precious enlightenment there.

In one of the commentaries in *In Alien Flesh*, Benford borrows an analogy applied by Robert Frost to the writing of free verse in order to characterise the writing of sf without a proper scientific conscience as "playing tennis with the net down". He is a writer who has always tried to play with the net up, but not to allow its presence to inhibit him in his stylistic experiments. It is as well to remember, though, that to think of any kind of conscience merely as a restriction is rather misleading. The point of a conscience is that it also works constructively towards the cause and security of some crucial good. The conscience of hard sf works towards the cause and security of enlightenment, and Benford's work in that cause can stand comparison with any modern writer in any field.

BRUCE STERLING

Michael Bruce Sterling was born in Brownsville, Texas on 14 April 1954. His parents moved to the gulf coast when he was three and he lived in various coastal refinery towns until he was fifteen. His father, a mechanical engineer, then obtained work in India, and Sterling spent a good deal of the following two-and-a-half years in various Far Eastern locations. He completed his formal education at his father's alma mater, the University of Texas, Austin, graduating in 1976 with a B.A. in Journalism. He married Nancy Baxter in 1979.

Sterling's first science fiction story, "Man-Made Self", appeared—somewhat mangled by the printer—in *Lone Star Universe* (1976), an anthology of Texan sf edited by George W. Proctor and Steven Utley. That anthology was introduced by Harlan Ellison, who was later to issue Sterling's first novel, *Involution Ocean* (1978 but dated 1977) in the short-lived "Harlan Ellison Discovery Series". Ellison explains in his introduction to the latter volume that in 1974, when he was a guest at one of the "Turkey City Workshops" in which Sterling regularly took part, he had also bought the first story Sterling ever sold. Unfortunately, he bought it for *The Last Dangerous Visions*, which has not yet seen print. In the intervening quarter-century Sterling has become one of the leading figures in the science fiction genre. He writes with admirable literary elegance and a fine wit; he is also a remarkably astute cultural commentator, second to none in his grasp of the keenness of the cutting edge of technological progress and the velocity with which that progress is likely to proceed. His passionate promotion of a new kind of science fiction adapted to a revolutionary new era in technology and popular culture enabled him to attain near-legendary status as the compiler of one of the key cultural products of the current *fin-de-siècle*, *Mirrorshades: The Cyberpunk Anthology* (1986).

* * * * * * *

Harlan Ellison's introduction to *Involution Ocean* records that the first version of the story was a novelette entitled "Moby Dust". The abandoned title acknowledges the story's formal debt to Herman Melville, although Ellison quotes the author's judgment that his principal influences in writing it were Clark Ashton Smith, Larry Niven, Samuel Taylor Coleridge, and Ellison himself. The novel is set on the colony world of Nullaqua, whose only habitable region lies at the bottom of a crater some five hundred miles across, in which ninety percent of the world's atmosphere is concentrated. This region consists of an "ocean" of extremely fine dust dotted with various island chains. The Nullaquan dustwhale is the only known source of the psychotropic drug syncophine, also known as Flare. Because Flare has been proscribed, the descendants of the religious fanatics who first settled the world have done their best to put an end to an era in which dust-masked privateers sailed the Sea of Dust in great trimarans in search of the alien leviathans—but the opportunity still remains for a group of ill-assorted travelers to undertake one last great adventure. The novel's plot is an account of the mixed motives and various fortunes of the expeditionaries.

Sterling's attempt to marry the imaginative adventurism of Clark Ashton Smith to the technophilic hardness of Larry Niven was typical of his ambition. Smith had taken the world-view of the French Decadent Movement of the nineteenth-century *fin-de-siècle* to the illimitable stages of cosmic fantasy and genre science fiction, while Niven, in the "Gil Hamilton" series, had been one of the first writers to attempt to analyze the social changes that were likely to flow from the combined effects of sophisticated biotechnology and information technology. *Involution Ocean* is a neo-Decadent fantasy of the far future, which owes far more to Smith than Niven, but the settings of Sterling's subsequent works of fiction were to move gradually closer to home. The majority eventually settled in a near future in which the social and political institutions of the present day are still struggling—with grotesque ineffectuality—to cope with a deluge of scientific innovations, but they never abandoned the colorful and ironic flamboyance of Decadent sensibility.

Sterling's second novel, *The Artificial Kid* (1980), is set on the watery but island-strewn world of Reverie. Its eponymous hero is a young "combat artist" whose adventures in a Decriminalized Zone where almost anything goes are assiduously chronicled by robot cameras. The resultant videotapes are edited for use as entertainment by legions of fans. Many of the elements of *Involution Ocean* reappear in *The Artificial Kid*, in much the same balance; drugs function as a double-edged means of liberation and religion as an essentially farcical but nevertheless powerful repressive force. The secrets of the Elder Culture, some of whose relics were marginally featured in the earlier novel, play a more prominent part here, refracted through the Gestalt theories of the protagonist's "tutor and mentor" Professor Crossbow. The climactic journey that takes the novel's leading characters into the heart of the alien Mass and out again is a baroque odyssey similar to that which supplied the plot of *Involution Ocean*.

The elaborate description of the protagonist provided in the first chapter of *The Artificial Kid* is strongly reminiscent of various heroes featured in the work of Samuel R. Delany, who were also deployed in exotic myth-infected milieux. The Kid dresses to impress, carries a customized weapon (a "nunchuck") which he uses artfully and judiciously, has a similarly quasi-fetishistic association with various other technical gadgets, moves with "resilient grace" and is irrepressibly precocious. He does not actually wear mirrorshades, but he is the kind of character custom-designed to fit almost everything that mirrorshades came to symbolize when it became the insiders' shorthand term for the literary movement whose prime movers were Sterling and William Gibson.

Sterling's own core contribution to the sf of the early 1980s was the Shaper/Mechanist series, whose earliest elements—"Spider Rose" (1982), "Swarm" (1982) and "Cicada Queen" (1983)—appeared alongside the story series which Gibson began with "Johnny Mnemonic" (1981). Sterling was later to recall that he had read Gibson's *Neuromancer* (1985) in manuscript "in 1982 or 1983" while he was guiding his own series towards the climax it eventually attained—following "Sunken Gardens" (1984) and the patchwork "Twenty Evocations" (1984)—in *Schismatrix* (1985; reprinted with the short stories as *Schismatrix Plus*, 1996).

Sterling's series details the rapid expansion through the solar system of various "posthuman" populations, loosely categorized as Shapers (a term of description applied to those groups who have remade themselves primarily by genetic engineering) and Mechanists (those groups who have remade themselves by extensive cyborgization). These main categories are elaborately subdivided into many splinter-societies organized according to a wide range of political and religious creeds. Their most extreme examples are very bizarre indeed, the ultimate mechanists being immobile and immortal "wireheads" equipped with all manner of mechanical senses while the most exotic Reshaped individuals are more alien than the actual alien species whose presence within and without the solar system complicates the human expansion into space.

The aliens provide important points of comparison throughout the series as Sterling and his many characters attempt to figure out what, if anything, is truly fundamental to the concept of "humanity"—and what, if anything, is worth preserving therefrom. The hive-intelligence of "Swarm" poses a challenge to a Shaper who believes that the preservation of individuality is both possible and desirable. The reptilean Investors, who barter artifacts and life-forms of many different kinds for human goods and art-works, offer a similar challenge the Mechanist protagonist of "Spider Rose", in the form of a carefully-tailored genetic artifact that eventually becomes reincarnate within her own flesh and mind.

A key location in the Shaper/Mechanist series is the space habitat C-K (Czarina-Kluster), whose central Palace is established to house the exiled Investor "Cicada Queen". It rapidly accumulates a host of "subbles" (bubble suburbs), eventually becoming host to a People's Corporate Republic. C-K, which is also an important setting in *Schismatrix*, becomes a temporary oasis of calm in the Shaper/Mechanist conflict, although it is by no means immune to the fallout of their various philosophical and commercial differences. Its moral and intellectual climate is advanced beyond those of the inner system's more tradition-bound locales, and although it is by no means a Utopia it represents Sterling's first major experiment in constructive social design. The ready access that C-K's inhabitants have to Investor technologies—by courtesy of the renegade Queen—places it at the cutting edge of the Posthumanist quest, providing a platform for the Lifesiders who oppose the more radical forms of Posthumanism and are intent on terraforming Mars—a project whose intermediate phases are described in "Sunken Gardens". C-K also offers a home to such extreme Mechanist sects as the Lobsters, the Spectral Intelligents and the Blood Bathers.

By the end of the extraordinarily complicated *Schismatrix*—whose hero's extended odyssey through the rapidly changing solar system covers 170 years of future history in less than 300 pages—humankind has broken up into a whole series of daughter species, or "clades", none of which can claim to be sole carrier of the torch of destiny. The odyssey of the novel's hero, Abelard Lindsay, takes him from the Mare Tranquillitatis People's Circumlunar Zaibatsu to the spaceship Red Consensus, the asteroid Esairs 89-XII, the Shaper "city-state" of Goldrich-Tremaine in the Rings of Saturn, an Investor trading ship and back to the asteroid belt's Dembowska Cartel before the plot revisits Czarina-Kluster. In the process, Lindsay witnesses and plays his own small part in the evolution of the Schismatrix: the system-wide society in which all the post-human factions can live in relative harmony.

In the final chapter of the novel Lindsay returns "home" to Earth, but that is only the opening of a final sequence of moves which takes him far abroad again. He visits the exhausted Earth—which has already begun its own process of self-renewal—merely in order to draw genetic material from its oceanic womb: material that will be transformed by the "angelic" Lifesiders to provide the Jovian satellite Europa with an ecosystem. The conclusion of the chapter is set in CircumEuropa as the new world awaits its transformation, and it finds Lindsay in the company of the mysterious Presence, looking outwards to "the final transcendance [sic]" and to the as-yet-unattained state of being in which it will not matter whether or not the Final Questions ever obtain the Final Answers.

* * * * * * *

It was Gardner Dozois, the editor of *Isaac Asimov's Science Fiction Magazine*, who popularized the term "cyberpunk" as a label for the kind of character that was foreshadowed in the Artificial Kid and became the symbol of the new sf that Sterling and William Gibson were trying to write. (In 1983 *Amazing* had published a story called "Cyberpunk" by Bruce Bethke which had applied the label to a different kind of individual, but Dozois might not have seen it.) Typically, Sterling had moved on so rapidly that he never used another leading character of the same caricaturish kind as the Artificial Kid, even in a carefully tuned-down version; Abelard Lindsay is cut from different cloth. Sterling left the sophistication of the new outlaw breed to William Gibson, whose "very technical boy" Johnny Mnemonic and cyberspace cowboy Bobby Quine became the archetypal cyberpunks. It is entirely appropriate to the nature of the movement that by the time Cyberpunk became firmly established as a key descriptive term, in 1985, all the writers involved were insistent that it was already obsolete.

Schismatrix is more ambitious in many ways than *Neuromancer*, and is certainly one of the landmark works of modern sf, but it is not entirely surprising that it was the latter novel that won the awards and attracted the lion's share of critical attention. While Gibson provided a generation of would-be cyberpunks with the vocabulary of ideas required to crystallize their image and creed, Sterling reached into more distant realms of possibility so strange and so discomfiting that the vast but safely-enclosed vistas of cyberspace seemed cozy by comparison.

Between 1984 and 1986 Sterling produced the fanzine *Cheap Truth*, where he pontificated extensively—employing the polemical persona of "Vincent Omniaveritas"—about the nature and significance of the Movement of which he and Gibson were a part, along with Lewis Shiner, John Shirley and Rudy Rucker. The climax of this endeavor—which established that although Gibson might be reckoned the Messiah of 1980s sf, Sterling was the hard-working Saint Paul who actually took the message on the road—was *Mirrorshades: The Cyberpunk Anthology*. This seminal collection featured all the aforementioned writers alongside Pat Cadigan, Tom Maddox and the more marginal figures of Greg Bear, James Patrick Kelly, Marc Laidlaw, and Paul Di Filippo.

Sterling's introduction to the anthology pays appropriate homage to cyberpunk's precursors within the sf field and draws crucial analogies to parallel cultural movements, especially those manifest in rock music, before providing the definitive explanation of the Movement's nature and ambitions:

> "Technical culture has gotten out of hand. The advances of the sciences are so deeply radical, so disturbing, upsetting, and revolutionary that they can no longer be contained. They are surging into culture at large; they are invasive; they are everywhere. The traditional power structures, the traditional institutions, have lost control of the pace of change.
>
> "And suddenly a new alliance is becoming evident: an integration of technology and the Eighties counterculture. An unholy alliance of the technical world and the world of organized dissent—the underground world of pop culture, visionary fluidity and street-level anarchy....
>
> "The hacker and the rocker are this decade's pop-culture icons, and cyberpunk is very much a pop phenomenon: spontaneous, energetic, close to its roots....
>
> "For the cyberpunks...technology is visceral. It is not the bottled genie of remote Big Science boffins; it is persuasive, utterly intimate. Not outside us, but next to us. Under our skin; often, inside our minds."
> (pp. x-xi)

The idea of cyberpunk fiction had an instant appeal to people ambitious to be the architects of a new "cyberculture", whose instruments of propaganda were such magazines as *Mondo 2000* and *Wired*. The former proclaimed Sterling a hero, while the latter welcomed his journalistic input. By 1987, however, the first issue of the fanzine *Science Fiction Eye* began its list of contents with a "Requiem for the Cyberpunks", reproduced a Science Fiction Research Association panel discussion of "Cyberpunk or Cyberjunk" (in which Norman Spinrad tried belatedly to secure his contention that "Neuromantics" would have been much a better label for the Movement's members) and promulgated "The Humanist Manifesto", issued in reaction against Sterling's *Mirrorshades* introduction by John Kessel, following a lead offered by Michael Swanwick. Sterling—whose interview with Takayuki Tatsumi was advertised as the last phase of the magazine's "cyberpunk autopsy"—agreed to serve as a regular columnist for *Science Fiction Eye*, but with characteristic insouciance he ignored the unfolding furore and devoted his opening contribution to a commentary on the works of Jules Verne.

The term "cyberpunk" also had an instant appeal to academics of a postmodernist stripe, who were anxious to get a fashionably-labeled theoretical grip on contemporary popular culture. Larry McCaffery, the editor of a massively comprehensive guide to *Postmodern Fiction* (1986), produced *Storming the Reality Studio: A Case Book of Cyberpunk and Postmodern Fiction* (1991), an anthology far more wide-ranging and far more grandiose than *Mirrorshades*, which mixed stories by the bona fide cyberpunks with fiction by the likes of Kathy Acker, J. G. Ballard, William S. Burroughs, Don DeLillo, and Thomas Pynchon, and non-fiction by Jean Baudrillard, Jacques Derrida, Timothy Leary, and others. The rapidity with which the movement was embalmed for academic inspection and critically dissected was entirely in keeping with its own theories about the flow of modern culture.

* * * * * * *

The Sterling novel of greatest relevance to the emergent cyberculture was *Islands in the Net* (1988). Like William Gibson's later work, however, it flatly refuses to become hung up on the idea of cyberspace as a magical frontier. Sterling is more concerned to explore the political implications of the global integration of the world's computers into a vast network. Although he is by no means the kind of naive technological determinist who imagines social change merely as a series of adaptations to technological innovation, Sterling is fascinated by the ways in which technological advancement opens up a host of new and various opportunities for different kinds of individuals and human groups. His travels in the Far East equipped him with the intellectual means to think on a global scale, and to consider the possible impact of new technologies on the balance of economic power dividing the First, Second and Third Worlds. He had previously addressed such questions in "Spook" (1983) and the novella "Green Days in Brunei" (1985), both of which made every effort to transcend the cultural insularity fostered by the American education system, but *Islands in the Net* developed them more seriously and more fully.

Islands in the Net is, in essence, a future-set thriller, but it deploys its far-flung settings with a casual profligacy that no genre thriller-writer had previously attempted. Its whole-world perspective offers an ambitious overview of the rigorous regime of natural selection to which existing political institutions will inevitably be subjected by new information technology: a regime in which rapid mutation is the only ward against gradual disintegration. Its hapless heroine, Laura Webster, is no cyberpunk; she has a good home, a nice family and a rewarding job, although her adventures bring all of these once-secure investments under dire threat. The idea of "the Net" has become so commonplace since 1988 that it is already difficult to understand that *Islands in the Net* was a work of considerable originality and ingenuity. It is not particularly "prophetic", in the vulgar sense, but the task of intellectually worthwhile science fiction is not so much to predict what will actually come to pass as to expose the whole range of realizable possibilities—and no one exposes possibilities in such reckless profusion as Sterling.

The novel's Net is the brain and nervous system of a global society, upon whose relatively smooth working the political health of the world depends. In such a world social stability is, virtually by definition, the controlled flow of information; the wilder excesses of "data piracy" constitute a blight that threatens universal social breakdown. The Net's "islands" are locations whose inhabitants will not subscribe to the royalty system that regulates the wealth of information; most of them are islands in the commonplace sense too, the ones which feature most prominently in the plot being Grenada and Singapore. Laura embarks upon an enforced and horribly uncomfortable educational odyssey through the highways and by-ways of this society, initially as an envoy but later as a kidnap-victim, political prisoner and pawn in schemes she is powerless to settle or convincingly upset. Roger Zelazny has observed that she has more in common with Candide than Odysseus, but hers is not a world from which anyone can sensibly retreat to tend his or her own garden; it is, to the contrary, a world in which no one can avoid claustrophobically intimate contact with everyone else's problems and everyone else's ambitions.

In view of the publicity given to Gibson's and Sterling's endeavors, and the fact that the cyberpunk writers were already accustomed to working in collaboration—Sterling had written "Red Star, Winter Orbit" (1983) with Gibson, "Storming the Cosmos" (1985) with Rudy Rucker, "Mozart in Mirrorshades" (1985) with Lewis Shiner, and "The Unfolding" (1985) with John Shirley—it is not surprising that Sterling and Gibson next undertook to write a novel together. The novel in question was, however, an alternative history to be set in Victorian England: a "steampunk" novel.

The baroque subgenre of "gonzo historical novels" is now primarily associated with a group of Californian writers consisting of K. W. Jeter, James Blaylock, and Tim Powers, who have provided some of the subgenre's most outstanding examples, but its roots lay in the work of two of Sterling's fellow participants in the "Turkey City Workshops", Howard Waldrop and Steven Utley, and key contributions to it have also been made by cyberpunks Rudy Rucker and Paul Di Filippo. Anyone interested in the power that technology has to transform society is likely to be interested in the "what ifs" of history as well as the "what ifs" of the near future, and Sterling had already written a handful of fantasies in which people in times past obtain supernatural insights into the incredible transformations that await them, including "Telliamed" (1984), "Dinner in Audoghast" (1985) and the beautifully tragic "Flowers of Edo" (1987). In *The Difference Engine* (1990) Gibson and Sterling raised the question of what might have happened if the revolution in information technology had taken place 150 years earlier than it actually did, when Charles Babbage, aided by Ada Lovelace (née Byron), first attempted to build a programmable mechanical computer.

As with most steampunk novels, the plot of *The Difference Engine* is a hectic adventure story in which a gang of villains with an exotic leader—in this case the neo-Luddite gangster Captain Swing—is engaged in a running battle with a band of stalwart heroes, avid to possess a McGuffin whose significance the reader should be better able to appreciate than they are. Real historical characters are, as per usual, relegated to cameo roles. Keats has a walk-on part as an operator of "kinotropes", while Byron—who has become prime minister following the sweeping political success of the technocratic "Rads"—remains in the wings; the only central role awarded to an actual writer is allotted to the far less famous Laurence Oliphant. The "Texian" exile Sam Houston has a substantial peripheral part, but Friedrich Engels—whose one-time associate Karl Marx is safely ensconced at the heart of the Manhattan Commune—barely rates a mention. The novel's true subject-matter is, however, neatly woven into the background, half-concealed in a welter of casual observation. The characters do sometimes have occasion to stand and stare at Babbage Engines, but for the most part, they simply take the presence of such entities for granted; the reader alone occupies the privileged position of being able to see what difference the engines have made to the fabric and thrust of nineteenth century society.

As an attempted best-seller *The Difference Engine* was a little too subtle for its own good—especially with respect to American readers, whose education in European history is likely to have been slight—but it features a wealth of deft and brilliant detail as well as a smog to rival the one that choked the population in Robert Barr's alarmist account of "The Doom of London". The story's conclusion is a neatly ironic nod in the direction of *Neuromancer*; its vaguely uplifting spirit provides some compensation for the cold cynicism that underlies the greater part of the text.

* * * * * * *

Although Sterling's second story collection, *Globalhead* (1992), was published only three years after his first, *Crystal Express* (1989), it is markedly different in tone and subject-matter. There are two interesting experiments in style that have no parallel in the earlier collection—"Our Neural Chernobyl" (1988) offers an indirect account of a fanciful future in the form of a book-review, while "The Sword of Damocles" (1990) takes postmodernist recursiveness to calculatedly absurd lengths—but the remainder of the collection has a distinctly darker edge.

"The Gulf Wars" (1988) juxtaposes the present and the distant past in a manner akin to that of "Dinner in Audoghast", but its moral applies an extra turn of a cruel screw. "The Shores of Bohemia" (1990) is a quasi-Utopian fantasy about artistry and decadence whose concerns echo the earlier volume's "The Beautiful and the Sublime" (1986), but it is markedly less flippant than its predecessor. A collaboration with Rudy Rucker left over from the earlier period, "Storming the Cosmos"—which describes the unhappy experiences of Russian cosmonauts whose search for the source of the Tunguska explosion is confused by the effects of psychotropic mushrooms—is followed by a much dourer collaboration with John Kessel, "The Moral Bullet" (1991), in which the inventor of a rejuvenation technology is pursued through a fragmented America future society so that he might be appropriately punished for his socially-disruptive sin.

The outlook that predominates in *Globalhead* is not entirely cynical, and certainly not unrelievedly callous, but it is determinedly jaundiced. The most sentimental story in the book is a small masterpiece of intimate alternative history, "Dori Bangs" (1989), which imagines that two lonely individuals who each died alone in our world might have found a tentative but rewarding companionship in another. It is saved for last, but, by the time the reader reaches it, its comforting quality has already been offset by a more extended description of the much more awkward relationship forged out of bitter necessity by the protagonists of "Jim and Irene" (1991).

In "We See Things Differently" (1990) an Arab assassin travels to a USA that has lost its political hegemony but still retains a stranglehold on the entertainment industry in order to carry the war against the Great Satan into its final and most ignominious phase. In "The Unthinkable" (1991), the juxtaposition of the implications attached to that word by H. P. Lovecraft with those attached to it by the hydrogen bomb puts Lovecraft's notion of the ultimate horror firmly in the shade. "Hollywood Kremlin" (1990) and "Are You for 86?" (original to the collection) both feature Leggy Starlitz, an opportunist wheeler-dealer of dubious origin and negligible moral commitment whose supernatural talent for evading the gaze of cameras assists him to carry out his scams anywhere in the world, from Afghanistan to Salt Lake City. He might be reckoned a cyberpunk of sorts, but there is a realpolitik grimness about his outlook and methods that puts as enormous a distance between him and the Artificial Kid as there is between Earth and Reverie.

The dourer stories in *Globalhead* were written alongside Sterling's first major exercise in popular non-fiction, *The Hacker Crackdown: Law and Disorder on the Electronic Frontier* (1992). This careful analysis of the over-reaction of law enforcement agencies to the rumor that clever PC-users were engaged in conspiracies to invade and subvert the systems of large corporations and government agencies contrasts somewhat with such exercises in alarmist sensationalism as *Cyberpunk* (1991) by Katie Hafner and John Markoff. Although Sterling is quoted on the jacket of the earlier book, lauding it as "the best book ever written on the computer underground, a marvel of lucidity and good sense" it is, in fact, considerably more melodramatic than his own study, which reported that the threatened apocalypse of outlawry had already been brutally aborted. There is a certain irony in the fact that the visionary science fiction writer was able to keep a better sense of proportion than the professional journalists.

The narrower focus of the later items assembled in *Globalhead* is also exhibited in the rather bleak novel *Heavy Weather* (1994), which extrapolates into an unsettled future the exploits of the real-world meteorologists who chase "twisters" along the American mid-West's "tornado alley". The principal plot-thread follows the zealous Storm Troupers to their dramatic encounter with the Holy Grail of weather-hackers, the F-6 supertornado, while the chief sub-plot tracks a group of government employees who know that the storm's unprecedentedly disruptive effect on electronic communication systems offers the only chance they are ever likely to get to slip the leash of close surveillance. Once the trough of low pressure has passed by, however, things begin to brighten up again.

The short stories that Sterling published after *Globalhead* reverted to a broader spectrum of concerns and a broader kind of comedy. In "Sacred Cow" (1993) an Indian film producer working in Britain extricates himself from his economic difficulties by a combination of luck and cunning while casually taking note of the devastations wrought by a human-infective form of B.S.E. which has devastated the hamburger-eating populations of the Western world. "Deep Eddy" (1993) introduces a cyberpunkish data-smuggler of a more colourful stripe than Leggy Starlitz, en route to Germany on a secret mission for the mysterious Cultural Critic (whose equally enigmatic adversary is the Moral Referee). His observations of the novelty-rich world within the text are aided by the computerized "spex" which add informational depth to his vision and serve as a translation device. The most extravagant of all Sterling's comedies is "Big Jelly" (1994), written in collaboration with Rudy Rucker, in which a young entrepreneur who needs a "killer app" for the artificial jellyfish he has invented teams up with an oil tycoon whose wells have started pumping a mysterious protoplasmic "urschleim". When the two men combine their resources, the jellyfish-inspired urschleim proves capable of very rapid and spectacular evolution.

The richly-detailed background of "Deep Eddy" is further elaborated in "Bicycle Repairman" (1996), in which an associate of Eddy's in Chattanooga accepts delivery on his behalf of a TV cable-box inhabited by a precocious Artificial Intelligence. Leggy Starlitz crops up again—this time in Finland—laundering money via the Internet and promoting a kiddipop band in "The Littlest Jackal" (1996). The imaginative labor that fed these relatively light-hearted exercises was, however, put to much more earnest use in the novel *Holy Fire* (1996). Like the short stories, this novel exploited the experience which Sterling had accumulated while carrying out journalistic assignments for *Wired* in various European locales.

Like most of Sterling's novels, *Holy Fire* is formulated as an odyssey of discovery, and is given direction by the promise of a transition from the human to the post-human condition. Unlike *Schismatrix*, however, which required its protagonist to maintain far more of his humanity than those around him, *Holy Fire* begins with a radical transformation of its aged heroine. Mia Ziemann has lived a quiet and docile existence as a medical economist until she volunteers for an experimental rejuvenation treatment—and having been the beneficiary of its staggering success, she immediately evades the grip of the interested experimenters. She goes in search of a new life, now calling herself Maya to distance herself from her cast-off larva. Cast adrift in Europe, Maya discovers the curious underworld inhabited by the disadvantaged young, who cannot compete with their increasingly-robust elders in an ever-shrinking job market where employability depends on experience and carefully refined skills. Ill-prepared for the gift of a second youth, Maya is continually in danger of frittering away her gift, but hidden opportunities await her in cyberspace, to which she is eventually led by a dutiful postcanine dog.

Holy Fire lacks a stirring climax, but that is not a weakness, because its message is that in the future life will go on, further than we can presently envisage, and that individuals will have to adapt themselves—along with their institutions—to infinite uncertainty. Although it is a much quieter novel than *Schismatrix* it is also much more controlled; although it cannot begin to match the earlier novel as a display of imaginative pyrotechnics it is, in its own way, equally inventive and equally impressive. It serves to confirm Sterling's reputation as the most prolifically inventive writer in the sf genre (although *Holy Fire* was not marketed as a genre work in the UK), while also demonstrating that his analytical powers are still continuing to mature. Although it does not quite fulfill the intention he declared in a *Locus* interview "to write about pleasure, the brighter aspects of life [and] creativity" it is a thoroughly constructive book, which takes care to emphasize that no matter how reckless and how disturbing the march of technology becomes, the likelihood is that it will offer more opportunities than threats even to those who are not naturally venturesome.

* * * * * * *

One of Sterling's greatest strengths as a science fiction writer is that he is more inclined than any other American working in the genre to take a global view of technological development. He was one of the first American writers to take a serious look at the cultural differences between the Russian and American space programs, more earnestly in "Red Star, Winter Orbit" than in "Storming the Cosmos", and he was one of the first to make convincing use of Third World settings. More recently, he has been one of the first to capture something of the cultural ambience of post-communist Eastern Europe. He has also tried to embrace Moslem perspectives—"We See Things Differently" was preceded by the brief but effective "The Compassionate, the Digital" (1985)—and Japanese perspectives, the latter with sufficient success to have had the Tokyo-set "Edo no Hano" ("Flowers of Edo") and "Maneki Neko" (1998) published in translation in *Hayakawa-SF* in advance of its first appearance in the USA.

The breadth of Sterling's concerns creates confidence in the firmness of his grasp of the issues he tackles, and there is no one whose images of possible near futures are worth more in the hard currency of pragmatic thought. Although he frequently uses comedy as a means of importing narrative verve into his stories his humor always has a serious edge. Were he to use melodrama instead he would have to invent villains to provide banishable threats, and that is the kind of cheap trickery of which he has usually tried to steer clear. Indeed, one of the strengths of cyberpunk fiction in general was its enthusiasm to avoid the mechanical plotting methods of the "technothriller" subgenre.

While his scientific and technological extrapolations have maintained the standards of realism expected of modern hard sf writers, Sterling has always brought to those extrapolations a sophisticated and distinctive aesthetic sensibility. Although it is comprehensively modernized, that sensibility is ultimately derived from those aspects of the Romantic theories of Coleridge that filtered into pulp fantasy writers by courtesy of the efforts of H. P. Lovecraft and Clark Ashton Smith. The strange combination of his influences has enabled Sterling to link his acute consciousness of the irredeemable obsolescence of a social order whose institutions have already been outstripped by technological opportunity to a fascination with the avid hunger for sensation that *ennui* and *spleen* sometimes impose upon the human mind. However odd this linkage may seem in the abstract, it is by no means inappropriate to the analysis of contemporary culture.

It is perhaps inevitable that Sterling's expertise as a cultural commentator should have deflected much of his recent effort into journalistic endeavors, but his work demonstrates that he has a very full appreciation of the unique value of speculative fiction as a medium of evaluative thought-experiments. In his preface to William Gibson's *Burning Chrome* (1986) he wrote:

> "If poets are the unacknowledged legislators of the world, science-fiction writers are its court jesters. We are Wise Fools who can leap, caper, utter prophecies, and scratch ourselves in public. We can play with Big Ideas because the garish motley of our pulp origins makes us seem harmless.
>
> "And Sf writers have every opportunity to kick up our heels—we have influence without responsibility. Very few feel obliged to take us seriously, yet our ideas permeate the culture, bubbling along invisibly, like background radiation."

All of this is true, although there is an element of bluff in stating it thus, because Sterling is the kind of writer who takes his responsibilities seriously, and tries his utmost to pack his calculated follies with as much wisdom as they can carry. If he takes great delight in whispering "Remember, thou must die!" into the ear of the global society established by American coca-colonization, he also takes great pride in trying to imagine as cleverly as possible the new order that will spring up in place of the old.

IAN WATSON

Ian Watson was born on 20 April 1943 in St Albans, while his father was engaged in war work. When the war ended the family returned home to North Shields, at the mouth of the River Tyne in North-East England. At Tynemouth School, Watson demonstrated prodigious intellectual ability, winning a scholarship to Balliol College, Oxford at sixteen. After leaving school, he hitch-hiked around Europe for a while, before taking up his university place in 1960. He married the painter Judith Jackson at the age of eighteen, while he was an undergraduate, and went on to take first class honors in English. His subsequent postgraduate research in comparative literature—examining the influence of various French writers of the nineteenth century on the aesthetic theories of Walter Pater—led to a B. Litt. in 1965, and he added the customary M.A. to his academic qualifications in 1966.

Watson's first teaching post was a two-year appointment at University College in Dar-es-Salaam, Tanzania. He then worked for three years at Tokyo University of Education, an experience of which he was to write that "although Africa made me aware of the Third World, and of politics, it was Japan which dosed me with future shock and made me become a science fiction writer." The legacy of his African experience is displayed in the "The Flags of Africa" (1970), and he published three fables in a Dar-es-Salaam University College magazine *Darlite* in 1966, but most of the writing he did there was academic criticism. In Japan, while his principal place of employment was strikebound, he began to write more variously and more prolifically. His first book was *Japan: A Cat's Eye View* (1969), a text intended for use in teaching English to Japanese students; by the time it was published he had begun to submit work to the British *avant garde* sf magazine *New Worlds*.

Watson's first story in *New Worlds* was "Roof Garden Under Saturn" (1969), which was rapidly followed by the quasi-documentary "Japan" (1970). Both items are surreal studies of life in the then-heavily-polluted atmosphere of the Japanese capital. The other stories he published before that incarnation of *New Worlds* died were a brief account of future alienation starring "The Sex Machine" (1970) and the offbeat political fantasy "The Tarot Pack Megadeath" (1971). The magazine's demise put a temporary brake on Watson's avantgardist experiments but he was to retain a taste for bizarre juxtapositions of subject-matter and a willingness to try out non-linear narrative techniques. When he resumed writing fiction he contributed offbeat pieces to other small press magazines, including the Japan-inspired fantasies "Programmed Love Story" (Transatlantic Review 1974) and "The Girl Who Was Art" (Ambit 1976). This aspect of his work is most abundantly represented in his small press collection of fiction and non-fiction *The Book of Ian Watson* (1985).

Watson returned to England in 1970, living in Oxford although he taught Complementary Studies at Birmingham Polytechnic's Art and Design Centre. He became involved with the Trotskyite political group that subsequently became the Workers' Revolutionary Party, wrote and distributed Situationist pamphlets, and experimented with LSD, also embarking on an extensive program of background research for his new novel, *The Embedding* (1973), which proved to be one of the most spectacular debut novels ever to appear in the science fiction field. It was published by Victor Gollancz, in the most prestigious sf list in Britain, to which Watson was to remain affiliated for the next 25 years. Its French translation, which appeared the following year, won the Prix Apollo.

The three plot-threads of *The Embedding* examine different aspects of the relationship between language and the human mind, extrapolating the psychlinguistic theories of Noam Chomsky. One thread describes an experiment in which children are taught an artificial language whose grammar is intricately "embedded", in order to investigate the mental consequences. A second describes anthropological investigations of an Amerindian tribe, the Xemahoa, who have two distinct languages, the second having been produced in connection with the altered states of consciousness induced by their use of psychotropic drugs. The third concerns the advent of alien visitors, the Sp'thra, who are interested in a more generalized study of human communication-systems, and who offer to trade new technology for experimental subjects.

The Embedding arrived at a time when linguistics was a newly-fashionable science, whose potential worth as a resource for sf writers had been demonstrated by Samuel R. Delany's *Babel-17* (1966), which had a far more exotic setting; Watson's decision to set his novel on Earth was a bold one, as was his use of a rather esoteric central notion which he had found during his researches in comparative literature, in *Nouvelles Impressions d'Afrique* by the French surrealist Raymond Roussel, a poem whose comprehensibility is severely compromised by its rigorously embedded form. The novel is further strengthened by a keen appreciation of the ecological and political implications of the exploitation of the Amazon rain-forest, and a similarly keen awareness of the ethics of experimentation with human subjects.

The result of this enterprise was an imaginative *tour de force*, which effortlessly surpasses in strangeness and complexity all previous sciencefictional depictions of alien thought. There had been other sf novels that drew on the resources of anthropological science to formulate images of alien society, but Watson was the first writer to emphasize a logical consequence of such extrapolations that his predecessors had often been careful to hide: the notion that humans are not so far removed from the alien, and that a transition from our familiar consciousness of the world to a radically different one might be achieved more easily than we care to suppose. The idea of an abrupt but extreme transformation of human consciousness—an existential breakthrough to a better way of seeing and thinking, and hence to a higher reality—was to remain central to Watson's work for many years, investing all his most important novels.

* * * * * * *

When *New Worlds* was reborn as a quarterly series of paperback anthologies Watson returned to its pages with "Thy Blood Like Milk" (1973), a novelette blending the imagery of futuristic speculation with that of ancient mythology—Aztec mythology in this case—in a manner which he was frequently to recapitulate, most immediately in "Sitting on a Starwood Stool" (1974), an anti-heroic version of the legend of Prometheus. *New Worlds* also reprinted "The Ghosts of Luna" (1973), one of two stories he published in the Oxford SF Group's *Sfinx*, but his shorter pieces of this early period are mostly trivial, the main focus of his attention being his novels.

Like *The Embedding*, *The Jonah Kit* (1975) entangles plot-threads that examine radically different aspects of the same question. One concerns the abstruse theoretical implications of astronomical observations made by a Nobel prize-winning physicist, which suggest that the observed universe is only a virtual echo of the Big Bang rather than the immediate object of Creation. The second concerns an experiment conducted by Soviet scientists in which "imprints" of the minds of a schizophrenic boy and a dead cosmonaut are superimposed on the brain of a sperm whale in order that the creature can be used as a spy on Western submarine movements. The communicative channel thus opened proves, however, to be more effective, as well as more problematic, than is required for such a mundane purpose.

As in *The Embedding*, the plot-threads of *The Jonah Kit* eventually form an unexpectedly awkward knot, because the news brought by the physicist—which seems pragmatically neutral within the Western world-view—has a devastating effect on the world-view of the whales, to whom it is communicated by the imprinted personalities. Again, Watson's use of politically-loaded settings in the Second and Third worlds gave the novel an internationalist flavor rarely seen in science fiction, and his strong commitment to socialist ideals added a further dimension of differentiation from typical products of the American-dominated genre.

The Embedding and *The Jonah Kit* were both reprinted in the USA by Scribner's, and both were rightly promoted as works of some importance. They appeared at a time when the science fiction genre was expanding rapidly in popularity and prestige, when work by the Polish writer Stanislaw Lem and the Russian collaborators Arkady and Boris Strugatsky were also attracting a good deal of attention and praise. For a few years in the mid-1970s it seemed that speculative fiction might break out of the parochial straitjacket imposed upon it by the routines of American genre marketing. Such prospects were ringingly endorsed by Watson in fanzine articles like "W(h)ither Science Fiction?" (1976) and "The Crudities of Science Fiction" (1978) and, less directly, in the unrepentantly esoteric talk he gave when he was the guest of honor at the Second French National SF Convention in Angoulême in 1975 on "Towards an Alien Linguistics". Alas, those hopes soon foundered—but not until Watson had resigned his teaching post to write full-time. He made that move in 1976, by which time he and his wife were parents of a three-year-old child.

Scribner's published only one more of Watson's novels, after which his American editions were mostly consigned to the narrower world of genre paperbacks, where literary sophistication was irrelevant, innovation largely unappreciated, and explicit socialist sympathies anathematized. Although his association with Gollancz in the UK provided some protection from the cold winds of change that swept continually through the sf marketplace after the slump of the late 1970s, the fact that there was never such a welcoming atmosphere as there had been when he produced his first two novels had a gradual but inexorable effect on Watson's literary ambitions. He was never to match the purchasing power of the advances or the enthusiasm of the critical acclaim that he was briefly able to obtain in the late 1970s; the products of his subsequent career as a freelance writer have to be examined in the context of a long struggle to maintain the aesthetic and intellectual standards of his work against the corrosions of commercial demand.

The first casualty of this long struggle was a novel that Watson had written in 1970, *The Woman Factory*, which he described as "a sarcastic deconstruction of pornography". It never appeared in English, although it was published in French translation as *Orgasmachine* (1976). The theme—the mass-production of female androids for sexual purposes—was unacceptable, even in what were supposedly taboo-breaking days, to mass-market publishers in Britain and America. He rewrote it as *The Woman Plant* in 1982, and this version—which he considered "far superior"—was sold to Playboy Press, but when that paperback line was sold to mass-market publisher Berkley it was deemed unpublishable, lest its satirical exaggeration of exploitation should be seen by unwary readers as exploitative. The only part of the revised text ever to see print in English was "Custom-Built Girl", an abridged version of the opening, which appeared in *Cybersex* (1996) edited by Richard Glyn Jones.

* * * * * * *

The first plot-thread of the third novel Watson published in his native tongue, *The Martian Inca* (1977), concerns events in Bolivia following the hard landing of an unmanned Russian space-probe carrying samples of Martian soil. The second follows an American manned mission to the red planet, whose prospects are seriously affected by the discovery that its soil is biologically and psychotropically active. Like the drug that bestowed a new understanding of the world upon the Xemahoa in *The Embedding*, the produce of the arid Martian surface awakens new potential in those exposed to it. One Bolivian obtains extreme delusions of grandeur, considering himself to be a new incarnation of the Inca, destined to recover the fortunes of his oppressed race.

It eventually transpires that evolution has worked differently on Mars, a planet of extremes whose ancient inhabitants had to rebuild their bodies, their minds and their culture from scratch with every new summer—and left that potential behind when conditions would no longer allow their recapitulative culture to flourish. The possibility remains for humankind to re-adopt the potentiality of Martian biology, using it as a progressive instrument in its own further evolution.

Alien Embassy (1977) is a similarly-themed novel in which humankind has run into ecocastastrophic difficulties on Earth but has seemingly opened communication with a number of alien races, employing mental disciplines of "astral travel" based on the Tibetan *Book of the Dead*. Watson had earlier written "On Cooking the First Hero in Spring" (1975), in which visitors to an alien world find the same text useful in figuring out alien Clayfolk, and had applied a similar form of communication to the plumbing of a black hole in "The Event Horizon" (1976).

The heroine of *Alien Embassy* leaves her African home to embark on a career in Astromancy. She eventually finds that, although no actual aliens are involved, the processes of "communication" in which she is involved are transformative experiences, in physical as well as mental terms--and that the transformations in question hold the key to the future evolution of humanity. Although it was published two years after Fritjof Capra's *The Tao of Physics* (1975)—and two years before Gary Zukav's *The Dancing Wu Li Masters* (1979)—*Alien Embassy*'s amalgamation of science and eastern mysticism seemed undesirably chimerical to many sf purists, and it received markedly less praise than its predecessors. At a later date it might have found a new audience, but it was too early to catch the wave of New Age enthusiasm that was to break on the Californian shore in the following decade.

The third book Watson published in 1977 was *Japan Tomorrow*, another work intended to help make learning English enjoyable for Japanese students. His next novel, *Miracle Visitors* (1978), followed *Alien Embassy* in anticipating subsequent developments in alternative belief systems, but treated them far too cleverly to appeal to true believers. It is the best science fiction novel ever written about UFOs, but it draws its principal inspiration from Carl Jung's study of *Flying Saucers* (1959), which interprets such sightings, and the elaborate fantasies grafted on to them, as a modern myth generated by the collective unconscious, Watson's book extrapolates the idea that the function of such hallucinations is to encourage, and perhaps to guide, mental evolution. He infuses an unprecedentedly-vivid account of alien abductions recalled under hypnosis with a strong dose of Sufist mysticism. Most UFO enthusiasts loathe the book because they are steadfast in clinging to crudely literal—and, ironically, far less complimentary—interpretations of their experiences.

The three central characters of *Miracle Visitors* are party to an absurd but magnificent voyage to the dark side of the moon by Ford Thunderbird, but on returning to normality—without any hard evidence of their adventure—they adopt radically different strategies of readaptation. One embraces denial, retreating into the world of "common sense"; the second continues to pursue a futile quest for the "proof" that will assimilate UFO-experiences to quotidian experience; the third—a psychologist researching altered states of consciousness—takes the Sufist route. The underlying argument of the book is not that any one of these strategies is correct, but rather that any mental instrument capable of fulfilling the kind of function Jung attributes to UFOs—science fiction itself being the most obvious example—can be dealt with by any of the strategies, and would be best served by the most productive one.

Watson's own science fiction is not entirely committed to the third strategy, but it generally proceeds from the supposition that critics who despise all speculative fiction for its unreality and critics who will only endorse the kinds of hard sf that aspire to rigorous realism may be missing out on the most interesting possibilities of the genre. He provided exuberant exemplary support for this approach to sf in such contemporary short stories as "The Very Slow Time Machine" (1978), in which the eponymous backward-traveling device offers its observers an opportunity for extravagant metaphysical speculation, and the briefly bizarre parable "My Soul Swims in a Goldfish Bowl" (1978). His first collection, *The Very Slow Time Machine* (1979), contains other stories thematically linked to his early novels, including "A Time-Span to Conjure With" (1978) and "Immune Dreams" (1978).

* * * * * * *

Watson followed *Miracle Visitors* with *God's World* (1979), which the market-conscious originating UK publisher chose to advertise on the cover as "his first novel of outer space". It failed to sell for more than a decade in the USA, presumably because publishers felt that it would not go down well in the Bible Belt. The story begins with an invitation to the people of Earth to visit God's World, issued by tall, shimmering "angels" which appear briefly in many locations, always adapting their form to fit local faiths and speaking in the native tongues of the people to whom they address their message. Those appointed to answer the summons embark upon the Pilgrim Crusader, which travels through the deceptive realms of "High Space". Those pilgrims fortunate enough to survive the ship's capture by the insectile Group-ones eventually arrive at their destination, the satellite of a gas-giant orbiting 82 Eridani, to find its indigenous angels living in intimate proximity to the borderlands of the other-worldly Askatharli: a "Heaven" to which they are gradually being assimilated. Having already been warned by the angelic broadcasts that there is a war in Askatharli space—also called "the Imagining"—they have to decide which side they are on.

Although it is stamped from a very similar template, his editor chose not to represent Watson's next novel as sf at all, issuing it in a short-lived "Gollancz Fantasy" series. *The Gardens of Delight* (1980) tells the story of an investigative mission conducted by the crew of the starship *Schiaparelli*, sent to find out what became of the *Copernicus*. They find a small planet, which keeps one side permanently turned towards the sun, whose land surface has been "terraformed" in the image of Hieronymus Bosch's triptych displaying Heaven, Hell and the Garden of Earthly Delights. All the distorted and chimerical monsters that Bosch had put into his surreal painting are here incarnate as living beings—as are Satan and God.

The key to this mystery is held by one Knossos, a former crewman on *Copernicus* and enthusiastic student of the esoteric artistry and symbolism of alchemy. Like Carl Jung, Knossos (whose name is a pun on Gnosis) has reformulated the failed science of alchemy and the entire "Hermetic tradition" as an allegory of human evolution, and he has persuaded the powerful entity which remade the planet for its colonists to remold human nature in such a way as to make that evolutionary allegory literal. The odyssey undertaken by the newcomers takes them from the Garden of Earthly Delights through Hell to a Paradise embodying and triumphantly celebrating a wholly new Enlightenment, unsuspected even by the world's makeshift god. The sciencefictional logic of the denouement is as well worked-out as in most of its predecessors, and it is slightly ironic that Watson's attempts to do that became increasingly tokenistic in subsequent works, which reverted to the protective umbrella of the sf label. In fact, *The Gardens of Delight* vies with *The Embedding* and *Miracle Visitors* for the privilege of being reckoned Watson's best sf novel.

Watson's fascination with religious ideas was further extrapolated in *Deathhunter* (1981), vastly expanded from "A Cage for Death" (1981). The story is set in a quasi-Utopian future whose angst-free inhabitants have reconciled themselves to the idea and experience of death—until they discover that the souls of the dead are carried into the unknown by a strange supernatural predator. When the hero sets off to follow this creature to its destination, however, the enlightenment vouchsafed to him by a drunken "angel" turns out to be rather derisory and—at least by comparison with the novel's immediate predecessors—distinctly unsatisfactory. A similar dismissive sarcasm is found in some of Watson's contemporary short stories, including the metaphysical fantasy "A Letter from God" (1981) and "Nightmares" (1981), in which benevolent aliens who save mankind from destruction are nevertheless reviled. "The World Science Fiction Convention of 2080" (1980) gave satirical vent to Watson's growing impatience with the genre marketplace, imagining sf fans doggedly pursuing the same old obsessions in a post-holocaust world.

All but the earliest of the more serious stories in *Sunstroke and Other Stories* (1982)—whose most notable inclusions are "Insight" (1980) and "The Milk of Knowledge" (original to the collection)—set aside the fascination with the esoteric and the outré that had inspired his earlier novels. His production of short stories increased markedly after 1979—the year in which he and his family moved from rented accommodation in Oxford to take up permanent residence in the Northamptonshire village of Moreton Pinkney—but much of that produce was calculatedly whimsical. "Jean Sandwich, the Sponsor and I" (1981), was expanded into *Converts*, a jocular and rather slapdash novel offering a fanciful account of the evolutionary possibilities open to mankind, but the novel was rejected by Gollancz. It eventually appeared as an original paperback in the UK in 1984, although its lack of seriousness helped it find a better US market than its predecessors.

Gollancz did publish *Under Heaven's Bridge* (1981), boldly advertised as the first transatlantic collaboration in the sf field. Indeed, Watson and his American co-author Michael Bishop had never met, conducting their collaboration entirely by mail. What had brought them together was a mutual fascination with Japanese society and a keen interest in the application of anthropology to the design of alien cultures. Bishop's classic of anthropological sf is *Transfigurations* (1979) but *Under Heaven's Bridge* owes more to his earlier novel, *A Little Knowledge* (1977), in which Cygnusian missionaries arrived on an Earth beset by Fundamentalist creeds. The plot of *Under Heaven's Bridge* is a conventional puzzle-story in which visitors from Earth bring very different spiritual resources to bear on the intractable problem of deciphering the culture of an enigmatic cyborg race whose homeworld orbits one element of a dangerously unstable binary star. The conditions under which the novel was written prevented its plot from becoming overly intricate, but it was still a little too esoteric to appeal to a wide audience. Watson and Bishop also collaborated in the editing of the anthology *Changes: Stories of Metamorphosis* (1983).

* * * * * * *

Watson's attempts to make his work more widely accessible continued in *Chekhov's Journey* (1983), an ingenious tale in which a Soviet film crew making a drama-documentary about Chekhov's investigation of the Tunguska explosion attempts to inspire its leading man by putting him in psychic touch with the great playwright. This ultimate extrapolation of Stanislavsky's "method" goes awry when the actor begins recapitulating an alternative history, generated by a disastrous timeslip experienced by the spaceship *K. E. Tsiolkovsky*. The story is well worked-out and elegantly-written, but again the book failed to find an immediate buyer in America, presumably because its Russian setting was considered likely to alienate some potential readers. It is hardly surprising that Watson then set out to make a deliberate compromise with public demand, producing a trilogy of novels set in a safely hypothetical milieu and cast in a mould much more familiar to genre readers than most of his early works.

The Book of the River (1984) describes two very different human societies living on opposite banks of a great river, separated by the seemingly-sentient "Black Current", whose intervention has secured female domination on one side while allowing males to retain more traditional roles on the other. Once the first volume had set the scene by means of a fairly conventional action/adventure plot the second volume, *The Book of the Stars* (1984), began to extrapolate the kind of metaphysical framework that Watson loved to design. Having established psychic contact with the Worm—the mind of the Black Current—the heroine, Yaleen, obtains intelligence of Eeden, from which the populations on either side of the river originally came, and to which their souls allegedly return after death. Enabled to test this second proposition, she travels through ka-space to discover that Eeden is Earth; there she begins to perceive—and to rebel against—the plan of destiny formulated by the Worm's great rival, the Godmind.

In *The Book of Being* (1985), the consequences of Yaleen's rebellion unwind. Having been reborn as her own sister she becomes a charismatic messiah, and dies again and again, experiencing life on a series of other worlds. Unlike the protagonists of *God's World*, she has no hesitation in siding with the "devil's party" in the apocalyptic cosmic conflict, and eventually fulfils a Promethean role in bringing light to a new Creation. Although the American critics Don D'Ammassa and Douglas A. Mackey have judged the trilogy to be Watson's most satisfactory realization of his philosophical concerns, the languid extrapolation of the story loses in subtlety and depth what it gains in clarity and conventional story-value; the third novel ends with a flippant and flagrantly-satirical coda.

In the introduction to *Slow Birds and Other Stories* (1985) Watson expressed a new affection for his shorter fiction, representing the items therein as products of a literary hothouse—"the orchids, the bonsai of a writer's creativity"—more closely regulated and more intimately meaningful than the novels he had "transplanted suddenly into the wild". Some of the stories feature abrupt and arbitrary transitions, like the one which drastically expands "The Width of the World" (1983) or the Change which separates the sexes in "Universe on the Turn" (1984). Others, including "The Mystic Marriage of Salome" (1981), the Joycean "The Bloomsday Revolution" (1984), and "Ghost Lecturer" (1984)—in which the Epicurean philosopher Lucretius is summoned from the depths of time to extend his discourse on the nature of the universe—revel unrepentantly, but not very earnestly, in esotericism. The 1983 title story, which was short-listed for the Nebula and Hugo Awards but won neither, is a relatively straightforward but perfectly-formed tale of computer-guided missiles, which are shifted into a parallel dimension in order to avoid detection.

Queenmagic, Kingmagic (1986) is an expansion of a playful novella featuring a universe whose laws of nature are modeled on the rules of chess. Its tendency to dissolve whenever a king is checkmated is inconvenient for its inhabitants, two of whom eventually contrive to escape. The expansion takes them into other, similarly board-game-based universes, including a snakes-and-ladders universe and a monopoly universe. The novel has little to recommend it except its panache in the face of absurdity—although the author liked the fundamental idea well enough to compose a further variant in "Jewels in an Angel's Wing" (1987)—and it seems that Watson had begun to feel that there was little scope left for the exercise of his talents in that fugitive sector of the science fiction field where metaphysical fantasies could be accommodated. His account of the brutal fate of "The People of the Precipice" (1985), although represented in the blurb of *Evil Water and Other Stories* (1987) as a political allegory, could also be construed as an extrapolation of his own sense of precariousness. There is little in Watson's own works of the time as zestfully adventurous as the contents of the anthology of (mostly original) stories of life after death that he co-edited with

Pamela Sargent, *Afterlives* (1986). For the next three years he diverted his principal efforts into horror fiction, which was then enjoying something of a boom in the British literary marketplace.

* * * * * * *

The Power (1986) and *Meat* (1988) attempt to use conventionally stomach-churning horror story formats to bolster two of Watson's pet political causes: nuclear disarmament and animal liberation. Both causes had come to seem acutely relevant by virtue of his experience of village life in Moreton Pinkney, which was a neighbor to both factory farms and American air-bases. He had long been active in the local Labour Party and the Campaign for Nuclear Disarmament. Although the two novels have a certain winning gruesomeness it is doubtful whether they excited much sympathy for their central causes among lovers of genre horror.

The shorter tales of supernatural evil "Jingling Geordie's Hole" (1986) and "Evil Water" (1987) are much more effective, being neatly-accomplished exercises in disturbing symbolism. Watson developed the former into an effective horror/sf novel, *The Fire-Worm* (1988), which offered him the opportunity to revisit some of his favorite themes. The old English legend of the Lambton Worm is here relocated to Watson's native Tynemouth and re-identified as the salamander featured in the alchemical writings attributed (falsely) to Raymond Lully. Gollancz published *The Fire-Worm* but would not take the more straightforwardly science-fictional The *Whores of Babylon* (1988), an expansion of the novelette "We Remember Babylon" (1984). The protagonists of the latter novel are visitors to a Babylon whose heyday has been re-created, ostensibly in the Arizona desert but actually in virtual reality; they find the business of adapting to their new environment more challenging than they had anticipated.

When it became clear that his horror fiction had not found a commercially viable audience Watson embarked upon a further experiment in popularization, writing tie-in novels for Games Workshop. Unlike most of the other writers who briefly formed the GW stable—including "Jack Yeovil" (Kim Newman), "Brian Craig" (Brian Stableford), and "David Ferring" (David S. Garnett)—Watson elected to use his own name, and while the other writers preferred the imaginary universes of GW's fantasy role-playing game Warhammer and the *Mad Max*-cloned board-game Dark Future he took on the more challenging task of working within the universe of GW's biggest-seller: the space-operatic war game Warhammer 40,000. Although his "Inquisition War" series", consisting of *Inquisitor, Harlequin* and *Chaos Child*—he also wrote *Space Marine*, set against the same background—was interrupted by the collapse of GW Books, it continued when the company franchised its literary offshoots to TV tie-in specialists Boxtree. It seemed set for success until the administrators of Games Workshop, in spite of its popularity, made the seemingly-paradoxical decision not to allow any more sales of the titles through the medium of their own shops.

While this fiasco was unfolding, Watson expanded the intriguing novella "The Flies of Memory" (1988) into a full-length novel of the same title, published in 1990. The original story explained how insectile aliens visiting the Earth seem at first to be mere tourists interested in seeing and memorizing the same sights as the domestic variety—until the attractions in question begin to vanish. The hero, an expert in non-verbal communication, goes in search of the missing monuments, some of which are becoming reincarnate in the Martian wilderness. Although the unwinding plot eventually makes its way back to the metaphysical bedrock of *The Gardens of Delight* it remains conscientiously quirky; even the heroine observes on the final page that its plot has had "too many Flies in the ointment".

The short fiction collected in *Salvage Rites and Other Stories* (1989), *Stalin's Teardrops and Other Stories* (1991), and *The Coming of Vertumnus* (1994), however, continued in the same determinedly idiosyncratic vein as their immediate predecessor, mingling science fiction, horror and exercises in surrealism with considerably artistry. Those stories that are pure science fiction, including "When the Timegate Failed" (1985) and "In the Upper Cretaceous with the Summerfire Brigade" (1990), are buoyantly inventive, but are perhaps less effective than such neat exercises in surrealism as "The Emir's Clock" (1987), "Stalin's Teardrops" (1990), "Gaudi's Dragon" (1990), and "The Odour of Cocktail Cigarettes" (1991), and such fine horror stories as "The Coming of Vertumnus" (1992) and "The Bible in Blood" (1994). The most adventurous sf story in these collections is the novella "Nanoware Time" (shorter version 1989; a longer version appeared as half of a Tor double in 1991), in which alien nanotechnology allows human brains to transcend their former limitations.

All Watson's novels of the 1970s and 1980s had been relatively short, but fashions in the marketplace had shifted to favor much longer works. Always willing to experiment, Watson set out to write the epic "Book of Mana", published in two volumes of more than 500 pages apiece: *Lucky's Harvest* (1994) and *The Fallen Moon* (1994). Like many other works responding to the same pattern of commercial demand, it employs sciencefictional ideas to complicate and enhance a story which follows the template of best-selling genre fantasies. Watson's long expertise in contriving such hybrids was turned to good advantage in producing an account of the world of Kaleva, whose design owes a good deal to the Finnish mythology set out in the Kalevala.

Kaleva has been settled by humans brought through mana-space by a mineral life-form called an Ukko, who have established a quasi-Feudal society. The dominant indigenes, the serpentine Isi, have domesticated the most human-like of the native species, the Juttahat. The Isi refer to the Ukkos as "the ears of the cosmos" and believed them to be important instruments of some kind of universal plan, but that does not prevent them from interfering with the people the Ukko has transplanted. The Ukko's human discoverer, Lucky Sariola, has been made immortal by the Ukko—a privilege shared by her mate and descendants, who are key pieces in the Ukko's schemes. Those schemes unfold in the leisurely and stately manner typical of this kind of work, never achieving the complexity of the trilogy begun with *The Book of the River* or the baroque intensity of Watson's early metaphysical fantasies, but the story is eminently readable and the intricately-woven backcloth of decoded myths adds a useful richness to the text. Watson did not abandon the setting when the novel was finished; "The Tragedy of Solveig" and "The Shortest Night" (1998) are further Kaleva stories.

Unfortunately, the Book of Mana was no more successful saleswise than Watson's other commercially-motivated experiment and he quickly moved on to a new phase, writing "technothrillers" of a kind which had become fashionable in the wake of best-sellers by Michael Crichton and others. *Hard Questions* (1996) features a supercomputer and a charismatic cult-leader engaged in industrial espionage, while *Oracle* (1997) involves an experiment in time-bending, funded by Military Intelligence, which displaces a Roman centurion from 60 A.D. into the present and entangles him with an IRA cell bent on assassinating the queen. Both novels are as skillfully executed and as readable as their immediate predecessors, but the thriller template operates in both as a narrative straitjacket which denies their sciencefictional ideas the room to develop beyond mere gimmickry.

* * * * * * *

"Being a freelance writer," Watson wrote in the Endnote to Douglas A. Mackey's 1989 bibliography of his works, "rather resembles walking a tightrope—without visible end—stretched over a dark abyss. Sometimes you're up on the rope; sometimes you're hanging on by your fingernails. But while you're up, you got to dance on that rope. You got to dance."

Watson's attempts to stay on that tightrope resulted in the wild ambition of his early novels being somewhat curtailed in later full-length works, but his remarkable inventiveness continued to shine in his shorter fiction, where he continues to trip the light fantastic without fear of falling. His frequent guest appearances at sf conventions in continental Europe—where his work has often been better-appreciated than in his homeland—have enabled him to research the international settings he is so fond of deploying, and his shrewd observations of the relevant locales help to sustain the remarkable range of narrative flavors exhibited in his work. "Secrets" (1997), a novella inspired by the Vigelund sculpture park in Oslo, is an excellent example of the methodology he employs in extrapolating art from experience.

Although many of Watson's short stories fall in or beyond the margins of the sf genre, the core of his work remains anchored therein. There are few writers who make use of sciencefictional devices as variously and as enterprisingly as he does in devising satires and allegories. Who but he would have enclosed a cycle of social history in the day-long time-loop of "Early in the Evening" (1996), or appointed the brother of the Son of God to be the pilot of the space probe to Tau Ceti III featured in "Such Dedication" (1996), or set the Space Navy to the work of intercepting the alien coffins projected into the solar system in "Ferryman" (1996)? In Watson's work brevity is no enemy of complexity, as demonstrated by such tales as "Nanunculus" (1997), in which the eponymous smart web-browser develops an agenda of its own while roaming cyberspace in the service of a Californian physicist, whose investigations of negative time are disturbed by bad dreams.

Watson's commitment to the sf genre has also been expressed in supportive activities. He served for some years on the council of the Science Fiction Foundation when it was based at the North East London Polytechnic and was the features editor of its journal, and he has also been the European representative of the Science Fiction Writers of America for many years. He has written numerous book reviews and contributed to several reference books on the field. There is no doubt, taking the full range of his endeavors into account, that he has risen above his difficulties to make a greater contribution to science fiction than any other British writer of his generation.

BIBLIOGRAPHY

Aldiss, Brian W. *Billion Year Spree: A History of Science Fiction.* London: Weidenfeld and Nicolson, 1973.
Amis, Martin. *Time's Arrow.* London: Jonathan Cape, 1991.
[Anon., ed.] *Fantasmagoriana.* Paris, 1812. Tr. as *Tales of the Dead.* London: White, Cochrane, 1813.
Asimov, Isaac. *Foundation.* New York: Gnome Press, 1951.
-------. The Rest of the Robots. Garden City, N.Y.: Doubleday, 1964.
Baxter, Stephen, with Arthur C. Clarke. *Light of Other Days.* New York: Tor, 2000.
Bear, Greg, with Martin H. Greenberg, eds. *New Legends.* New York: Tor, 1995.
Bellamy, Edward. *Looking Backward, 2000-1887.* Boston: Ticknor, 1888.
Benford, Gregory. *Across the Sea of Suns.* New York: Simon & Schuster, 1984. Revised ed. New York: Bantam, 1987.
-------. *Against Infinity.* New York: Simon & Schuster, 1983.
-------. *Artifact.* New York: Tor, 1985.
-------. *Beyond the Fall of Night* (with *Against the Fall of Night* by Arthur C. Clarke). New York: Ace, 1990.
-------. *Chiller* (as Sterling Blake). New York: Bantam, 1993.
-------. *Cosm.* New York: Avon, 1998.
-------. *Deeper than the Darkness.* New York: Ace, 1970. Revised as *The Stars in Shroud.* New York: Berkley, 1978.
-------. *Find the Changeling* (with Gordon Eklund). New York: Dell, 1980.
-------. *Foundation's Fear.* New York: HarperPrism, 1997.
-------. *Furious Gulf.* New York: Bantam, 1994.
-------. *Great Sky River.* New York: Bantam, 1987.
-------. *Heart of the Comet* (with David Brin). New York: Bantam, 1986.
-------. *If the Stars are Gods* (with Gordon Eklund). New York: Berkley, 1977. Revised, New York: Bantam, 1989.

-------. *In Alien Flesh*. New York: Tor, 1986.
-------. *In the Ocean of Night*. New York: Dial Press, 1977.
-------. *Jupiter Project*. Nashville: Nelson, 1975. Revised as *The Jupiter Project*. New York: Berkley, 1980.
-------. *Matter's End*. New York: Bantam, 1994. Expanded ed. London: Victor Gollancz, 1996.
-------. *Sailing Bright Eternity*. New York: Bantam, 1995.
-------. *Shiva Descending* (with William Rotsler). New York: Avon, 1980.
-------. *Tides of Light*. New York: Bantam, 1989.
-------. *Timescape*. New York: Simon & Schuster, 1980.
Beresford. J. D. *The Hampenshire Wonder*. London: Sidgwick & Jackson, 1911.
-------. "*What Dreams May Come...*" London: Hutchinson, 1941.
-------, with Esmé Wynne-Tyson. *The Riddle of the Tower*. London: Hutchinson, 1944.
Bester, Alfred. *The Stars my Destination*. New York: New American Library 1957.
[Béthune, Chevalier de]. *Relation du monde de Mercure*, 2 vols. Geneva: Barillot, 1750.
Bilderdijk, Willem. *A Short Account of a Remarkable Aerial Voyage and Discovery of a New Planet*. Paisley: Wilfion, 1989. {Originally published in Dutch in 1813.]
Bishop, Michael. *A Little Knowledge*. New York: Berkley 1977.
-------. *Transfigurations*. New York: Berkley, 1979.
Bleiler, Everett F. *Science-Fiction: The Early Years*. Kent, Ohio & London: Kent State University Press, 1990.
Blish, James. *Black Easter; or, Faust Aleph Null*. Garden City, N.Y.: Doubleday, 1968.
-------. *A Case of Conscience*. New York: Ballantine, 1958.
-------. *Cities in Flight*. New York: Avon, 1970.
-------. *The Day After Judgment*. Garden City, N.Y.: Doubleday, 1971.
-------. *Doctor Mirabilis*. London: Faber, 1964.
-------. *The Duplicated Man* (with Robert A. Lowndes). New York: Avalon, 1959.
-------. *Earthman, Come Home*. New York: Putnam, 1955.
-------. *Fallen Star*. London: Faber, 1957; as *The Frozen Year*. New York: Ballantine, 1957.
-------. *Galactic Cluster*. New York: New American Library, 1959.
------. (as William Atheling Jr.) *The Issue at Hand*. Chciago: Advent, 1964.
-------. *Jack of Eagles*. New York: Greenberg, 1952.

-------. *A Life for the Stars*. New York: Putnam, 1962.
-------. *Midsummer Century*. Garden City, N.Y.: Doubleday, 1972.
-------. *The Night Shapes*. New York: Ballantine, 1962.
-------. *The Quincunx of Time*. New York: Dell, 1973.
-------. *The Seedling Stars*. New York: Gnome Press, 1957.
-------. *Spock Must Die!* New York: Batam, 1970.
-------. *The Star Dwellers*. New York: Putnam, 1961.
-------. *Star Trek 1*, New York: Bantam, 1967.
-------. *They Shall Have Stars*. London: Faber, 1956.
-------. *Titan's Daughter*. New York: Berkley, 1961.
-------. *A Torrent of Faces* (with Norman L. Knight). Garden City, N.Y.: Doubleday, 1967.
-------. *The Triumph of Time*. New York: Avon, 1958; as *A Clash of Cymbals*. London: Faber, 1959.
-------. *VOR*. New York: Avon, 1958.
-------. *The Warriors of Day*. New York: Galaxy, 1953.
-------. *Welcome to Mars*. London: Faber, 1967.
Borel, Pierre. *Discours nouveau prouvant la pluralité des mondes; que les astres sont des terres habités, at la terre un estoile, etc.* Geneva, 1657.
Bradbury, Ray. *Fahrenheit 451*. New York: Ballantine, 1953.
Burroughs, Edgar Rice. *The Master Mind of Mars*. Chicago: McClurg 1928.
Butcher, William. Verne's *Journey to the Center of the Self: space and time in the voyages extraordinaires*. London: Macmillan, 1990.
Butor, Michel. "The Golden Age in Jules Verne" in *Inventory*. London: Cape, 1970.
Campbell, John W, Jr. *The Best of John W, Campbell*. ed. Lester del Rey. New York: Ballantine, 1976.
-------. *The Black Star Passes*. Reading, Penn,: Fantasy Press, 1953.
-------. *Cloak of Aesir*. Chicago: Shasta, 1952.
-------. "Concerning Science Fiction" in *The Best of Science Fiction* ed. Groff Conklin, New York; Crown, 1946.
-------. *The Incredible Planet*. Reading, Penn.: Fantasy Press, 1949.
-------. *Invaders from the Infinite*. Hicksville, N.Y.: Gnome Press, 1961.
-------. *Islands of Space*. Reading: Penn.: Fantasy Press, 1956.
-------. *The Mightiest Machine*. Providence, R.I.: Hadley, 1947.
-------. *The Moon is Hell!* Reading, Penn.: Fantasy Press, 1951.
-------. *The Planeteers*. New York: Ace, 1966.
-------. *The Ultimate Weapon*. New York: Ace, 1966.

-------. *Who Goes There? Seven Tales of Science Fiction.* Chicago: Shasta, 1948.
Capra, Fritjof. *The Tao of Physics.* Berkeley, Cal.: Shambhala, 1975.
Carr, Terry. *Universe 1.* New York: Ace, 1971.
Clarke, Arthur C. *Against the Fall of Night.* New York: Gnome Press, 1953. Revised as *The City and the Stars.* London: Muller, 1956
-------. *Childhood's End.* New York: Ballantine, 1953
Clement, Hal. "Proof" *Astounding Science Fiction*, June 1942. pp.101-109.
Clifton, Mark, with Frank Riley. *They'd Rather be Right.* New York: Gnome Press, 1957.
Cole, Robert W. *The Struggle for Empire: A Story of the War of 2236.* London: Stock, 1900.
Constantine, Murray. *Proud Man.* London: Boriswood, 1934.
Crichton, Michael. *Jurassic Park.* Franklin Center, Penn.: Franklin Press, 1976.
Cyrano de Bergerac, Savinien. *Histoire comique contenant les états et empires de la lune.* Paris: Charles de Sercy, 1657; tr. by Richard Aldington in *Voyages to the Moon and Sun.* London: Routledge & New York: Dutton, 1923; tr. by Geoffrey Strachan in *Other Worlds: The Comic History of the States and Empires of the Moon and Sun.* London: Oxford University Press, 1963.
-------. *Fragment d'histoire comique contenant les états et empires du soleil.* Paris: Charles de Sercy, 1662; trs. as above.
Daniel, Gabriel. *Voyage du monde de Descartes.* Paris: S. Bernard, 1691; tr. as *A Voyage to the World of Cartesius.* London: T. Bennet, 1694.
Darwin, Erasmus. *The Botanic Garden, a Poem, in Two Parts. Part I Containing the Economy of Vegetation. Part II The Love of Plants.* London: J. Johnson, 1791.
Davy, Humphry. *Consolations in Travel: The Last Days of a Philosopher.* London: John Murray, 1830.
Delany, Samuel R., with Marilyn Hacker, eds. *Quark* 1-4. New York: Paperback Library, 1970-71.
Dick, Philip K. *Counter-Clock World.* New York: Berkley, 1967.
-------. *Eye in the Sky.* New York: Ace, 1957.
Dumas, Alexandre. *The Count of Monte Cristo.* London: Chapman and Hall, 1846.
Ellison, Harlan, ed. *Again, Dangerous Visions.* Garden City, N.Y.: Doubleday, 1972.
Eshbach, Lloyd Athur, with E. E. Smith. *Subspace Encounter.* New York: Berkley, 1983.

Evans, Arthur B. *Jules Verne Rediscovered: Didacticism and the Scientific Novel*. Westport, Conn.: Greenwood Press, 1988.

Faulkner, William. *As I Lay Dying*. New York: Jonathan Cape, 1930.

-------. "The Bear" in *The Best American Short Stories 1943* ed. Martha Foley. Boston: Houghton Mifflin, 1943.

Figuier, Louis. *La Terre avant le deluge*. Paris: Hachette, 1963. Revised ed. 1867.

Finney, Jack. *The Body Snatchers*. New York: Dell, 1955.

Fitting, Peter, ed. *Subterranean Worlds: A Critical Anthology*. Middletown, Conn.: Wesleyan University Press, 2004.

Flammarion, Camille. *Astronomie populaire: description générale de ciel*. Paris: Marpon et Flammarion, 1880; tr. by J. Ellard Gore as *Popular Astronomy: A General Description of the Heavens*. New York: Appleton, nd; London: Chatto & Windus, 1894.

-------. *L'Astronomie et ses fondateurs: Copernic et la découverte du systeme du monde*, Paris: Marpon et Flammarion, 1891.

-------. *L'Atmosphère: description des grands phénomènes de la nature*. Paris: Hachette, 1871; tr. by C. B. Pitman (edited by James Glaisher) as *The Atmosphere*. London: Sampson Low, Marston, Low & Searle, 1873.

-------. *Clairs de lune*. Paris: Flammarion, 1894.

-------. *Contemplations scientifiques, Première série*. Paris: Hachette, 1869; *deuxième série*, 1887.

-------. *Contes philosophiques*. Paris: La Revue, 1911.

-------. *Dans le ciel et sur la terre: tableaux et harmonies*. Paris: Marpon et Flammarion, 1886.

-------. *Dieu dans la nature; ou le Spiritualisme et le Matérialisme devant la Science moderne*. Paris: Didier er cie, 1867.

-------. *L'Éruptions volcanique et et les tremblements de terre: Krakatoa—La Martinique—Espagne et Italie*. Paris: Flammarion, 1902.

-------. *Les Étoiles et les curiosités du ciel: description complète du ciel visible ... l'oeil nu et de tous les objéts célestes faciles à observer; supplement de l'astronomie populaire*. Paris: Marpon et Flammarion, 1882.

-------. *La Fin du Monde*. Paris: Flammarion, 1894; tr. by J. B. Walker as *Omega: The Last Days of the World*. New York: Cosmopolitan, 1894.

-------. *Des Forces naturelles inconnues ... propos des phénomènes produits par les frères Davenport et les mediums en générale: étude critique*. (as by Hermès) Paris: Didier et cie, 1865; reprinted as by Camille Flamarion, Paris: Flammarion, 1907; tr. as

Mysterious Psychic Forces: An Account of the Author's Investigations in Psychical Research, together with those of other European savants. Boston: Small & Maynard, 1907.
-------. *Les Habitantes de l'autre monde, révélations d'outre-tombe.* Paris: Ledoyen, 2 vols., 1862-3.
-------. *Histoire du Ciel et des différents systèmes imaginés sur l'univers.* Paris: Bibliothéque d'éducation et récréation, 1872; tr. (edited by J. F. Blake) as *Astronomical Myths, Based on Flammarion's "History of the Heavens".* London: Macmillan, 1877.
-------. *L'Inconnu et les problèmes psychiques.* Paris: Flammarion, 1900; tr. as *L'Inconnu, the Unknown.* London & New York: Harper, 1900.
-------. *Lumen.* Paris: Marpon et Flammarion, 1887; expanded edition, 1906.
-------. *Les maisons hantées, en marge de la mort et son mystère.* Paris: Flammarion, 1923; tr. as *Haunted Houses.* London: Unwin, 1924 & New York: Appleton, 1924.
-------. *Memoires biographiques et philosophiques d'un astronome.* Paris: Flammarion, 1912.
-------. *Les Merveilles célestes; lectures du soir.* Paris: Hachette, 1865; tr. by Mrs. Norman Lockyer as *The Wonders of the Heavens.* New York: Scribners, 1871 and as *The Marvels of the Heavens.* London: Bentley, 1872.
-------. *Le Monde avant le création de l'homme; origines de la terre, origines de la vie, origines de l'humanité.* Paris: Marpon et Flammarion, 1885.
-------. *Les Mondes imaginaires et les mondes réels: voyage pittoresque dans le ciel et revue critique des théories humaines, scientifiques et romanesques, anciennes et modernes sur les habitants des astres.* Paris: Didier et cie, 1864; expanded ed., Paris: Marpon et Flammarion, 1892.
-------. *La mort et son mystère.* Paris: Flammarion, 2 vols, 1920-22; tr. by Latrobe Carroll & E. S. Brooks as *Death and its Mystery.* New York: Century, 3 vols, 1921-3.
-------. *La Planète Mars et ses conditions d'habitabilité.* Paris: Gauthier-Vilars, 1892; expanded edition 1909.
-------. *La Planète Venus, discussion générale des observations.* Paris: Gauthier-Villars, 1897.
-------. *La Pluralité des mondes habitées: étude où l'on expose les conditions d'habitabilité des terres célestes, discutées au point de vue de l'astronomie, de la physiologie et de la philosophie naturelle.* Paris: Didier, 1862.

-------. *Récits de l'infini: Lumen; Histoire d'une comète; Dans l'infini*. Paris: Didier et cie, 1872; tr. by S. R. Crocker as *Stories of Infinity: Lumen; The History of a Comet; In Infinity*. Boston: Roberts Bros, 1873; expanded ed. as *Récits de l'infini: Lumen, histoire d'une âme; Histoire d'une comète; La Vie universelle et eternelle*. Paris: Marpon et Flammarion, 1892.

-------. *Rêves étoilés*. Paris: Flammarion, 1914; tr. by E. E. Fournier d'Albe as *Dreams of an Astronomer*. London: T. Fisher Unwin, 1923.

-------. *Stella*. Paris: Flammarion, 1897.

-------. *Les Terres du ciel: description astronomique, physique, climatologique, géographique des planètes qui gravitent avec la terre autour du soleil et l'état probable de la vie à leur surface*. Paris: Didier, 1877.

-------. *Uranie*. Paris: Marpon et Flammarion, 1889; tr. by Mary J. Serrano as *Uranie*. New York: Cassell, 1890; tr. by Augusta Rice Stetson as *Urania*. Boston: Estes & Laurist, 1890 and London: Chatto & Windus, 1891; tr. by E. P. Robins as *Urania*. Chicago: Donohue, Henneberry & Co, 1892.

-------. *Voyages aériens: impressions et etudes*. Paris: Marpon et Flammarion, 1881.

-------. [Translator] *Les derniers jours d'un Philosophe; Entretiens sur la Nature et sur les Sciences, de sir Humphry Davy* tr. by Camille Flammarion. Paris, Didier et cie, 1869.

Foigny, Gabriel de. *La Terre australe connu: c'est ... dire, la description de ce pays inconnu jusqu'ici*. Geneva: 1676; tr. as *A New Discovery of Terra Incognita Australis, or the Southern World, by James Sadeur, a French-man*. London: J. Dunton, 1693.

Fontenelle, Bernard le Bovier de. *Entretiens sur la pluralité des mondes*. Paris: C. Blageart, 1686; tr. by Sir W. D. Knight as *A Discourse of the Plurality of Worlds*. Dublin: William Norman, 1687.

Forster, E. M. "The Machine Stops." *Oxford and Cambridge Review*, Michaelmas 1909.

Franklin, H. Bruce. *War Stars: The Superweapon and the American Imagination*. New York: Oxford University Press, 1988.

Gautier, Théophile Gautier. "Le Roi Candaule" (1844) in *Nouvelles*, Paris: Charpentier, 1845.

[Godwin, Francis] *The Man in the Moone or a Discourse of a Voyage Thither by Domingo Gonsales, the Speedy Messenger*. London: Kirton & Warre, 1638.

Gernsback, Hugo. *Ralph 124C41+: A Romance of the Year 2660.* Boston: Stratford, 1925.

--------. *Ultimate World.* New York: Walker, 1972.

Gloag, John. *Tomorrow's Yesterday.* London: Allen & Unwin, 1932.

-------. *Winter's Youth.* London: Allen & Unwin, 1934.

Goethe, J. W. von. *Die Leiden des Jungen Werther.* Lepizig: Weygand'sche, 1774.

Greenberg, Martin S., with Robert Silverberg, eds. *Murasaki: A Novel in Six Parts.* New York: Bantam, 1992.

Griffith, George. *The Angel of the Revolution.* London: Tower, 1893.

Haldane, J. B. S. *The Inequality of Man and Other Essays.* London: Chatto & Windus, 1932.

-------. *Possible Worlds.* London: Chatto & Windus, 1927

Haldeman, Joe. *The Forever War.* New York: St. Martin's Presss, 1975.

Hamilton, Cicely. *Theodore Savage.* London: Parsons, 1922.

Hamilton, Edmond. *The Star Kings.* New York: Signet, 1949.

Healy, Raymond J. *9 Tales of Space and Time.* New York: Holt, 1954.

Heard, Gerald. *Doppelgangers: An Episode of the Fourth, the Psychological Revolution.* London: Cassell, 1948.

Heinlein, Robert A. *Assignment in Eternity.* Reading, Penn.: Fantasy Press, 1953.

-------. *Between Planets.* New York: Scriber, 1951.

-------. *Beyond This Horizon.* Reading, Penn.: Fantasy Press, 1948.

-------. *The Cat Who Walks Through Walls.* New York: Putnam, 1985.

-------. *Citizen of the Galaxy.* New York: Scribner, 1957.

-------. *The Door into Summer.* Garden City, N.Y.: Doubleday, 1957.

-------. *Double Star.* Garden City, N.Y.: Doubleday, 1956.

-------. *Farmer in the Sky.* New York: Scribner, 1950.

-------. *Farnham's Freehold.* New York: Putnam, 1964.

-------. *Friday.* New York: Holt Rinehart, 1982.

-------. *Glory Road.* New York: Putnam, 1963.

-------. *The Green Hills of Earth.* Chicago: Shasta, 1951.

-------. *Grumbles from the Grave*, edited by Virginia Heinlein. New York: Ballantine, 1989.

-------. *Have Space Suit—Will Travel.* New York: Scribner, 1958.

-------. *I Will Fear No Evil.* New York: Putnam, 1970.

-------. *Job: A Comedy of Justice.* New York: Ballantine, 1984.

-------. *The Man Who Sold the Moon.* Chicago: Shasta, 1950.

--------. *The Menace from Earth*. Hicksville, N.Y.: Gnome Press, 1959.
--------. *Methuselah's Children*. Hicksville, N.Y.: Gnome Press, 1958.
--------. *The Moon Is a Harsh Mistress*. New York: Putnam, 1966.
--------. *The Number of the Beast*. New York: Fawcett, 1980.
--------. *Orphans of the Sky*. London: Gollancz, 1963.
--------. *Podkayne of Mars*. New York: Putnam, 1963.
--------. *The Puppet Masters*. Garden City, N.Y.: Doubleday, 1951.
--------. *Red Planet*. New York: Scribner, 1949.
--------. *Requiem: New Collected Works by Robert A. Heinlein and Tributes to the Great Master*, edited by Yoji Kondo. New York: Tor, 1992.
--------. *Revolt in 2100*. Chicago: Shasta, 1953.
--------. *Rocket Ship Galileo*. New York: Scribner, 1947.
--------. *The Rolling Stones*. New York: Scribner, 1952.
--------. *Sixth Column*. New York: Gnome Press, 1949. As *The Day After Tomorrow*. New York: Signet, 1951.
--------. *Space Cadet*. New York: Scribner, 1948.
--------. *The Star Beast*. New York: Scribner, 1954.
--------. *Starman Jones*. New York: Scribner, 1953.
--------. *Starship Troopers*. New York: Puntam, 1959.
--------. *Stranger in a Strange Land*. New York: Putnam, 1961. Restored text, 1990.
--------. *Take Back Your Goverrnment: A Practical Handbook for the Private Citizen Who Wants Democracy to Work*. Riverdale, N.Y.: Baen, 1992.
--------. *Time Enough for Love: The Lives of Lazarus Long*. New York: Putnam, 1973.
--------. *Time for the Stars*. New York: Scribner, 1956.
--------. *To Sail Beyond the Sunset: The Lives and Loves of Maureen Johnson*. New York: Putnam, 1987.
--------. *Tunnel in the Sky*. New York: Scribner, 1955.
--------. *The Unpleasant Profession of Jonathan Hoag*. Hicksville, N.Y.: Gnome Press, 1959.
--------. *Waldo & Magic, Inc.* Garden City, N.Y.: Doubleday, 1950.
Herbert, Frank. *Dune*. Philadelphia: Chilton, 1965.
Hilliard, A. Rowley. "Death from the Stars" *Wonder Stories* October 1931, pp.612-623.
Hinton, C. H. *Scientific Romances*. London: Swan Sonnenschein, 2 vols, 1884-5.
--------. *Scientific Romances, Second Series*. London: Swan Sonnenschein, 1902.

Hodgson, William Hope. *The House on the Borderland.* London: Chapman & Hall, 1908.
[Holberg, Ludvig]. *Nicolai Klimii iter subterraneum.* Leipzig: J. Preussii, 1741; tr. as *A Journey to the World Under-Ground* by Nicholas Klimius. London: Astley & Collins, 1742.
Hope, Anthony. *The Prisoner of Zenda.* Bristol: Arrownsmith, 1894.
Hunting, Gardner. *The Vicarion.* Kansas City, Miss.: Unity School of Christianity, 1926.
Huxley, Aldous. *Brave New World.* London: Chatto & Windus, 1932.
Huygens, Christian. *Cosmotheoros, sive de Terris coelestibus earumque ornatu conjecturae.* The Hague: A. Moetjens, 1698; tr. as *The Celestial World discover'd, or Conjectures concerning the inhabitants, plants and products of the worlds in the planets.* London: T. Childe, 1698.
Jaeger, Muriel. *The Question Mark.* London: Hogarth Press, 1926.
Joncquel, Octave & Varlet, Théo. *L'agonie de la terre.* Amiens: E. Malfère, 1922.
-------. *Les titans du ciel.* Amiens: E. Malfère, 1921.
Jones, Richard Glyn, ed. *Cybersex.* London: Robinson, 1996.
Kant, Immanuel. *Allgemeine Naturgeschichte und Theorie des Himmels.* Königsberg & Leipzig: J. F. Petersen, 1755.
Kepler, John. *Joh. Keppler Mathematici Olim Imperatorii. Somnium se opus posthumus de astronomia lunare.* Frankfurt, 1634; tr. by Everett F. Bleiler as "Somnium: or the Astronomy of the Moon, An Allegory of Science by Johannes Kepler" in *Beyond Time and Space* ed. August Derleth. New York: Pelegri & Cudahy, 1950; tr. & annotated by Edward Rosen, *Kepler's Somnium. The Dream, or Posthumous Work on Lunar Astronomy.* Madison, Wis.: University of Wisconsin Press, 1967.
Ketterer, David. *Imprisoned in a Tesseract: The Life and Work of James Blish.* Ohio: Kent Statue University Press, 1987.
Kipling, Rudyard. *Kim.* London: Macmillan, 1901.
Kircher, Athanasius. *Itinerarium Exstaticum quo mundi opificium,* etc. Rome: V. Mascardi, 1656.
Lake, David. *The Right Hand of Dextra.* New York: DAW, 1977.
Lamarck, Jean-Baptiste, Chevalier de. *Philosophie Zoologique, ou Exposition des considérations relatives ...l'histoire naturelle des animaux.* Paris: Dentu, 2 vols., 1809.
[Lewis, Matthew Gregory]. *The Monk.* London: J. Bell, 1796.
Lofficier, Jean-Marc & Lofficier, Randy. *French Science Fiction, Fantasy, Horror and Pulp Fiction.* Jefferson, NC: McFarland, 2000.

Lowell, Percival. *Mars*. Boston: Houghton MIffin, 1895.

-------. *Mars as the Abode of Life*. New York: Macmillan, 1909.

Mackey, Douglas A. *The Work of Ian Watson: An Annotated Bibliography and Guide*. San Bernardino. California: Borgo Press, 1989.

Maturin, Charles. *Melmoth the Wanderer*. London: Hurst & Robinson, 1820.

McCaffery, Larry, ed. *Postmodern Fiction*. Westport, Conn.: Greenwood, 1986.

-------, ed. *Storming the Reality Studio: A Casebook of Cyberpunk and Postmodern Science Fiction*. Durham, North Carolina: Duke University Press, 1991.

Merritt, A. *The Metal Monster*. New York: Avon, 1926.

Miles *The Gas War of 1940*. London: Scholartis, 1931. Reprinted as *Valiant Clay* by Neil Bell,.

Moskowitz, Sam. *Explorers of the Infinite: Shapers of Science Fiction*. Cleveland: World, 1963.

-------. *Seekers of Tomorrow: Masters of Modern Science Fiction*. New York: Ballantine, 1967.

Nau, John-Antoine. *Force ennemie*. Paris: Éditions de la Plume, 1903.

Niven, Larry, "creator". *The Man-Kzin Wars VI & VII*. New York: Baen, 1994-1995.

Niven, Larry, with Jerry Pournelle. *Lucifer's Hammer*. Chicago: Playboy Press, 1977.

Odle, E. V. *The Clockwork Man*. London: Heinemann, 1923.

Orwell, George. *Nineteen Eighty-Four*. London: Secker and Warburg, 1949.

Panshin, Alexei. *Heinlein in Dimension: A Critical Analysis*. Chicago: Advent, 1968.

Perry, Thomas. "An Amazing Story: Experimenter in Bankruptcy" *Amazing Stories* May 1978. [Supplement to letter in the July 1977 issue.]

-------. "Ham and Eggs and Heinlein" Monad 3 (September 1993). pp.91-128.

Poe, Edgar Allan. "The Conversation of Eiros and Charmion." *Burton's Gentleman's Magazine* December 1839, reprinted in *Tales of the Grotesque and Arabesque*.

-------. *Eureka, a prose poem*. New York: G. P. Putnam, 1848; reprinted as *Eureka—An Essay on the Material and Spiritual Universe* in *Complete Works of Edgar Allan Poe in 10 Volumes*, Vol. X; New York: Fred de Fau & Co, 1902; French tr. by Charles Baudelaire as *Eureka*. Paris: Michel Lévy frères, 1864.

---------. "Hans Phaal." *Southern Literary Messenger*, June 1835, reprinted in *Tales of the Grotesque and Arabesque*; most reprints retitled "The Unaparalleled Adventure of One Hans Pfaal".
---------. *The Narrative of Arthur Gordon Pym of Nantucket*. New York: Harper, 1838.
---------. "Sonnet—To Science" in *Al Aaraaf, Tamerlane and Minor Poems*. Baltimore: Hatch & Durning, 1829.
---------. *Tales of the Grotesque and Arabesque*. Philadelphia: Lea and Blanchard, 1840.
Radcliffe, Ann. *The Mysteries of Udolpho*. London: G.G. and J. Robinson, 1794.
Restif de la Bretonne, Nicolas-Edmé. *La Decouverte Australe par un homme volant ou la Dédale français*, 4 vols. Paris: Veuve Duschesné, 1781.
---------. *Les Posthumes, lettres réçues après la mort du mari par sa femme, qui le croit en Florence*. Paris: Duchêne, 1802.
Rhine. J. B. *Extra-Sensory Perception*. Boston: Boston Society for Psychic Research, 1934.
Robida, Albert. *L'Horloge des siècles*. Paris: F. Juven, 1902.
Rosny, J. H. aîné. *La Mort de la terre*. Paris: Plon, 1910.
---------. *Les Navigateurs de l'infini*. Paris: Oeuvres Libres, 1925.
---------. *Les Xipéhuz*. Paris: Savine, 1887.
Roumier, Marie-Anne de [Mme. Robert]. *Voyages de Mylord Céton dans les sept planètes, ou le nouveau mentor*, 7 vols. Paris: La Haye, 1765-6.
Roussel, Raymond. *Nouvelles Impressions d'Afrique*. Paris: Lemerre, 1932.
Sand, George. *Laura: Voyage et impressions*. Paris: Michel Lévy, 1865.
Scoggins, C. E. *The Red Gods Call*. Indianapolis, Ind.: Boobs-Merrill, 1926.
Shanks, Edward. *The People of the Ruins*. London: Collins, 1920.
Shaw, Bob. *Other Days, Other Eyes*. London: Gollancz, 1972.
Shaw, George Bernard. *Back to Methuselah: A Metabiological Pentateuch*. London: Constable, 1921.
Shelley, Mary. *Frankenstein; or, The Modern Prometheus*. London: Lackington Hughes, 1818. Revised ed. London: Colburn and Bentley, 1831.
---------. *The Last Man*. London: Colburn, 1826.
Sherred, T. L. "E for Effort," *Astounding Science Fiction*, May 1947, p.119-162.
Shiel, M. P. *The Yellow Danger*. London: Grant Richards, 1898.
---------. *The Young Men Are Coming!* London: Allen & Unwin, 1937.

Simak, Clifford D. [actually by John W. Campbell, Jr.] *Empire*. New York: Galaxy, 1951.
Smith, Edward E. *Children of the Lens*. Reading, Penn.: Fantasy Press, 1954.
-------. *First Lensman*. Reading, Penn.: Fantasy Press, 1950.
-------. *Galactic Patrol*. Reading, Penn.: Fantasy Press, 1950.
-------. *The Galaxy Primes*. New York: Ace, 1965.
-------. *Gray Lensman*. Reading, Penn.: Fantasy Press, 1951.
-------. *Second Stage Lensman*. Reading, Penn.: Fantasy Press, 1953.
-------. *Skylark DuQuesne*. New York: Pyramid, 1966.
-------. *The Skylark of Space*. Providence, R.I.: Buffalo, 1946.
-------. *Skylark of Valeron*. Reading, Penn: Fantasy Press, 1949.
-------. *Skylark Three*. Reading, Penn.: Fantasy Press, 1948.
-------. *Spacehounds of I.P.C.* Reading: Penn.: Fantasy Press, 1947.
-------. *Subspace Explorers*. New York: Canaveral, 1965.
-------. *Triplanetary*. Reading, Penn.: Fantasy Press, 1948.
-------. *The Vortex Blaster*. New York: Gnome Press, 1960.
Spengler, Oswald. *The Decline of the West*. New York: Knopf, 1926.
Stapledon, Olaf. *Last and First Men*. London: Methuen, 1930.
-------. *Star Maker*. London: Methuen, 1937.
Sterling, Bruce. *The Artificial Kid*. New York: Harper, 1980.
-------. *Crystal Express*. Sauk City, Wisconsin: Arkham House, 1989.
-------. *The Difference Engine* (with William Gibson). London: Victor Gollancz, 1990.
-------. *Globalhead*. Shingletown, California: Mark V. Ziesing, 1992.
-------. *The Hacker Crackdown: Law and Disorder on the Electronic Frontier*. New York: Bantam, 1992.
-------. *Heavy Weather*. New York: Bantam, 1994..
-------. *Holy Fire*. New York: Bantam, 1996.
-------. *Involution Ocean*. New York: Jove, 1977 [actually 1978].
-------. *Islands in the Net*. New York: Arbor House, 1988.
-------. *Schismatrix*. New York: Arbor House, 1985.
-------. *Schismatrix Plus*. New York: Ace, 1996.
-------. (editor) *Mirrorshades: The Cyberpunk Anthology*. New York: Arbor House, 1986.
Swedenborg, Emanuel. *Arcana coelestia quae in Scriptura sacra seu verbo Domini sunt detecta, etc.* (written 1749-56), 13 vols. Tubingen, 1833-42.
Swift, Jonathan. *Travels into Several Remote Nations of the World in Four Parts by Lemuel Gulliver, first a Surgeon, and then a*

Captain of Several Ships, 2 vols. London: Bejamin Motte, 1726. Often reprinted as *Gulliver's Travels*.
Taine, John. *The Time Stream*. Providence, R.I.: Buffalo, 1946.
Tennyson, Alfred Lord. *In Memoriam*. London: Edward Moxon, 1850.
Tennyson, Alfred Lord and Charles. *Poems by Two Brothers*. London: W. Simpkin, R. Marshall & J. Jackson, 1827.
Tolkien, J. R. R. *The Lord of the Rings*. London: Allen & Unwin, 3 vols., 1954-1955.
Uris, Leon. *Battle Cry*. New York: Putnam, 1953.
Varlet, Théo. *La Grande panne*. Paris: Portique, 1930.
Versins, Pierre. *Encyclopédie de l'Utopie, des voyages extraordinaires et de la science fiction*. Lausanne: L'Age d'Homme, 1972.
Verne, Jules *Voyage au centre de la terre*. Paris: Hetzel, 1863. Revised ed. 1867. Translated as *Journey to the Centre of the Earth*. London: Griffin and Farran, 1872 [corrupt translation].
Voltaire. *Le Micromégas de mr. de Voltaire*. Londres (so advertised, but probably Berlin), 1752; tr. as *Micromegas, A Comic Romance. Being a Severe Stire upon the Philosophy, Ignorance, and Self-Conceit of Mankind*. London: Wilson & Durham, 1753.
[Walpole, Horace]. The Castle of Otranto. London: Tho. Lownds, 1765.
Watson, Ian. *Alien Embassy*. London: Victor Gollancz, 1976.
-------. *The Book of Being*. London; Victor Gollancz, 1985.
-------. *The Book of Ian Watson*. Willimantic, Connecticut: Ziesing, 1985.
-------. *The Book of the River*. London; Victor Gollancz, 1984.
-------. *The Book of the Stars*. London; Victor Gollancz, 1984.
-------. *Chaos Child*. London: Boxtree, 1995.
-------. *Chekhov's Journey*. London; Victor Gollancz, 1983.
-------. *The Coming of Vertumnus and Other Stories*. London; Victor Gollancz, 1994.
-------. *Converts*. London: Panther, 1984.
-------. *Deathhunter*. London; Victor Gollancz, 1981.
-------. *The Embedding*. London: Victor Gollancz, 1973.
-------. *Evil Water and Other Stories*. London; Victor Gollancz, 1987.
-------. *The Fallen Moon: The Second Book of Mana*. London; Victor Gollancz, 1994.
-------. *The Fire-Worm*. London; Victor Gollancz, 1988.
-------. *The Flies of Memory*. London: Victor Gollancz, 1990.
-------. *The Gardens of Delight*. London; Victor Gollancz, 1980.
-------. *God's World*. London; Victor Gollancz, 1979.

------. *Hard Questions*. London; Victor Gollancz, 1996.
------. *Harlequin*. London: Boxtree, 1994.
------. *Inquisitor*. Brighton: GW Books, 1990.
------. *Japan: A Cat's Eye View*. Osaka: Bunken Shuppan, 1969.
------. *Japan Tomorrow*. Osaka: Bunken Shuppan, 1977.
------. *The Jonah Kit*. London; Victor Gollancz, 1975.
------. *Lucky's Harvest: The First Book of Mana*. London; Victor Gollancz, 1993.
------. *The Martian Inca*. London; Victor Gollancz, 1977.
------. *Meat*. London: Headline, 1988.
------. *Miracle Visitors*. London; Victor Gollancz, 1978.
------. *Oracle*. London; Victor Gollancz, 1997.
------. *Orgasmachine*. Paris: J.-C. Lattès, 1976.
------. *The Power*. London: Headline, 1987.
------. *Queenmagic, Kingmagic*. London; Victor Gollancz, 1986.
------. *Salvage Rites and Other Stories*. London; Victor Gollancz, 1989.
------. *Slow Birds and Other Stories*. London; Victor Gollancz, 1985.
------. *Space Marine*. London: Boxtree, 1993.
------. *Stalin's Teardrops and Other Stories*. London; Victor Gollancz, 1991.
------. *Sunstroke and Other Stories*. London; Victor Gollancz, 1982.
------. *Under Heaven's Bridge* (with Michael Bishop). London; Victor Gollancz, 1981.
------. *The Very Slow Time Machine*. London; Victor Gollancz, 1979.
------. *Whores of Babylon*. London: Grafton, 1988.
Wells, H. G. "The Land Ironclads." *The Strand*, December 1903.
------. "The Man of the Year Million" *Pall Mall Gazette*, 6 November 1893.
------. *The Shape of Things to Come*. London: Hutchinson, 1933.
------. *The Time Machine*. London: Heinemann, 1895.
------. *The War in the Air*. London: G. Bell, 1908.
------. *The War of the Worlds*. London: Heinemann, 1898.
------. *The World Set Free*. London: Macmillan, 1914.
[Wilkins, John]. *The Discovery of a World in the moone, or a discourse tending to prove that 'tis probable there may be another habitable world in that planet*. London: M. Sparks & E, Forrest, 1638; Book II as *A Discourse Concerning a New World and Another Planet*. London: John Maynard, 1640.

Wollheim, Donald A. *The Universe Makers*. New York: Harper, 1971.
Wright. S. Fowler. *The New Gods Lead*. London: Jarrolds, 1932.
-------. *The World Below*. London: Collins, 1929.
Zukav, Gray. *The Dancing Wu Li Masters*. New York: Morrow, 1979.

FILMOGRAPHY

Destination Moon. dir. Irving Pichel, 1950.
Frankenstein. dir. James Whale, 1931
Invasion of the Body Snatchers. dir. Don Siegel, 1956.
The Thing. dir. Christian Nyby, 1951.
2001: A Space Odyssey. dir. Stanley Kubrick, 1968

INDEX

Acker, Kathy 146
Across the Sea of Suns 124, 130, 133-134
Adler, Alfred 73
Adventures of Three Russians and Three Englishmen in South Africa, The 48
Afterlives 166
"After Such Knowledge" trilogy 118
Again, Dangerous Visions 124
Against Infinity 124, 130
Against the Fall of Night 126, 133, 135
Agonie de la terre, L' 45
"Al Aaraaf" 22
Aldiss, Brian W. 11
Alien Embassy 160
"All" 78, 98
"All You Zombies—" 99, 102
"Alphas" 133
Amazing Stories 65-69, 71, 74, 76, 83-84, 89, 122-124, 144
Amazing Stories Annual 66
Amazing Stories Quarterly 66
Ambit 156
American Legion Magazine, The 100
Analog 74, 82, 123, 126
Anaxagoras 33
Anderson, Poul 91, 115
"—And He Built a Crooked House" 99
"…And Searching Mind" 79
"And the Sea Like Mirrors" 124, 130
Angel of the Revolution, The 57
Annuaire de cosmos 25
Anvil, Christopher 78
"Anvil of Jove, The" 125

Aquinas, Thomas 29
Arena, The 44
"Are You for 86?" 150
Argosy 100
Ariosto, Ludovico 29
Around the Moon 48
Around the World in Eighty Days 48
Artifact 130-131
Artificial Kid, The 141-142
"Art-Work" 120
"As Big as the Ritz" 132
As I Lay Dying 132
Asimov, Isaac 11, 27, 78, 81, 91, 115, 129, 133
Assignment in Eternity 97, 101
Astounding Science Fiction 68, 79-81, 87, 89, 94-96, 98-99, 101-102, 109, 114, 133
Astounding Stories of Super-Science 67-69, 74, 84, 86-87
Astronomie, L' 26
Astronomie populaire 26
"At Death's End" 115-116
Atheling, William Jr. 112, 117
Atmosphère, L' 26
Attila the Hun 33
"At War with the Invisible" 64
Autour de la lune 48
Aventures de Capitaine Hatteras, Les 48
Aventures de trois russes et de trois anglais dans l'Afrique australe 48
Babbage, Charles 148
Babel-17 156
Babylon-5 84
Back to Methuselah 76
Bacon, Roger 117-118
Ballard, J. G. 146
Banks, Iain M. 91
"Baron Muenchhausen's Scientific Adventures" 64
Barr, Robert 149
Bates, Harry 86
Battle Cry 105
"Battleground" 122
Baudelaire, Charles 39
Baudrillard, Jean 146
Baxter, Nancy 140

"Beanstalk" 112
"Bear, The" 130
Bear, Greg 137
"Beautiful and the Sublime, The" 149
"Beep" 119
Bell, Eric Temple 68, 83
Bell, Neil 57
Bellamy, Edward 98
Benford, Gregory 121-139
Benford, James 121-122
Beresford, J. D. 58
Bester, Alfred 103
Best of Science Fiction, The 80
Bethke, Bruce 144
Between Planets 102-103
"Beyond Grayworld" 126
"Beyond the Fall of Night" 133, 135
Beyond This Horizon 95, 99, 101
"Bible in Blood, The" 167
"Bicycle Repairman" 151
"Big Jelly" 151
Bilderdijk, Willem 11
Billion Year Spree 11
"Bindlestiff" 115
Bishop, Michael 163-164
Black Easter 118-119
Black Star Passes, The 75
Blake, Sterling 131, 137
Blake, William 12
Blaylock, James P. 148
Bleiler, Everett F. 64-65
Bleiler, Richard 8
Blish, James 7, 11-120
Blockade Runners, The 48
"Bloomsday Revolution, The" 165
"Blowups Happen" 97, 109
Blue Book 100
Boëx, Joseph-Henri 44
Book, David L. 122, 128
Book of Being, The 164-165
Book of Ian Watson, The 156
Book of the River, The 164, 168
Book of the Stars, The 164

Borel, Pierre 29-30
Bosch, Hieronymus 162
Boucher de Perthes, Jacques 51
Boy's Life 100, 103
Bradbury, Ray 106, 132
Brandt, C. A, 66
Brave New World 58
"Bridge" 115
Brin, David 122, 131-132, 137
Bruno, Giordano 29
Buck, Doris Pitkin 122
Buffon, Comte de 54
Burks, Arthur J. 79
Burning Chrome 154
Burroughs, Edgar Rice 66
Burroughs, William S. 146
"But the Secret Sits" 123
"By His Bootstraps" 98-99, 102
Byron, Lord 16, 148
"Cadenza" 127
"Cage for Death, A" 162
Caidin, Martin 130
"Calibrations and Exercises" 129
Calling All Girls 100
"Cambridge, 1.58 A.M." 123
Campbell, John W. Jr. 7, 59, 68, 72-82, 85, 89, 94-98, 100-103, 106, 114, 128, 133
Capra, Fritjof 160
Captain Video 112
Carr, Terry 121, 123
Carter Paul A. 122, 132-133
Cartmill, Cleve 97
"Case of Conscience, A" 112, 117-118
Cassini, Jean-Dominque 33
Castle of Otranto, The 10
"Cathedrals in Space" 117
Cat Who Walks Through Walls, The 95, 109
"Celestial Love, A" 44
"Centigrade 233" 132, 137
Chandler, Raymond 113
Changes: Stories of Metamorphosis 164
Chaos Child 167
Cheap Truth 145

Chekhov's Journey 164
Childhood's End 125
Children of the Lens 86-88
Chiller 131
Chomsky, Noam 156
"Cicada Queen" 142-143
Cinq semaines en ballon 47-48
Cities in Flight 112, 115-116
Citizen of the Galaxy 102-105, 109
City and the Stars, The 126, 135
Clairmont, Claire 16
Clairs de lune 43
Clarke, Arthur C. 27, 103, 110, 124-126, 132-133
Clash of Cymbals, A 116
Clewiston Test, The 128
"Cliff and the Calories" 100
Clifton, Mark 79
Clipper of the Clouds, The 48
Cloak of Aesir 77
"Cloak of Aesir" 78
Clockwork Man, The 58
Coblentz, Stanton A. 68, 83
"Cold, Dry Cradle, A" 138
"Cold Equations, The" 79
Cole, Robert W. 83
Coleridge, Samuel Taylor 141, 153
Collier's 94
Comète, La 31
"Coming of Vertumnus, The" 167
Coming of Vertumnus, The 167
"Common Sense" 99, 101
"Common Time" 112, 120
"Compassionate, the Digital, The" 153
Conklin, Groff 80
Consolations in Travel; or, The Last Days of a Philosopher 28, 33-36
Constantine, Murray 58
Contes philosophiques 44
"Conversation avec un Marsien" 44
Conversations on the Plurality of Worlds 30
Converts 163
Cook, Robin 130
Cornelius Agrippa 13

Cosm 138-139
Cosmologie Universelle 24
Cosmos, Le 26
Cosmotheoros 32
Count of Monte Cristo, The 103
"Coventry" 97
Craig, Brian 166
"Creation Took Eight Days" 99
Crichton, Michael 130-131
Cromwell, Oliver 33
"Crudities of Science Fiction, The" 158
Crystal Express 149
Cummings, Ray 65, 68
"Custom-Built Girl" 159
Cuvier, Georges 54
"Cyberpunk" 144
Cyberpunk 150
"Cyberpunk or Cyberjunk" 146
Cybersex 159
Cyrano de Bergerac, Savinien 29-30
Dalgleish, Alice 103, 105-106, 108
D'Ammassa, Don 165
Dancing Wu-Li Masters, The 160
Daniel, Gabriel 32
Dans le ciel et sur la terre 43
"Dans l'infini" 29
Dante Alighieri 29
"Dark Backward, The" 137
"Darker Geometry, A" 138
"Dark Sanctuary" 127
Darlite 155
Darwin, Charles 21
Darwin, Erasmus 21-22
Davy, Humphry 28, 33-36, 38, 42
Day After Judgment, The 118-119
Day After Tomorrow, The 78
Deathhunter 162-163
de Camp, L. Sprague 79
Decline of the West, The 115
"Deep Eddy" 151
"Deeper Than the Darkness" 122-123
Delany, Samuel R. 123, 142, 156
De la terre à la lune 48

DeLillo, Don 128, 146
Delmas, Léon 51
Derrida, Jacques 146
Descartes, René 31, 33, 38
Désert de glace, Le 48
Desert of Ice, The 48
"Desperate Calculus, A" 137
Destination Moon 100
"Devil Makes the Law, The" 98
"Dialogue entre deux Acaémiciens et deux insects stercoraires" 44
Dick, Philip K. 96
Dieu dans la nature 28
Difference Engine, The 148-149
Di Filippo, Paul 148
"Dinner in Audoghast" 148-149
Disch, Thomas M. 105
Discours nouveau prouvant le pluralité des mondes 30
Discover of a New World in the Moon, A 29
"Dr. Hackensaw's Secrets" 65
Doctor Mirabilis 117-118
"Doing Alien" 133
"Doing Lennon" 126
Doppelgängers 58
"Doom of London, The" 149
Door into Summer, The 101-103
"Dori Bangs" 150
Doubleday 101
Double Star 101-102, 109
Doyle, Sir Arthur Conan 27
Dozois, Gardner 144
Dreams of an Astronomer 43
Dumas, Alexandre 47, 103
Dune 79
Duplicated Man, The 111
"Early Bird" 132
"Early in the Evening" 169
"Earthman, Come Home" 114-115
Earthman, Come Home 115-116
Edison, Thomas Alva 64
Eklund, Gordon 90, 121-125, 127
Einstein, Albert 36
"Elder Gods, The" 78
Electrical Experimenter, The 64-65

Ellern, William B. 90
Ellison, Harlan 121, 124, 140-141
"Elsewhen" 96-97, 101
"Elsewhere" 97
Embedding, The 156-159, 162
"Emir's Clock, The" 167
Empire 78
Enfants du Capitaine Grant, Les 48
Engels, Friedrich 149
English at the North Pole, The 48
Entretiens sur la pluralité des mondes 30-32, 36-37
EPIC News 93-94, 96, 98
Eshbach, Lloyd Arthur 90
Eureka—An Essay on the Material and Spiritual Universe 21, 23, 33, 39-42
Evans, E. Everett 90
"Event Horizon, The" 160
"Evil Water" 166
Evil Water and Other Stories 165
Experimenter Publishing Company 66-67
Explorers of the Infinite 62
"Exposures" 126
Extra-Sensory Perception 76
Eye in the Sky 96
Faber 116, 118
Fahrenheit 451 132
Fallen Moon, The 167-168
Fallen Star 119-120
Fantasmagoriana 16
Fantastic Stories 122
Fantasy Press 78, 101
Farnham's Freehold 108
Faulkner, William 129, 132
Ferring, David 166
"Ferryman" 169
Fézandie, Clement 65-66, 68
Figuier, Louis 50-53
Find the Changeling 127
Fin du monde, La 41-44
Finney, Jack 103
Fire-Worm, The 166
First Lensman 86-87
Fitzgerald, F. Scott 132

"Flags of Africa, The" 155
Flammarion, Camille 8, 24-46, 83
Flammarion, Ernest 26
"Flattop" 122
"Flies of Memory, The" 167
Floating City, A 48
"Flowers for Algernon" 71
"Flowers of Edo" 148, 153
Flying Saucers 160
Fontenelle, Bernard de 30-32, 36-39
Force ennemie 45
Forces naturelles inconnues, Des 25
Forecast 70
Forever War, The 105-106
"Forgetfulness" 77, 80
Forster, E. M. 76
Foundation (journal) 129
Foundation series 81
Foundation's Fear 133
Franson, Donald 121-122
Frankenstein; or, The Modern Prometheus 9-19
Franklin, H. Bruce 88
Friday 109
From the Earth to the Moon 48
Frost, Robert 138
Frozen Year, The 119-120
Fur Country, The 48
Furious Gulf 135-136
Galactic Odyssey, A 135
Galactic Patrol 86-87
"Galaxia" 133
Galaxy Primes, The 89-90
Galileo Galilei 29
Games Workshop 166-167
Gardens of Delight, The 162, 167
Garnett, David S. 166
Garnier, Charles 33
Garrett, Randall 78
Gas War of 1940, The 57
"Gaudi's Dragon" 167
Genesis 51
Gernsback, Hugo 7, 62-72, 74, 80
Gernsback, Sidney 66-67

"Ghost Lecturer" 165
"Ghosts of Luna, The" 157
Gibson, William 142, 144-148, 154
"Girl Who Was Art, The" 156
Glen or Glenda 70
Gloag, John 57-58
Globalhead 149-151
Glory Road 108
Gnome Press 101
God's World 161-162, 164
Godwin, Francis 29
Godwin, Tom 79
Goethe, J. W. von 15
"Goldfish Bowl" 99
Goldin, Stephen R. 90
Gollancz, Victor 101, 156, 158
Gourmont, Remy de 18
Gravity's Rainbow 128
Gray Lensman 86-87
Great Sky River 134
Greenberg, Martin H. 136
"Green Days in Brunei" 146
"Green Hills of Earth, The" 100
Griffith, George 57
Grumbles from the Grave 94-95, 99, 103, 107
Guevara, Che 128
"Gulf" 100-101
"Gulf Wars, The" 149
Habitants de l'autre monde, Les 25
Hacker, Marilyn 123
Hacker Crackdown, The 150
Hafner, Katie 150
Haldane, J. B. S. 57, 75
Haldeman, Joe 105-106
Halley, Edmond 51-52
Hamilton, Cicely 57
Hamilton, Edmond 84-85, 88, 103
Hampdenshire Wonder, The 58
Hard Questions 168
Harlequin 167
Have Space Suit—Will Travel 105
Hayakawa-SF 153
Healy, Raymond J. 78

Heard, Gerald 58
Heart of the Comet 131
Heavy Weather 151
Hector Servadac 48
Heimskringla 49
Heinlein, Robert A. 78-79, 93-110, 115, 121, 124
Heinlein, Virginia (née Gerstenfeld) 93, 95, 99, 107
Heinlein in Dimension 93
"Hellas Is Florida" 125
Hemingway, Ernest 128
Herbert, Frank 79
Heroes in Hell 128
Hetzel, P.-J. 47-48, 51, 53
"High Abyss" 137
"Hiss of Dragons, A" 127
Histoire des états et empires du soleil 30
Histoire des oracles 31
"Histoire d'une comête" 29, 41
"History of a Comet, The" 29
Hodgson, William Hope 45
Hoffmann, E. T. A. 18
Holberg, Ludvig 32
"Hollywood Kremlin" 150
Holy Fire 151-152
"Homemaker" 129
Homer 33
Hope, Anthony 103
Hornig, Charles 68
"Hour After Earthrise, The" 120
House on the Borderland, The 45
Howard, Robert E. 90
"How It All Went" 128
How to be a Politician 100
Hubbard, L. Ron 78
Huet, Mademoiselle 25
"Humanist Manifesto, The" 145
Huxley, Aldous 58
Huxley, Julian 57
Huygens, Christian 32
Huysmans, Joris-Karl 45
"Icarus Descending" 124-125, 127-128
Iceborn 132
If 84, 90

"If This Goes On—" 97
"If the Stars are Gods" 124-125
If the Stars are Gods 125, 138
"Immersion" 133
"Immortal Night" 124
"Immune Dreams" 161
"Imperial Stars, The" 90
Imprisoned in a Tesseract 114
"Inalienable Rite" 123-124
"In Alien Flesh" 127
In Alien Flesh 127, 138
Incredible Planet, The 78
"In Infinity" 29
Inquisitor 167
In Search of the Castaways 48
Interzone 7
"In the Ocean of Night" 124-125, 127
In the Ocean of Night 122, 124, 126, 129, 133
"In the Upper Cretaceous with the Summerfire Brigade" 167
Intransigéant, L' 26
Invaders from the Infinite 75
Invasion of the Body-Snatchers 103
Involution Ocean 140-141
"Irrelevant, The" 78
Isaac Asimov's Science Fiction Magazine 144
Islands in the Net 146-147
Islands of Space 75
Issue at Hand, The 112, 115, 119
Itinerarium Exstaticum 30
I Will Fear No Evil 107-109
Jack of Eagles 113
Jackson, Judith 155
Jaeger, Muriel 58
"Japan" 155
Japan: A Cat's Eye View 155
Japan Tomorrow 160
Japan 2000 135
"Jeanne" 70
"Jean Sandwich, the Sponsor and I" 163
Jeter, K. W. 148
"Jewels in an Angel's Wing" 165
"Jim and Irene" 150
"Jingling Geordie's Hole" 166

Joan of Arc 125
Job: A Comedy of Justice 109
"John of the Apocalypse" 127
"Johnny Mnemonic" 142
Jonah Kit, The 157-158
Joncquel, Octave 45
Jones, Richard Glyn 159
Journey to the Center of the Earth 47-53
Jung, Carl 160, 162
Jungle Stories 120
Jupiter Project 124, 129
Jurassic Park 19
Kant, Imanuel 32
Kardec, Allan 25
Karloff, Boris 9
Keats, John 148
Keller, David H. 68-69
Kelly, Frank K. 68
Kepler, John 29, 39
Kessel, John 146
Ketterer, David 114, 120
Keyes, Daniel 71
Kidd, Virginia 112
Kim 103
Kipling Rudyard 103
Kircher, Athanasius 30
Knight, Damon 112, 120
Knight, Norman L. 119
"Knowing Her" 127
"Kollapse" 137
Kornbluth, Cyril M. 120
Kuttner, Henry 79
Kyle, David A. 90
Laidlaw, Marc 122, 127
Lamarck, Chevalier de 38
"Land Ironclads, The" 56
La Rochefoucauld, Baron de 33
Lasser, David 68
Last and First Men 58-59, 75
Last Dangerous Visions, The 140
"Last Evolution, The" 75-77, 80-81
"Last Judgment, The" 75
Last Man, The 10

Latham, Philip 126
Laura 51
"Lazarus Rising" 130
Leary, Timothy 146
Légende sceptique, La 44
Le Guin, Ursula K. 91
Leiber, Fritz 78-79
Lem, Stanislaw 158
Lennon, John 126
"Letter from God, A" 163
"Let the Finder Beware" 112-113
"Let There be Light" 96
Le Verrier, Urbain 24
Lewis, Matthew Gregory 10
Lewis, Sinclair 98
Library Journal 103
"Life-Line" 94
Life for the Stars, A 116
"Lion and the Lamb, The" 78
Littenburg, Lawrence 121
Little Knowledge, A 163
"Littlest Jackal, The" 151
Locus 152
"Logic of Empire" 99
Lone Star Universe 140
Looking Backward, 2000-1887 98
Lord of the Rings, The 79, 90
"Lost Legacy" 96, 101
"Lost Legion" 96
Louis Napoléon 47
Louis XIV 31
Lovecraft, H. P. 150, 153
Lovelace, Ada 148
Lovelock, James 138
Loves of the Plants, The 21
Lowell, Percival 62
Lowndes, Roberet A. W. 111
Lucifer's Hammer 128
Lucky's Harvest 167-168
Lumen 8, 28-30, 33-34, 36-42, 44-46
Lyon, Charlees W. 94
McCaffery, Larry 146
McCarthy, Joseph 94

MacDonald, Anson 98-99
MacDonald, Leslyn 93, 100
"Machine, Stops, The" 76
Mackey, Douglas A. 165, 168
Mad Max 166
Magasin d'Éducation et de Récréation, Le 48
Magasin pittoresque, Le 25
Magazine of Fantasy & Science Fiction, The 102, 122, 129
"Magic, Inc." 98, 101
Maisons hantées, Les 27
"Maître Zacharius" 47
Malartre, Elisabeth 122, 138
"Maneki Neko" 153
"Man in a Vice" 124
Man-Kzin Wars, The 138
"Man-Made Self" 140
"Man of the Year Million, The" 54
Manson, Charles 107
"Man Who Stole the Moon, The" 101
Margulies, Leo 74
Markoff, John 150
"Marooned" 78
Martian Chronicles, The 106
Martian Epic, The 45
Martian Inca, The 159-160
Martin, Mark O. 122, 138
Marx, Karl 149
Master-Mind of Mars, The 66
"Matter's End" 132
Maturin Charles 10
Measuring a Merdian 48
Meat 166
"Me/Days" 130
Melmoth the Wanderer 10
Melville, Herman 141
Meredith, Scott 112, 117
Merlyn, Arthur 113, 120
Merritt, A. 66
"Metal Emperor, The" 66
"Metal Horde, The" 75
"Metal Monster, The" 66
Methuselah's Children 99, 101, 109
"Microcosmic God" 79

Micromégas 32
Midsummer Century 119
Mightiest Machine, The 76, 78
"Milk of Knowledge, The" 163
Miracle Visitors 160-162
Mirrorshades: The Cyberpunk Anthology 140, 145-146
"Misfit" 96, 99
"Mistake Inside" 120
"Moby Dust" 141
Modern Electrics 63-64
Monde avant le création de l'homme, Le 24, 42
Mondes imaginaires et les modes réels, Les 25, 29-33, 39
Mondo 2000 146
Monk, The 10
Monroe, Lyle 96
Montaigne, Michel de 29
Montesquieu, Baron de 33
Moon is a Harsh Mistress, The 108
Moon is Hell, The 78
Moorcock, Michael 80
Moore, C. L. 79
"Moral Bullet, The" 149-150
Morgan, Jacques 64
"Mort de la terre, La" 44
Mort et son mystère, La 26
Moskowitz, Sam 7, 62, 66-67, 69-73, 76, 93
"Movement, The" 123
"Mozart in Mirrorshades" 148
"Mozart on Morphine" 126
Murasaki 136
"My Soul Swims in a Goldfish Bowl" 161
Mysteries of Udolpho, The 10
"Mystic Marriage of Salome, The" 165
"Nanoware Time" 167
"Nanunculus" 169
Napoleon 13
Nau, John-Antoine 45
Navigators de l'infini, Les 44-45
Neuromancer 142, 144, 149
Newcomb, W. A. 128
New Gods Lead, The 76
New Legends 137
Newman, Kim 166

Newton, Isaac 33-34, 128
"Newton's Sleep" 128
New Worlds 155-157
New York Times 67
Nicholas of Cusa 29
Nicholls, Peter 114
"Night" 77
"Nightfall" 78
"Nightmares" 163
Night Shapes, The 120
Nils Klim 32
"Nine Billion Names of God, The" 132
9 Tales of Space and Time 78
Nineteen Eighty-Four 59
Niven, Larry 128, 138, 141
"Nobody Lives Around Here" 123
"Nobody Lives on Burton Street" 123
"Nooncoming" 129
"Not for an Age" 136
Nouveau Petit Larousse 44
Nouvelles Impressions d'Afrique 157
Number of the Beast, The 109
"Oath, The" 120
Odle, E. V. 58
"Odorchestra, The" 70
"Odour of Cocktail Cigarettes, The" 167
"Of Space/Time and the River! 125
"Okie" 114-115
Oliphant, Laurence 148
"Old Legends" 137
"Old Woman By the Road" 132
Omniaveritas, Vincent 145
"On Cooking the First Hero in Spring" 160
Oracle 168
Orgasmachine 159
Orphans of the Sky 101
Orwell, George 59
"Other Side of the River, The" 130
"Our Neural Chernobyl" 149
"Out of Night" 77-78
Pal, George 99
Palmer, Ray 74
Panshin, Alexei 93

Paracelsus 13
Paris au XXe siècle 47
"Paris Conquers All" 137
Paris in the Twentieth Century 47
Partners in Wonder 121
Pascal, Blaise 33, 41
Pater, Walter 155
Paul, Frank R. 65
Pays de fourrures, Le 48
"People of the Precipice, The" 165
People of the Ruins, The 57
Perry, Tom 67, 93-94, 108
Petrarch 20
Philadelphia Evening Telegraph 50
Physical Review 128
"Piracy Preferred" 75
Planète Mars et ses conditions d'habitabilité, La 26
Plato 33
Pluralité des mondes habités, La 24-25, 28
Podkayne Fries 106
Podkayne of Mars 106
Poe, Edgar Allan 8, 20-23, 33, 39-41
Poems by Two Brothers 20
Pohl, Frederik 96, 111
Polidori, John W. 16
Pol-Just, René 51
"Poor Daddy" 100
Popular Detective 100
Posthumes, Les 33-34
Postmodern Fiction 146
Pound, Ezra 111
Pournelle, Jerry 128
Power, The 166
Powers, Tim 148
Pringle, David 7
Prisoner of Zenda, The 103
Proctor, George W. 140
"Profession of Science Fiction, The" 129
"Programmed Love Story" 156
"Proselytes" 125
"Proserpina's Daughter" 132, 138
Proud Man 58
Puppet Masters, The 101-103

Pynchon, Thomas 128, 146
Pythagoras 33
Quark 123
Queenmagic, Kingmagic 165
Question Mark, The 58
Quincunx of Time, The 119
Rabelais, François 29
Radcliffe, Ann 10
Radio-Electronics Magazine 69-70
Radio News 65
Ralph 124C41+ 63-64, 69
Ratner's Star 128
Reagan, Ronald 110
Récits de l'infini 29, 41
Red Gods Call, The 76
Red Planet 103
"Red Star, Winter Orbit" 148, 153
"Relativistic Effects" 130
"Requiem" 97, 99
"Requiem for the Cyberpunks" 146
Restif de la Bretonne, Nicolas 33
Rêves étoilés 43-44
Reynolds, Mack 78
Rhine, J. B. 76
Richardson, Robert S. 126
Riddle of the Tower, The 58
Riley, Frank 79
Riverside, John 99
"Roads Must Roll, The" 97, 109
Robur le conquérant 48
Roche, Wiliam 62
Rocket Ship Galileo 100
Rolling Stones, The 103
"Roof Garden Under Saturn" 155
"Rose and the Scalpel, The" 125
Rosny, J. H. aîné 44-45
Rotsler, William 122, 127
Roumier, Mare-Anne de 32-34
Roussel, Raymond 157
Rucker, Rudy 145, 148-149, 151
Russell, Eric Frank 79
"Sacred Cow" 151
Sailing Bright Eternity 135-136

Salvage Rites and Other Stories 167
Sand, George 52
"Sargasso of Lost Cities" 115
Sargent, Pamela 166
Saturday Evening Post 100
Saunders, Caleb 97
"Scarred Man, The" 124
Schismatrix 142-144, 152
Schismatrix Plus 142
Schmitz, James H. 78
Science and Invention 65-66, 71
Science Fiction Eye 146
Science-Fiction Plus 69
Science Fiction: The Early Years 64
Science Illustrée, La 52
"Science in SF, The" 122
Science Wonder Stories 68
Scoggins, C. E. 76
"Seascape" 127
Second-Stage Lensman 86-87
"Secrets" 169
Seed, David 8
Seedling Stars, The 113-114, 119
Seekers of Tomorrow 73, 93
Senior Prom 100
"Sex Machine, The" 156
Sexology 69-70
Sfinx 157
"Shakers of the Earth" 127
Shakespeare, William 20
"Shall We Take a Little Walk?" 124
Shanks, Edward 57
Shape of Things to Come, The 56
Shaw, George Bernard 76
Shelley, Mary 9-19
Shelley, Percy Bysshe 12, 14, 16-18, 22
Shiel, M. P. 57-58
Shiner, Lewis 145, 148
Shirley, John 145, 148
Shiva Descending 127
"Shores of Bohemia, The" 149
Short Account of a Remarkable Aerial Voyage, A 11
"Shortest Night, The" 168

Siècle, Le 26
Siegel, Don 103
Silverberg, Robert 136
Simak, Clifford D. 78-79
Sinclair, Upton 93-94
"Sitting on a Starwood Stool" 157
Sixth Column 78, 98, 101
Skylark DuQuesne 84, 90
Skylark of Space, The 75, 83-85
Skylark of Valeron 84-85
Skylark Three 76, 84
"Sleepstory" 124
"Slices" 129
Sloane, T. O'Conor 66, 68, 83
Slow Birds and Other Stories 165
Smith, Clark Ashton 76, 141, 153
Smith, Edward E. 7, 68, 75-76, 83-92
Smith, George O. 79
"Snark in the Night, A" 125
"Snatching the Bot" 129
Socrates 34
"Solarite" 75
"Solution Unsatisfactory" 99
Somnium 29
"Sonnet—to Science" 8, 20-23
"Sons of Man" 122, 125, 132
Sophocles 33
Sorrows of Young Werther, The 15
Space Beyond, The 78
Space Cadet 100, 102
Spacehounds of I.P.C., The 86
Space Marine 167
Spengler, Oswald 115
"Spider Rose" 142-143
Spock Must Die! 119
"Spook" 146
Stableford, Brian 166
"Stalin's Teardrops" 167
Stalin's Teardrops and Other Stories 167
"Stand-In" 122
Stapledon, Olaf 46, 58, 75
Star Beast, The 102-103
"Star Crossing" 122, 127

Star Kings, The 103
"Star Lummox" 102
Star Maker 46, 58
Starman Jones 103
Starship Troopers 105-107, 109
Stars in Shroud, The 123
Stars my Destination, The 103
"Starswarmer" 127
Star Trek 84, 119
Star Trek: The Next Generation 135
Stella 41, 43
Sterling, Bruce 140-154
"Storming the Cosmos" 148-149, 153
Storming the Reality Studio: A Case Book of Cyberpunk and Postmodern Fiction 146
Stories of Infinity 29
"Story of the Machine, The" 77
Stranger in a Strange Land 106-109
Strugatsky, Arkady and Boris 158
Struggle for Empire, The 83
Stuart, Don A. 76-78
Sturgeon, Theodore 79, 132
Subspace Explorers 90
"Subspace Survivors" 90
"Such Dedication" 169
Summa Theologica 29
"Sunken Gardens" 142-143
"Sunken Universe" 113
Sunstroke and Other Stories 163
Super Science Stories 96
"Surface Tension" 112-114
Swanwick, Michael 146
"Swarm" 142-143
"Swarmer, Skimmer" 124, 130
Swedenborg, Emmanuel 32
Swift, Jonathan 11, 32
Swiss Family Robinson, The 108
"Sword of Damocles, The" 149
"Tachyonic Anti-Telephone, The" 128
Taine, John 68, 83
Take Back Your Government 100
Tao of Physics, The 160
"Tapestry of Thought, A" 137

"Tarot Pack Megadeath, The" 156
Tatsumi, Takayumi 146
Television 66
"Telliamed" 148
Tennyson, Alfred, Lord 20
Tennyson, Charles 20
Terre avant le déluge, Le 50-51
"Tête de Mimers, La" 51
Theodore Savage 57
"There Shall Be No Darkness" 120
"They" 99
"They Do it With Mirrors" 100
They'd Rather be Right 79
They Shall Have Stars 115-116
Thing, The 77
"Thing in the Attic, The" 113
Things to Come 56
"Threads of Time" 122, 125
"3.02 P.M. Oxford" 123
Thrill Book 66
Thrilling Wonder Stories 74, 76, 94
"Thunder and Roses" 132
"Thy Blood Like Milk" 157
Tides of Light 127, 133-135
Time Enough for Love 109
Time for the Stars 103
"Time Guide" 129
Time Machine, The 54-56
Timescape 123, 128-129
"Time Shards" 127
"Time-Span to Conjure With, A" 161
Time Stream, The 83
"Time to Survive, A" 114
"Titan Falling" 125
Titan's Daughter 114, 119
Titans du ciel, Les 45
Tolkien, J. R. R. 90-91
Tom Corbett—Space Cadet 100
Tomorrow's Yesterday 58
Tomorrow, the Stars 101
Torquet, Eugène 45
Torrent of Faces, A 119
To Sail Beyond the Sunset 109

"To the Stars" 78
"To the Storming Gulf" 132
"Touch, The" 130
"Touches" 130
Tour de monde en quatre-vingt jours, Le 48
"Towards an Alien Linguistics" 158
Town and Country 100
"Tragedy of Solveig, The" 168
Transatlantic Review 156
Transfigurations 163
Travels into Several Remote Nations of the World by Lemuel Gulliver 11, 32
Tremaine, F. Orlin 76-77, 79, 86
Triplanetary 86
Triumph of Time, The 116
"Trojan Cat, The" 138
Tunnel in the Sky 103
Twain, Mark 136
"Twenty Evocations" 142
Twenty Thousand League Under the Sea 48
"Twilight" 76-77
Tycho Brahe 22
Ultimate World 70
Under Heaven's Bridge 163
"Unfolding, The" 148
"Universe" 99, 101
Universe 123-124
Universe Makers, The 80-81
"Universe on the Turn" 165
Unknown 78-79, 98
"Unparalleled Adventure of One Hans Pfaall" 33
"Unpleasant Profession of Jonathan Hoag, The" 99, 102
"Unthinkable, The" 150
Uranie 41-45
Uris, Leon 105
Utley, Steven 140, 148
Van Campen, Karl 78
Van Vogt, A. E. 79, 90, 113, 115
Varlet, Théo 45
Verhoeven Paul 105
Verne, Jules 8, 28, 47-53, 62-63, 66, 137
Vertex 122
"Very Slow Time Machine, The" 161

Very Slow Time Machine, The 161
Ville flottant, Un, suivi Les Forceurs du Blocus 48
Vingt mille lieues sous les mers 48, 51
"Voice, The" 137
"Voice of the Void, The" 75-76, 81
Void 121-123
Voltaire 32, 125
Vortex-Blaster, The 86
Voyage au centre de la terre 47-53
Voyage du monde de Descartes 32
"Voyage extatique aux régions lunaires, correspondence d'un philosophe adolescent" 24
Voyages de Mylord Céton sans les sept planets 32-33
"Waldo" 99, 101-102
Waldrop, Howard 148
Walpole, Horace 10
Wandrei, Donald 76
War in the Air, The 56-57
War of the Worlds, The 39, 45, 137
War Stars 88
"Warstory" 124
"Watershed" 113
Watson, Ian 155-169
"We Also Walk Dogs—" 100
Weird Tales 66, 84
Weird Tales from Shakespeare 136
Welcome to Mars! 120
Wells, H. G. 8, 28, 39, 45, 49, 54-63, 66, 137
Wentz, Elma 96
Wentz, Roby 96
"We Remember Babylon" 166
"We See Things Differently" 150, 153
"West Wind Falling" 123, 131
"What Dreams May Come...?" 58
"When the Atoms Failed" 75
"When the TImegate Failed" 167
"Where Did You Go Last Year?" 127
White, Ted 121-12
"White Creatures" 126
"W(h)ither Science Fiction?" 158
"Who Goes There?" 77
Whores of Babylon, The 166
"Why is There So Little Science in Literature?" 129

"Width of the World, The" 165
Wilhelm, Kate 128
Wilkins, John 29, 31
Williamson, Jack 68, 79, 85
Winter's Youth 57
Winthrop, R. and C. 64
Wired 146, 152
Wollheim, Donald A. 72, 80, 111
Wood, Ed 70
Wolfe, Charles 658
Wolfe, Gary K. 132
Woman Factory, The 159
Woman Plant, The 159
Wonder Stories 67-69, 71, 74
"Work of Art, A" 120
World Before the Deluge, The 50
World Below, The 58
World Science Fiction Convention of 2080, The" 163
World Set Free, The 56, 60
"World Vast, World Various" 136
"Worm in the Well, The" 132
Wright, S. Fowler 58, 76
Wynne-Tyson, Esmé 58
"Xipéhuz. Les" 44
Year 2018! 116
Yellow Danger, The 57
Yeovil, Jack 166
Young Men Are Coming, The 58
Zelazny, Roger 147
"Zoomers" 137
Zukav, Gary 160

Lightning Source UK Ltd.
Milton Keynes UK
05 August 2010

157977UK00001B/28/P